An American Scholar Recalls Karl Barth's Golden Years as a Teacher (1958-1964)

The Mature Theologian

A Theology
of
Playful Freedom and Radiant Joy

AN AMERICAN SCHOLAR RECALLS KARL BARTH'S GOLDEN YEARS AS A TEACHER (1958-1964)

The Mature Theologian

Raymond Kemp Anderson

With a Foreword by
Herbert Richardson

The Edwin Mellen Press
Lewiston•Queenston•Lampeter

Library of Congress Cataloging-in-Publication Data

Library of Congress Control Number: 2013935935

Anderson, Raymond Kemp.
  An American scholar recalls Karl Barth's golden years as a teacher (1958-1964) : the mature theologian / Raymond Kemp Anderson ; with a foreword by Herbert Richardson.

1. Religion--Christian life--spiritual growth. 2. Religion--Christian life--personal growth. 3. Biography--philosophers.

  p. cm.
  Includes bibliographical references and index.
  ISBN-13: 978-0-7734-4467-6 (hardcover)
  ISBN-10: 0-7734-4467-X (hardcover)
  I. Title.

hors série.

A CIP catalog record for this book is available from the British Library.

The Edwin Mellen Press   The Edwin Mellen Press
Box 450   Box 67
Lewiston, New York   Queenston, Ontario
USA 14092-0450   CANADA L0S 1L0

The Edwin Mellen Press, Ltd.
Lampeter, Ceredigion, Wales
UNITED KINGDOM SA48 8LT
Printed in the United States of America

To Erik and Jennifer

In Memory of Martin

Table of Contents

GEHORSAM

A Personal Memory

"As a child of the American West, I felt Barth's continual call to "obedience" smacked of abject submission to authority and mechanical conformity. [As I had] always used the term, "obedience" connoted an abject subservience. [So during] one Colloquium I took Professor Barth to task: Wouldn't his emphasis on obedience imply we must repress the truth of who we are and act hypocritically, as we were being ordered around by a domineering autocrat?

After [the next meeting of the Colloquium], Barth with a shy smile handed me a palm-sized slip of paper. In his tightly crabbed hand it was headed, "Word-study for Americans." It outlined how the German verb, <u>gehorchen</u>, parallel to its Latin equivalent, <u>obedire</u>, derives from the root meaning, <u>hören</u>, to hear, or even more positively, to listen.

Barth's point: the theological term "obedience" means, at root, to have been rendered wholeheartedly attentive—i.e., inwardly attuned to another person—through a free, love-motivated holistic abandon. So this is something quite opposite from going against one's emerging inclination or desire. A person can no more be <u>ge-**hor**-sam</u> by an act of self-repressive will, than you can attach new ears to your head. [<u>hor</u>→<u>hören</u>, to listen]

i

As a heartfelt, personal response to Christ, Karl Barth's "obedience" was intended as something quite opposite to the reluctant, duty-bound subservience we were prone to associate with the term. From first to last any true obedience is—and can only be—itself a gift, a freedom.

[So if] being ourselves, we find we've become deeply attentive to the Lord, we may believe his own initiative to be behind it; he will have already touched us inwardly with his grace."

Raymond Anderson

The above is an edited excerpt from pages 108-110

Foreword

Professor Raymond Anderson's mixed-genre narrative weaves together contemporary church history, constructive theology, and the autobiographical quest for the meaning of life.

On the last page Dr. Anderson describes his "strange dream of breathing life into my son's prone body, a dream that was still vivid when we learned of his tragic death a few days later."

There had been not the slightest hint of this son in the author's 400 pages of previous narrative. So my shock at reading these words made me reconsider the meaning of everything in this book that I had previously read.

Throughout his manuscript, the author continuously reminds us that "*Alles ist Gnade.*" This means that everything happens through an act that is initiated and guided by the grace of God. Therefore, because everything is grace, we live by "gehorsam." "Gehorsam" means experiencing and responding to the graceful activity of God that is manifested in everything around us.

"Gehorsam" means that we are opened out to life itself as the center of life, and we do not live as if life is centered in us. Judged by this measure, even the death of a loved son is God's grace.

This book begins by describing Professor Anderson's educational journey from his early life in California to his doctoral studies with Professor Karl Barth. What makes these six chapters both lovable and of immense historical value is its vivid description of Barth as a teacher.

The early chapters are filled with detailed reminiscences about Barth's interaction with particular students (many of whom later became renowned theologians). In these reminiscences, the author captures smells and sounds of Barth's colloquia both at the University of Basel and in Basel cafes.

But what is most valuable is the author's transcriptions of actual questions, answers, and discussions between Karl Barth and his many students. (The author even notes when Barth signals with a wink or a smile that his words are to be taken lightly.) There is nothing else in the history of Christian theology to compare with these transcriptions other than Martin Luther's *Table Talk*.

What I myself most appreciated was Professor Anderson's discussion of the relation between Karl Barth and his female collaborator, Fraulein Charlotte von Kirschbaum. She and Professor Barth lived together in the same house with Nelly, who was Karl Barth's wife and the mother of his five children. Over the years I've heard many insinuations about the unusual relationship among these three people. But, I found the author's extensive and nuanced account to be a vindication of the integrity of their life together.

The second part of this book describes the influence of Karl Barth on Professor Anderson's own life and thought. It discusses the range of issues that have preoccupied American theologians during the last half of the 20th century: (1) how to speak about grace to a society that emphasizes creative freedom, (2) how to speak about the particularity of faith in Jesus Christ to people whose highest moral value is universality, (3) how to speak about loving forgiveness to a society that is preoccupied with revengeful justice, (4) how to speak about revelation to a society that finds a natural religion in everything, (5) how to find one's identity in community rather than in one's own individuality, and (6) how to find God through suffering and death rather than through health and happiness.

This book is also a history of the Protestant intellectual conversation in the last half of the 20th century. It includes the names of dozens of thinkers who have contributed to that story.

Herbert Richardson

LIST OF CHARACTERS

THE DOZENS OF THINKERS
WHO ARE MENTIONED IN THIS STORY

Hans Urs von Balthasar
Gyula Barczay
Marcus Barth
Donald Bloesch
Dietrich Bonhoeffer
Henri, Bouillard
John Wick Bowman
Carl E. Braaten
Robert MacAfee Brown
Rudolf Bultmann
Joseph Burgess
Eberhard Busch
Samuel Calian
Georges Casalis
John B. Cobb Jr.
Arnold Come
Marion Conditt
Oscar Cullmann
Johannis Dantini
Hermann Diem
C. H. Dodd
Gary Dorrien
Bart D. Ehrman
Ludwig Feuerbach
Joseph Fletcher
Grover Foley
Paul Frelick
Jacob Friedrich Fries
Dan Fuller
Max Geiger
David Gibson
Theodore Gill

David Gilson
John D Godsey
Billy Graham
Gustavo Gutiérrez
Niel Hamilton
Adolf von Harnack
Stanley M. Hauerwas
Elizabeth Haug
Heinrich Heppe
Wilhelm Hermann
Frederick Herzog
I. John Hesselink, Jr.
George Hunsinger
William James
Robert W. Jenson
Paul Dafydd Jones
Søren Kierkegaard
Charlotte von Kirschbaum
Renate Köbler
Al Krass
Wolf Krötke
Hans Küng
Franz Leenhardt
Paul L. Lehmann
Auguste LeMaître
J. Gersham Machen
Helmut Mach
John Macmurray
Ulrich Mann
Tuomo Mannersmaa
Richard McConnell
Bruce L. McCormack

Alexander J. McKelway
Gerald P. McKenny
Donald K. McKim
Stuart A. McLean
Jürgen Moltmann
Henri Mottu
Reinhold Niebuhr
Anders Nygren
Colm O'Grady
Douglas F. Ottati
Rudolf Otto
Todd B. Pokrifka
Gilles Quispel
Joseph Ratzinger
Bo Reicke
Benjamin Reist
Herbert Richardson
Dietrich Ritschl
R. H. Roberts
John A.T. Robinson
H. M. Rumscheidt
Petruschka Schaafsma
Friedrich Schleiermacher
Jacques de Senarclens

Robert D. Shofner
Donald Shriver
Surjit Singh
James Smart
Ernst Staehelin
Daniel Strange
William Stringfellow
S. W. Sykes
Eduard Thurneysen
Paul Tillich
Thomas F. Torrance
Hendrik Van Oyen
Cornelius Van Til
Allen Verhey
Wilhelm Vischer
Howard Vogel
James Wagner
Hans Emil Weber
John Webster
Amos Wilder
Garry J. Williams
Willimon Williams
Christian T. Winn

Prologue

After a paper on John Calvin I read at the meeting of the Society of Christian Ethics in Chicago in 2009, Herbert Richardson of the Mellen Press challenged me to write a retrospective on the Reformed theologian, Karl Barth with whom I had done my Calvin study at the University of Basel in Switzerland during the 1960s. How had American doctoral candidates studying under him during the last period of his long life experienced the man who even popes have come to recognize as the most significant theologian since St. Thomas Aquinas? Well aware of Barth's mixed reception in England and America[1] and especially of how often the heightened human concern of his mature years has been slighted, I was emboldened to undertake this.

I have done so with some hesitancy, however, since my study in Basel was a half century ago, and I never thought of myself as a complete devotee of Barth. I write simply as one who has been occupied over the years with the similar theological subjects and who, though I was never exclusively

---

[1] S.W. Sykes gives a summary sketch of the desultory reception of Barth in the English-speaking world: See "The Study of Barth," in his essay collection, *Karl Barth* (Oxford: Clarendon Press, 1979), pp. 1-16.

his disciple, was fortunate to benefit from his personal critique and support as my doctoral advisor during the five or six years when he was at the culmination of his own theological journey.

I hear some teacher in an American seminary has said derisively that "Barth never had an unpublished thought." Such a stereotype is unkind, for there was enormous labor and careful planning behind all of Barth's publications. But his voluminous work stands on its own, and my purpose here is not to present anything resembling another systematic approach to or summation of his thought. Many have attempted that and will be doing so for generations to come. My intent is to portray something of the elderly man as teacher and of his focal Church teachings during the golden years (1958-64) that capped the period that Arnold Come described as the "decade of Barth's maturity."[2] Although Barth continued to claim unbroken continuity with his earlier writings (with their one-sided sharp defense against the humanistic challenges of his day), he was at this time unfolding their fuller, grace-centered and human-shaped positive implications.

This retrospective is offered in the hope that my memories of a six-year association with Karl Barth and his literary partner, Charlotte von Kirschbaum, may shed light on the latter years of this celebrated thinker, about whom so much

---

[2] *An Introduction to Barth's "Dogmatics" for Preachers* (Philadelphia: Westminster, 1963), pp. 59-62.

has already been written. To this I have added reflections on the continuing challenges that their spirit and the Christ-responsive intellect they envisioned have brought to our own later work as scholars and church leaders in America.

When citing Barth, I record my recollections of what impressed itself upon me in conversation at the time. This means that, except where indicated otherwise, the statements ascribed to Barth are the substance of what he said and not in every instance his exact words. I attest to the tenor and meaning of what transpired, but occasionally cite from memory and depend on notes, which are sometimes summary in form. I have limited myself largely to direct impressions, however, without much recourse to the secondary literature that has accumulated around his name, though that inevitably will have had some effect upon what and how one remembers.

I did not go to Basel specifically to study Barth's own work, as did a number of international students. Rather, I was interested in exploring the roots of Reformed faith and ethics—especially our traditional notions of virtue—under the tutelage of this man who was purported to be our Presbyterian tradition's greatest living exponent. So I sought to do my post-graduate doctoral project on Reformed theological ethics under his guidance and critique; and he generously committed himself to act as my mentor and discussion partner or *"Doktor-Vater,"* as the German students liked to call this relationship. As said, although I have a great indebtedness to him, I never thought of myself as a "Barthian" in any intentional sense, but have made my own way as a free biblical theologian. (Of course, I suppose that in itself puts me in accord with this man who, as Paul Tillich once said, "refused to become his own follower.")

It is true however, that my respect for Barth and sense of indebtedness has only increased through the years. Much of what one heard in Basel has, in fact, worn well in the American classroom and pulpit and could have great importance for our times. I try to suggest this especially in the last part of this book, where I touch thematically on particular issues where I have found Barth's thought especially cogent in our own unfolding situation.

INNOCENT ABROAD

Since this book is to be a retrospective of Barth's last years, as seen through the eyes of an American student, it may be useful to preface with a brief explanation regarding what in my own background brought me to study under the man who has come to be recognized as the most prolific Protestant-Reformed writer of the twentieth century, and one of the most circumspect Christian thinkers of all time.

My first awareness of Karl Barth, I think, was in 1952, when my eye was caught by a shelf of his massive books in a young chaplain's office at U.C.L.A. Bound in white linen with the jagged title, *Kirchliche Dogmatik* and volume numbers emblazoned across their spines, they declared a weighty intent, such as I had seen manifest only on lawyers' or physicians' shelves. My curiosity was captive.[3] In retrospect, I suppose I may have been predisposed towards Barth's thought by my early experience in the Church, for there was an underlying simplicity at the core of his immense work. Years later, while this author of thousands of pages of critical analysis of Church teaching was on his sole tour in America and was being portrayed on a 1962 cover of *Time* magazine as a scowling prophet, he was asked by a reporter if he could characterize his theology in a single sentence. Grinning, he said, "Jesus loves me this I know, for the Bible tells me so!"[4]

As it happens, one of my earliest memories—I must have been four or five at the time—is of being taught those words of a nursery song at a vacation church school in the citrus oasis of my birth, Fillmore, California. In those days, church dogmatics for us were largely the province of earnest women volunteers, mostly of Midwestern pioneer stock, who ran our Sunday schools. During the more recent women's movement,

---

[3] This was in the office of a German student pastor, who had come as assistant to Cecil Hoffman, the Presbyterian minister who had organized a thriving Westminster Fellowship within the newly built inter-faith Conference Center serving the University of California at Los Angeles.

[4] Other oral tradition recounts this as a response to a Seminar student in Virginia. (See, Stanley Hauerwas, *With the Grain of the Universe*, p. 182). It is quite likely that, Barth, as was his habit, used this rejoinder more than once.

which was made strident by dissidents such as the radical Catholic feminist, Mary Daly, I often wondered how significant it is that the faith we absorbed as children had been mediated mainly by women and not by dominant males. My mother took it upon herself to read a larger part of the Bible to me in delicious quiet times together. She lived and breathed an unquestioned puritan piety from Western Kansas where frontier revivalism had been a tangible reality and the godless dance hall a threat to ordered family existence. Her relaxed way of pointing to a golden thread of God's nurturing grace that was gradually emerging against the macho, often bloody background of the Old Testament world would find a resonance in Karl Barth's *Church Dogmatics.*[5]

Perhaps quite as telling, was something very simple Barth said to me some years into my doctoral studies with him I lamented that I had run through three or four post-graduate scholarships and was not finished, but feeling guilty still to be so financially dependent upon others.

"Herr Anderson," he said, *"Alles ist Gnade!"* [Everything is grace.] Everything! Every last thing is part of a positive gift of someone else's kindness—finally of God's own. There was nothing casual about those three words for him.

---

[5] G. C. Berkouwer, gave an early, rather grudging summary of this line under title of *The Triumph of Grace in the Theology of Karl Barth* (Grand Rapids: Eerdmans, 1956).

Everything is gifted, nested somehow in grace.[6] He had rediscovered that belief in the revelation of Christ and in the Apostle Paul, in Augustine and in the great Reformers. There was nothing really new in that either. Many of us had already heard it from our first theologians, our mothers. But for Barth, if you uncover the how and why of it, all of life takes on a zestful tone, the pressure's off; and a sense of spontaneous freedom and nestling gratitude begins to reshape your perceptions and soften everything you do. No matter how complicated and unhappy life becomes, there is the underlying assurance, all is well, for its ending well has already been brought about. Despite all its tragedies then, life is truly *comedy*—in the deepest sense of that word—to be lived with relaxed good humor and radiant joy.

Now, given these hints of an inner dramatic unity at the core of Barth's thought, it would completely misrepresent the tenor of his life work should anyone assume that he was antirational or simply a card-carrying member of one or another of the sects that push similar slogans.

There was nothing simplistic, naïve or uncritical about Barth. That his thought can engage and satisfy the most critical mind was brought home to me by recent conversations with a brilliant young mathematician who grew up in Red China and

---

[6] In his *Call for God* Barth tells us, the Bible's four "words, 'My grace is enough' say much more and say it better than [my] whole pile of paper—something that I am very far from being able to say about my books" (p. 78): cited by E. Busch, *The Great Passion*, p. 38).

teaches at Beijing University. He told me that, despite his hard-nosed scientific background, he became a Christian solely by having begun out of curiosity to read *The Church Dogmatics*.

It has often struck me as almost bizarre, that the distance Barth and company gradually won from the anthropocentric "liberal" speculations they had received in the European universities of their student days is nearly always described as an earth-shaking revolution. Whereas, in fact, the stance that emerged is simply a clarification of what many of us had heard from the first as basic teaching in our churches. (One often meets the assumption that academic fashion had been steering the Christian community's thought, though this notion is far from accurate.) The intellectual clubbishness of European liberal scholarship with its almost idolatrous preoccupation with human culture and moral progress had remained peripheral and alien to many of us. And where Barth had only gradually separated himself from that milieu through a new appreciation of christocentric revelation and growing biblical attentiveness, the theological ground where he struggled to regain his footing was not really beyond the terrain where those at the moderate grassroots of our churches had stood all the while.

In retrospect I also recall two moments in my university formation that paralleled Barth's own: a tussle with Immanuel Kant's moral philosophy and the discovery of Søren Kierkegaard's astringent epistemology. Overcome by west-of-the-Rockies wanderlust, in the fall of 1952 I went to Scotland for my junior year of university. In Edinburgh right alongside philosopher John Macmurray's personalism, one was immersed in Kantian moral philosophy (which seemed to have provided an ethical orientation for the colonialism that was only then beginning to wane). So confronted by the mechanical cool of Kant's rationalistic duty ethic, I found myself forced to re-think with new appreciation the contrasting affective wholeness of a grace-responsive life viewed in Pauline terms.

Then, during a senior year back at U.C.L.A., I was introduced to the book which was to become seminal in my thinking: Kierkegaard's *Philosophical Fragments*, where he gives the Unknown (with capital "U") his utter seriousness and unfolds the Absolute Paradox, whereby, as far as we know, the Unknown, while not discernible in nature or natural experience, is not necessarily (as far as we *know*) unknowable. Thus our intelligence must include the possibility that the Unknown *might* be able to take the initiative to make itself known, giving both the occasion and the content for a crucial advance in our knowledge (and inducing in us the requisite condition of mind to grasp it rationally).

This became the background for my own openness to the effort to take revelation seriously that was nurtured at San Francisco Theological Seminary alongside a fully scientific use of historical-critical method. There, under title of "Prophetic

Realism," John Wick Bowman, Arnold Come and Surjit Singh were bringing such affirmation and critical thought together in biblical studies, systematic theology and Christian philosophy. They claimed affinity with other scholars who *within an atmosphere of critical study*, took scriptural revelation or *Heilsgeschichte* seriously, under title of Neo-Orthodoxy or dialectic theology—such people as Emil Brunner, the brothers, Reinhold and Richard Niebuhr, Gustaf Aulen, Nels Ferré and of course, Karl Barth.

Professor Arnold Come was writing a book on Barth's theology "for preachers," but the volumes of the *Church Dogmatics* were too hefty to figure much in our course work. This, it seems, was true of the American theological scene at large. Barth was caricatured through a series of clichés more often than he was actually read and understood, though the grand scale and apparent seriousness of his work seemed to beckon and command an almost reluctant respect.

That the fields of theology and philosophy were given prominence alongside the natural sciences at Basel University was one of the things that attracted me there as an American. There is a well-known saying from Barth that "theology is *the* beautiful science," *die schöne Wissenschaft*. This could mean that, as with other sciences, theology is to be shaped inductively, always responsive to its subject. But one notices that the word, "*Wissenschaft*" carries a much broader meaning than hard "science" does in English. The German word connotes the craft that seeks understanding in any area of enquiry, and as used here does not carry the same meaning of universal empirical verifiability.[7]

Along with Barth's grasp of theology as the beautiful science one should notice that it is in his final view "*die dankbare und darum fröliche Wissenschaft*," the grateful and thereby joyful way of knowing, in which the appropriate mood is that of free play in grace,[8] and perhaps we should add, the grace freely to play.

Neil Q. Hamilton, who had come to our seminary as a young instructor with a newly minted doctorate from Basel, fired some of us with the possibility of going there ourselves. Hamilton assured us that one could work with Barth partly in English, though German in those days was still regarded as the primary language for theological research, alongside of Latin, Greek and Hebrew. I had had no German in school but purchased a small lexicon of theological terms which I began to memorize.

Upon graduation in 1957, scholarship prizes and a fellowship from the Council of Churches enabled further study including a year at the University of Tübingen which is not terribly distant from Basel. There I threw myself into courses of

---

[7] The German term can just as well refer to faith claims regarding the non-empirical and possible self-disclosure of the Unknown.

[8] *Einführung...*, *S*.18 & 121. See further in Chapter 13.

German theology; but found myself a victim of having believed the myth, that if you immerse yourself for a time in a foreign culture, the language becomes easy. My struggle was complicated by the heavy Swäbisch dialect of the local students. Fortunately, German words are spelled almost exactly as they are pronounced; so I could try to scribble down the entire lectures verbatim each day, then go to my room and decipher them word by word. I mention this because it became the note-taking habit that enabled me to keep the rather exact records I have of some of Barth's unpublished Colloquia.

The Tübingen professor, Hermann Diem, like Barth, had been an active pastor and was deeply influenced by him. Diem, too, was working out a serious, but critical approach to biblical revelation.[9] Diem engaged a couple of us from America to proofread some translations of his work; and in the course of conversation, told about how as a German soldier, drafted into the artillery, he spent a furlough backpacking through the Alps to re-establish an escape route for Jewish refugees into Switzerland. The contact at the other end of this mountainous Underground Railroad, he told us, had been none other than Professor Karl Barth.[10]

---

[9] *Was Heisst Schriftgemäss?* (Neukirchen Kreis Moers: Verlag der Buchhandlung der Erziehungsvereins, 1958); *Theologie als Kirchliche Wissenschaft* (Münich: Chr. Kaiser Verlag, 1951).

[10] Compare E. Busch, *The Great Passion*, p. 34.

The following school year I began my doctoral studies under Barth himself in Basel. Later, after a prescribed period of residency at the University there, I was called to assist Paul Frelick, Director of Foyer John Knox, in Geneva.[11] For many months then, while also attending university lectures in Geneva, I travelled across Switzerland to Barth's fortnightly English colloquia and some of his lectures on dogmatics. This entailed a twisting 200-kilometer trip, sometimes by car, but more often by rail, returning on a slow milk train that creaked through the wee hours, clattering to stop to load clanging canisters at the smallest villages en route to arrive, just as French Switzerland was shaking itself awake. Another year, while still knitting on my dissertation, I was employed half-time as assistant pastor near the U.C.L.A. campus in Westwood, California, before returning to Basel for my culminating study with Barth. Thus my contacts were spread across six years from 1958 through 1964.

I gratefully acknowledge my debt to Herbert Richardson for challenging me to write this retrospective and to my wife, Gunlög, for her loving support as it was taking shape. My

---

[11] The Foyer John Knox, a fraternal work project of the American Presbyterian and Swiss Churches, was essentially a mission experiment, asking students to commit themselves to seeking true community while confronted with the tensions of international living.

heartfelt thanks also go out to Stanley Hauerwas, John Hesselink, Donald Shriver, Eberhard Busch and all the others who have cheered me on my way or taken a hand with the manuscript and. I am especially indebted to Marie Lanser Beck and Carole Gallagher for their expertise and thoughtful assistance in manuscript preparation.

Note On Language Usage

Masculine pronouns and fatherhood imagery in references to God are used advisedly throughout, not just because Karl Barth used them in the traditional way, but with the historical-critical understanding that in previous eras a father's commitment to his recognized children was widely supposed to have had a more freely elective character than a mother's. In the popular mind, at least, to acknowledge one's own fatherhood had to be covenantal in character, and this is what made *"father"* appropriate in reference to the covenant-making God.[12]

---

[12] The mother's connection to her offspring (according to pre-Freudian notions, at least) was regarded as more automatic, determined by womb-feeling, birth pangs and breast-bonding. Committed fatherhood, by contrast, was manifestly a freely intentional undertaking. (There was even a widespread ceremony [the *sublatio* in Rome] whereby a good father, by lifting the newborn on high, made public his assumption of permanent, loyal responsibility.) Use of the masculine for God, did not imply either naïve anthropomorphism or mean-spirited male-dominance. Historically, fatherhood was simply the readiest available symbol for the gentle freedom

Evocative of Barth's European scene a number of Latin and other foreign expressions are included in this retrospective, but care has been taken to provide English translations even for common theological terms when the meaning is not clear from context.

Abbreviations

CD = Karl Barth's *Church Dogmatics* in its standard. English edition: *Church Dogmatics*, G.W. Bromiley *et al.* (Edinburgh: T&T Clark, 1957-1977).

KD = Karl Barth's *Kirchliche Dogmatk* in the original or my own fresh reading directly from it: *Kirchliche Dogmatik* (Zollikon-Zürich: Evangelischer Verlag, 1932-1967).

S (or SS) indicates page (*Seite*) number[s] in German editions to distinguish them from page references in English or French translations.

---

whereby a person-affirming God was believed to have pledged gratuitous loyalty to all. In this spirit we may continue the thoughtful Early Christian practice of referring to God as "he" or "him."

Chapter 1

Pilgrimage to Basel

As a World Council of Churches fellow at Tübingen (1957-58), I felt at the heart of Europe. I lived in the *Evangelische Stift*, a large monastery of Pre-Reformation times that served as a center for Württemberg's theology students. The teaching assistants there chuckled about how Georg Wilhelm Friedrich Hegel's papers that survived in the cellar show the great philosopher to have been a rather mediocre student. The half-timbered hall where Martin Luther's associate, Philip Melanchton, taught was but a stone's throw away overlooking the promenade- and garden-flanked Neckar River which wends its lazy way northwest through beautiful Heidelberg to join the Rhine. My window opened onto a charming scene, romantic at night with its lantern-lit boatloads of singing students, but I tried to stick to my desk, absorbing German language and theology, word by word.

In February 1959, while still at Tübingen, I was invited to Basel to visit my seminary friend, Vern Clark, who with his wife, Doni, had scrimped and saved to spend some months there. He agreed to take me to visit Karl Barth's English Colloquium and meet the professor for the first time. So I found myself on a bus to Basel that halted long enough in the town of Donau-Eschingen for me to wash my hands in the bubbling wellspring that purports to be the ultimate source of the Danube, flowing away eastwards, in the opposite direction from the Neckar. So this really was the watershed mid-point of Europe. Through parts of the Black Forest the road became steep and snowy enough for the bus to skid off the pavement in an alarming way. When I later found myself, as a guest walking up Bruderholzalle in Basel to Karl Barth's Colloquium, I felt I had made a long, rather twisting pilgrimage to the center of European theology as well.

FIRST IMPRESSIONS

Barth and his assistant, Charlotte von Kirschbaum, who by all accounts was always at his side, walked the short distance from his home on Bruderholzallee up to the Bruderholz Restaurant, where on alternate weeks he met his evening colloquia with English- and French-speaking students. This engagingly smiling gentleman who was nearly seventy-two years old and walked with a stoop that made him appear shorter than he was . . . Could this retiring man be the lion of European theology, who in his writings had taken on the leading minds of the age with such impassioned force and fairly roared, "Let God be God!"? Was this the fiery antagonist, who had emblazoned a huge "NEIN!" across the front of his response to the rather mild natural-order ethic of his erstwhile Zürich proponent, Emil Brunner, and who proclaimed that God's Word descends like a lightning bolt "*senkrecht von oben nach unten*"?

I hesitate to voice my first impression that there was an elfin, teddy bear quality about him, a harmless, almost shy openness—not in the least frightening, though the students, daunted by the astounding mass of his writings, did surround him with an aura of deference. The following semester, as an American student in Basel, I was continually struck by how different was this affable gentleman from the assumptions generally made about him back home. There was nothing strident or overbearing about Karl Barth.

His suits usually looked a bit rumpled, and he would wear a limp, nondescript tie. Even in bad weather, he would come on foot to his colloquia, heavy-vested, with muffler and a beret. The fragility of his years showed in his cautious gait, his tufted hair, the slightest of tremors in his voice and the tobacco-stained teeth behind his ready smile.

3

His eyes, at first glance owlish behind heavy-rimmed glasses, one soon discovered, were always dancing with amused warmth. His sense of humor seemed indomitable, and his conversation was constantly salted with puckish repartee. It was evident that his mind remained astonishingly fresh and agile— free of the lapses most of us experience with advancing age.

Eberhard Busch, in his biography, tells us that Barth would suffer from near exhaustion in his latter years. But during the time I knew him, you saw no trace of that. Even in the colloquia he continued after retiring from the task of lecturing at the University, he showed the same sprightly good humor. In the course of discussion, he spoke with an amazing grasp of the history of dogma, as well as of current trends. But his genius seemed to lie in his analytic and creatively analogical thinking, rather than in a truly exceptional memory. During colloquia we occasionally witnessed his amused toleration of Grover Foley, an American student gifted with near total recall. Foley, in his punctilious way would confront Professor Barth with some long-forgotten comment he had made years before.

"But as you said in 1930 . . ."

Barth's eyes twinkled with humor and were ringed with lines that suggested a quizzical anticipation: as if he were curious and expected to receive something new from this exchange with you. It's an expression I've noticed in other Reformed teachers as well; until I've found myself wondering, whether a peculiar combination of humorous warmth and quizzically open-ended anticipation could actually reflect an added dimension their particular world view brings into each new encounter.

Barth's single glass of white wine was a *sine qua non* at his evening English and French Colloquia and German *Societät* at the Bruderholz Restaurant. The briar he fussed with, as a bit of theatrical business while he gathered his thoughts in discussion, was not only a stage prop, but his constant companion. He had once teased Thomas Torrance, "You can't be a theologian if you don't smoke a pipe!"[1] Years later, the early manuscripts of my own writing bore not just the minuscule lines he put in the margins, but the faint odor and grains of tobacco from his pipe. Turning the pages, I could close my eyes and be transported back through time by the distinctive fragrance.

The European university provided little academic advising, and international students were bound to feel some isolation and cultural friction that within a year or so tends to occasion a nasty syndrome known as cultural shock. One could feel reduced to Lilliputian scale in the presence of the recognized giants in our disciplines who were patient enough to work with us. Some of the fifty or sixty Americans who had participated in

---

[1] Anecdote shared by Torrance's ex-student, Prof. Andrew Purves of Pittsburgh Seminary.

Barth's English Colloquium must have appeared rather naïve in European perspective. Eberhard Busch tells us how Barth, amused that one American student lacking a baby-sitter had brought her small child along to his English Colloquium, quipped that no doubt, "next time, some baby or other will certainly appear in order to be informed about the basic concepts of ethics."[2] Naïve or not, we, of course, took advantage of the offerings of the other notable scholars at Basel[3] as well as Barth's university lectures and seminars.

"HERR PROFESSOR DOKTOR"—

A FIELD MARSHAL'S ROLE

The enormously prestigious position that was afforded European professors, especially in Germany, had always been a subject of bemusement to Americans. Continental students had little or no sense of school loyalty, no sense of *alma mater* or *in loco parentis,* to bind them to a single institution. Instead, they lived entirely on their own (or sometimes in a foundation facility)[4] as independent scholars, always quite separate from the

---

[2] *Karl Barth*, p. 462.

[3] Notably, Oscar Cullmann, Bo Reicke and Mathias Rissi, in New Testament, Hendrik van Oyen and Heinrich Ott, in theology, Ernst Staehelin and Max Geiger in Church History.

[4] I stayed first in the *Evangelische Stift* in Tübingen and then *Das Theologische Alumneum* in Basel which were both supported by the church-

school. Even undergraduates in preparation for future licensure exams would move between several universities in order to study under three or four of those professors reputed to be cutting-edge figures in their chosen field. This pattern fostered a kind of academic Darwinism that was promoted both by scholars and their publishers, who reinforced the myth that human development and intellectual evolution are so intense that students should seek out the foremost figures in their field, sit at their feet and soak up their latest innovations.

In this environment a well-known professor would be elevated to a status analogous to that of a military general. His role was to marshal the current knowledge in a field and establish a front line of intelligibility to be reinforced and held against all comers. The overblown importance given to *Herr Professor Doktor's* position harbored a status-sharing place for assistants and colleagues, who would entrench themselves to assist him—most frequently a *him*—in holding the line on his enormously responsible academic front.

In the European academy, professors' personal contacts with individual students or even with each other were not especially frequent. Karl Barth was no exception there; but he was always relaxed, responsive and genteel at the semi-formal ap-

---

es to provide living accommodations for ministerial students.

pointments one would set up when one felt ready to present a draft or seek his perspective. Yet, our situation—having travelled so far, struggled with the language and immersed ourselves in advanced studies—often evoked in me the prior anxiety of an oral exam before such appointments, even though this was quite irrational, since the avuncular gentleman was good at putting you at your ease. Such meetings would be scheduled at his home, at 26 Bruderholzallee. If the weather was fine, his collaborative assistant, Fraülein von Kirschbaum, would have put some chocolate covered jelly candies on a patio table for him to offer along with the tea she would pour into fancy little glasses of the Russian type, cradled in silver filigree. But beyond such conferences, we international students were, as a rule, quite on our own in Europe.

Since we had little personal contact with our professors outside the classroom, our hunger to know the more human side of Barth led us to pass around anecdotes about him. We had our own oral tradition and, for example, would retell one student's memory of coming upon Barth crawling about on all fours while regaling his grandchildren with the grunts, quacks and snorts of various farm animals and, again, how the professor began barking like a dog to amuse a student's small child. It was reassuring to know his homespun reality corresponded to the affable persona we met in the academic setting. So we

8

treasured such lore, and much of it has found its way into print. Of course, we also savored already widely publicized stories, such as how Barth had answered his Nazi inquisitors in Bonn by pulling a copy of Plato's *Apology* from his pocket and reading from Socrates's defense when accused of corrupting the youth of Athens.

My first conference with Barth upon moving to Basel as an international student was mediated (inevitably, as I was to learn) by Fraülein von Kirschbaum, Barth's close co-worker for over thirty years, who always accompanied him to his lectures at the University and handled most of his scheduling, routine correspondence and manuscript preparation.

During my first post-seminary fellowship in Europe I had written about my growing desire to do a study testing "the systematic bases [if any] of the concept of Christian virtue." I was hoping, as I put it at the time, to fight against "a superficially pragmatic or legalistic morality rampant in the American churches."[5] So now, at this first appointment, I approached Barth about my desire to deal with the theologically incongruent pursuit of individual merit and virtue often associated with a dualistic legalism in our churches. His response, as I would

---

[5] R[aymond Kemp] Anderson, "Christianity is caught, not taught," in *Leibhaftige Ökumene: Berichte ausländischer Mitarbeiter und Studenten in unserer Kirche* (Berlin/Stuttgart:Lettner Verlag, 1963), S. 154.

learn, was typical of his academic approach: "*Herr* Anderson, when you are as old as I am, you may be ready to write your doctrine of virtue, but what you need now is a historical hook-up [*eine geschichtliche Anknüpfungspunkt*]." Theology for him was to be pursued in deep conversation with those who have gone before us, as well as with those in the living Church.

For reasons I did not yet fully appreciate, he suggested that, if I were to settle on such a study, I take John Calvin as my historical focus. But before we agreed to that, he broached a telling interest of his own. I was astonished when he suggested that he would be especially gratified if someone would undertake to do a study on "the American Way of Life." (This, remember, was toward the end of the 1950s, several years before Barth became notorious for counseling East German churchmen against hankering back to the "*flesh-pots of the West*" and urged them to dig in instead and strive to serve Christ in the godless Communist environs where they found themselves.)

I hadn't come all the way to Basel to study an American theme, however, so I chose to immerse myself in the interpretation of the Reformer, who I already knew, though "the American Way of Life" surely would have had greater curb appeal back home. He graciously agreed to be mentor for my dissertation on Calvin and the encroaching virtue concept.[6]

AN EXISTENTIAL SEARCH FOR MEANING

You never heard Barth speak of a moment of conversion in his own experience. For him the reorientation and personal relationship that makes you a Christian is a gift one may, thank God, receive anew every ordinary day. If there is such a thing as particularly religious experience, it is not the essential basis of Christian faith or the stuff of theology.

Barth did, however, describe his own struggle as pastor and teacher in vivid images—some of them often cited and familiar. More than once I heard him refer to his experience as a young minister in writing his *Römerbrief*, as having been like that of a man dizzied in the darkness of a steeple, reaching out, to grab hold of something to steady himself, only to discover, to his stunned surprise, that he had latched onto a bell rope and awakened the whole town. ("Let God be God!") In the mature Barth we came to know, that initial peal had mellowed to an even deeper appeal to let God be himself, *human as well,* in the most unexpected ways.

---

[6] Raymond K. Anderson, *Love and Order—the Life-Structuring Dynamics of Grace and Virtue in Calvin's Ethical Thought: An Interpretation, 1973.*

11

The pursuit of theology is personal. You are trying to stabilize your own grasp of life itself and to speak about your vision. But by its nature Christian theology bonds you into the community of faith and never becomes individualistic. Thus for Barth the root concern is *Church* teaching; and theology is essentially a living conversation within a community.

The seriousness of a real search for meaning at Basel is one of the things that counted most for me. Barth would often describe his relation to his subject as always being like tracing the flight of a bird across the sky. The living subject of theology can be expected always to take the initiative. God has spoken to a people. The Spirit leads. We hear. We follow.

Barth said that in beginning with each new topic, he always felt as if he were standing at the bottom of a fluid sea, and had to snorkel again up toward light at the surface. Because of his conviction that theology should remain for everyone a dynamic, Spirit-responsive conversation in community, he grew fearful that some might try to make of his tentative work a kind of self-contained *summa* cast in bronze. Nothing bothered him more than the first symptoms of a complaisant attitude among some who so disregarded his openness that they could think of entrenching themselves within his dogma, or pin themselves with the tag of being *Barthians*. "The *Church Dogmatics* did not drop down from heaven," he would caution and insist that he intended it to spark real discussion.

He could speak with great irony of the reputation some of his students had garnered of being cocksure of themselves: "the legendary pitilessness of a genuine *Basler Doctorandus* [who always seems ready] to separate the sheep from the goats." He would hope, instead, to stimulate his readers to play out their own dynamic response to liberating apostolic claims. He once expressed to me real dismay over how his one-time student, Edinburgh's Thomas Torrance, had begun to interpret John Calvin, as if the Reformer himself had been a proto-Barthian. Although my own theological quest would also uncover an unexpectedly positive dynamic in Calvin's ethics, Barth was insistent that I think of my dissertation (and entitle it appropriately) as "an interpretation," and not as a settled last word.

To be regarded as the harbinger of an ironclad Neo-Orthodoxy was anything but a compliment for Karl Barth. In his *Kleiner Kreis*[7] we heard how a Dutch enthusiast, introducing him at a birthday festival in the most glowing terms, spoke of his white-bound *Kirchliche Dogmatik* as an immense finished

_____

[7] Barth's "Smaller Circle": an intimate discussion group of nine or ten advanced theological students and other friends invited to meet intermittently, usually around themes uppermost in his thought and writing at the time.

creation—comparing it to the huge white whale in *Moby Dick*. Barth came to his feet protesting that the whole thing might be done much better and quite differently—nothing absolute or finished about it—everything in flux! The speaker, evidently feeling quite let down, told a friend afterwards, that Barth had placed his whole *system* in question. It was not Barth's goal to uncover a putative fixed system or to create one.

After completing my residency requirements at Basel University, and my further years of commuting thither from French-speaking Switzerland, I spent another year as assistant pastor back home near U.C.L.A. and along the way I had to tussle with the Swedish spoken by my young wife's family in Finland. So when I returned to Basel, my own German remained ragged. But Barth generously invited me to join his more intimate *"Kleiner Kreis."*

BARTH'S MATURITY AS TEACHER—
AN UN-AMERICAN ACTIVITY

Students in the European system were supposed to be looking toward their own ultimate grasp of life and developing world view. It was a given that they were committed to their preparation for final career exams, so they were not continually subjected to the hassle of short–term exams—a practice too prevalent in America. Frequent tests, such as our wearisome spot-quizzes and semester finals were considered appropriate only for ground-level "pro-seminars" in preparatory subjects, such as language study. For better or for worse—and sometimes tragically so—students were assumed to be professionals, who are ethically mature, responsible citizens, self-motivated and completely on their own. As mentioned above, the *in-loco-parentis* role of American colleges, which was being disputed at the time, was simply unheard of—totally foreign to the European academy.

Karl Barth had been an ordained pastor and had not followed the usual post-graduate route, but had been awarded his doctoral degrees on the basis of his independent study and writings. Yet he came from an academic family and with relish and a grain of self-irony lived out the role of doughty professor that had been thrust upon him. He certainly knew how to balance the short class semesters with the long retreats for research and course preparation which came with that role. (I had noticed in Tübingen a kind of unwritten law that the status of a professor was suggested by how late the date he might deign to begin the semester's lectures.) Time for research was obviously of paramount concern.

Over some thirty years until his final retirement in 1962, every theology lecture for Barth was a new creation, the draft, in fact, for the next unit in his *Church Dogmatics*. Though his lectures had a pastoral edge and frequently addressed current events and social issues, right down to the rumpus surrounding recent football matches, they remained in formal European style, and were always strictly discursive in format.

The standard lecture or *Vorlesung*, was, as the word's roots denote, a *reading forth* of the professor's portrayal of the state of his field of enquiry and of his own perspective and most recent contributions to it. There was almost no place here for free exchange, no question-and-answer sessions and little spontaneous, extempore content. However dry, this format avoided the time-consuming costs of a more Socratic method, which severely limits the ground a teacher can cover. The lecturer was expected to make it part of his task to open and formulate the great unanswered questions in his field while leaving dialogue for another occasion. It was understood that students were hearing in advance the manuscript for what might, after a time, follow as the most recent publication in their field. This advance-hearing function of the traditional lecture, of course, is being overtaken today by the potential for immediate electronic communication, which renders this *latest-word* aspect of the formal, set lecture less important. Barth himself came to question the apodictic lecture format and felt it could become outmoded for the Church, where teaching might best be more interactive and conversational. [8]

At the time, the German students I had known at
Tübingen found it an unusual indulgence that their ex-pastor-
professor, Hermann Diem, himself a supporter of Barth, actually came down off the podium sometimes to respond to questions and engage his students in direct dialogue—something we
Americans took for granted. Although Barth clearly thrived on
student interchange, there was none of that accompanying his
formal Dogmatics lectures in Basel's large, bright, marble-clad
lecture hall. I know he worked half the night sometimes getting
the day's offering into final shape, and his associate, Fraülein
von Kirschbaum, was always there to catch any emendations
inspired during his actual presentation before she typed up the
material in publishable form.

For a different perspective, we could attend the late af-
ternoon philosophy lectures of Karl Jaspers, the famed existential philosopher. Jaspers would descend on the University in a
stiffly square, high-cabbed, chauffeur-driven black motorcar,
from which he would descend like a dark-winged Gabriel, with
white mane flowing. You could imagine the trumpets blowing.
A flutter of culture-hungry Basel housewives, who swelled the
audience, almost swooned at his silver-voiced, sibilant North

---

[8] See E. Busch, *Karl Barth*, p. 464.

17

German elegance and would nod to each other knowingly as he gave a psychiatrist's panache to his reading of how religious concepts are mere "ciphers" that we project to stand in for realities beyond our human intelligence. We couldn't help but be entertained by the contrast of styles between him and the playful, almost baroque swirls of Barth's earthy, incarnation-based and history-steeped thought.

Although Barth obviously had fun with the comedic role of frumpish European professor, he styled himself as a most ordinary man, taking the tram back and forth to his modest villa in Bruderholzallee. Most have heard the anecdote he liked to tell on himself: When asked by a tram conductor whether he knew the famous Professor Barth, who was supposed to live up that street, he had exclaimed, "Know him? Why, man, I give him his shave every morning!" [The word, "*Bart*," of course, means "beard" in German.] When someone would refer to him as a theological giant, he would slump down into his most crooked stoop and exclaim, "Giant? Just look at me!"[9]

Barth's thematic academic seminars in the ancient classroom on the Rhine, and his additional evening German language *Sozietät*, and French and English Colloquia at the Bruderholz Restaurant were a complete departure from his for-

---

[9] For Barth's own disclaimer here see his Preface to the American edition of *Evangelical Theology*, p. x.

18

mal, discursive lecture style. Here a modified Socratic method reigned. It was obvious that during his last years at the University, almost all his waking moments were either directly or indirectly devoted to teaching; and he engaged an astounding variety of students in direct discourse. Others have characterized his teaching style aptly—I think especially of Alexander McKelway, who studied under Barth after having been pastor in the American Church in Vienna—but I will add my own impressions.[10]

BARTH IN COLLOQUY AND CLASSROOM

Barth's voluntary evening colloquia in French and in English, which alternated, bi-weekly, were largely focused on successive chapters of his published *Dogmatics*, as was his German-speaking *Sozietät*. At each session, one student would be responsible for providing in his or her own words a brief summary or précis of the next section and then lead off with a carefully prepared set of reactions and critical questions. These would spark Barth's response and evoke further questions and

---

[10] Alexander J. McKelway, "*Magister Dialecticae et Optimarium Partium*: Recollections of Karl Barth as Teacher," *Union Seminary Quarterly Review*, Vol. XXVIII, No. 1, Fall, 1972; John D. Godsey, "Reminiscence of Karl Barth," *Theology Today,* Vol. 43/3, *Oct, 1986.* For the ambivalence felt by a Lutheran student, see also Robert W. Jenson "In Memoriam Karl Barth," Lutheran Theological Seminary, *Summer Bulletin, 1969,* p. 9ff.

reactions from the group at large. (When possible, the student leader's work was mimeographed to be studied by all.) To Barth's amusement, I varied that format once by styling my set of questions as those John Calvin assuredly would have thrown at him.

His spoken English, though self-taught, was quite adequate. (English detective stories and Civil War novels had occupied his spare time. "You can't do theology all the time," he would laugh.) His effort to restate his key ideas in his straightforward, but somewhat limited English, gave Barth's Colloquia special interest since here he was epitomizing his thought in basic language. [For full examples see Chapter 6.[11]] His fluency in French came from the trilingual upbringing common to the Swiss upper classes and his first post had been in French-speaking Geneva. Even his academic German, of course, was tinged with a broad Swiss accent; for the softened dialect of his Basel homeland differs from High German almost as widely as Dutch.

Barth's pipe and the single glass of white wine that the restaurant always set before him enhanced a kind of mellowness

---

[11] Examples from Barth's Colloquia are transcribed in Chapter 6. For similar examples from the early 1950s see John D. Godsey, *Karl Barth's Table Talk* (Richmond VA: John Knox Press), 1963. I am currently editing for Mellen Press a larger set of those I attended (1958-64).

that marked these conversations. I mentioned previously how he used his omnipresent briar, as do many pipe smokers, to punctuate his meaning. He would fill moments of reflection by scraping at its bowl, tamping in tobacco, applying fire, and sucking it to a savory glow, then wave it and finally speak, enwreathed in smoke.

Indeed, a reflective dialogic interchange was Barth's main method in teaching smaller groups, and this, to be sure, was a *kind* of practical dialectic in action, but the *"dialectic-theology"* tag commonly applied to his work was something he had come to decry (though he had occasionally used the term early on). He clearly loved to listen closely, puffing quietly on his pipe and taking an occasional sip of his wine. But as we shall see, such mutual dialogue between those who find themselves more or less positively responding to Christ had little in common with any set methodology or theory, such as Hegel's, that truth emerges through dialectic antitheses. That was something Barth had early left behind and finally forcefully rejected.[12]

Often there were guests present from far and wide, so some of the questions thrown at him represented antagonistic extremes of fundamentalism or of liberal humanism. Yet, over

---

[12] Recorded by John Godsey (*Op. cit.*, p. 24).

several years, I never heard him fail to take a question or challenge respectfully under consideration. Even when something struck the rest of us as puerile or vapid, he made a real effort to understand where the question was coming from. He would engage his questioners where he found them to be in their own life pilgrimage. Something of the pastor always remained.

To Barth there was no such thing as a bad question—if it represented a person's heart and mind. We came to realize this was more than civility. Barth actually believed that questions from all sides—especially perhaps, from anyone trying to be responsive to the believed Word in the Church, but also from other perspectives—are always fruitful as a means through which the Holy Spirit focuses faith's search for understanding. In the spirit of Calvin, he was intent on setting his students on the way for their own explorations, "to use their own eyes and ears," rather than trying to mold what their thought should be.[13]

We noticed, however, that he needed to sense that their queries or objections were authentic. Sometimes one of us would cook up a set question just to draw his typical response. When, already knowing the questioner, he could not see why this particular person would ask just this question, he would become flummoxed. And then, when he discovered that it did not

---

[13] Compare Busch, *Karl Barth*, p. 439.

express actual puzzlement or curiosity in the questioner's mind, but had only been handed him as a stick of academic chewing gum, he would be visibly disappointed. For him the "beautiful *Wissenschaft*" is always at one level the drive of our own living faith to find its intelligence and *in that sense* is to be a shared existential quest.

These colloquia pulsed with give and take and frequent laughter. Naturally some of his favorite anecdotes and examples had already or would later find their way into his voluminous writings, but they had a special amused and amusing charm, as he applied them to issues in spirited, living dialogue.

As I have mentioned, there was also a *Kleiner Kreis* or "Smaller Circle" of advanced students and other discussion partners who he invited into his home, partly to explore background for his upcoming topics. Prof. Arnold Come once had told us that European scholars are in the habit of piggy-backing on the research of a whole stable of subservient graduate students.[14] If this was to any extent true of Barth, I was never aware of it. He did take his mature students' findings into serious consideration; but he was simply including them in the wide circle of discussants, both modern and ancient, whom he felt

---

[14] Professor Come made this supposition long before he actually came to spend a sabbatical in Basel, where I had managed to locate a house rental for him and his wife.

called to hear responsively. His astounding output came finally from his own delving in the widest community of scholarship.[15]

Barth's more formal University Seminars were conducted in a completely different setting. Huddled by the Rhine, sagging with age, the theological classroom facility leaned out toward the passing tugs and barges, just below the *Rheinbrücke*. There, clanging green trams, trucks and pedestrians surged across the bridge to Klein Basel with its medieval river-frontage, ultra-modern chemical factories, ancient convent and red-light district. I retain impressions from an interior of white woodwork, layered thick with centuries of glossy enamel paint, and airy windows opening onto the river traffic below. One could imagine the ghosts of Erasmus, Nietzsche and other Basel greats hovering nearby. On the other side, where the building protruded over the narrow *Gasse*, facing the Seminar was a strange establishment for cleaning pillows and goose-down bedding. It was fronted by a large-windowed chamber where millions of drying feathers were to be seen eternally swirling about in a cloud of hot air—like a warning metaphor for the danger of vacuous discussions across the way.

---

[15] Max Zellweger, tells us how Karl immersed himself in background sources for his writing on eighteenth and nineteenth century theologians, where, if anywhere, one might well expect him to have employed research assistants.

For his university seminars in this ancient setting, Barth had come to use a partially student-led format; but he always came primed to supply short framing statements and a wealth of information regarding the content, motivation, background and theological significance of the particular text or subject in question, and finally to share his own perspective. This, of course, was especially rich when the stated subject of the seminar corresponded to that of one of his own writings, such as our 1959 exploration of Anselm's *Proslogion,* the subject of the book Barth considered key among his own writings, *Fides quaerens intellectum.*[16]

At the beginning of the semester he would take time to ask each student where she or he had studied previously, which, of course, in Europe was tantamount to asking which theologians had most engaged each one. Answering at my first seminar, I unrolled my own spotty list: University of California at Los Angeles, University of Edinburgh, San Francisco Theological Seminary, University of Tübingen, and short stints at Bonn and the Sorbonne. I remember Barth's affable grin, "*Es gibt nichts was nicht gibt!*" (Nothing's too strange to be true)— an impression I suspect he may have retained in my regard.

---

[16] I.e, "Faith Seeking Rational Intelligence. This *Systematisches Seminar* was billed as "*Anselms Beweis der Existenz Gottes*" [Anselm's Demonstration (or proof) of the Existence of God].

To participate in Barth's classroom was for us some-times to feel as though we were participating in a great work in progress. There could be little doubt that whether consciously or not, his teaching style was reflective of his grace-centered chris-tology: relaxed and confident despite his rather amused acknowledgement of his own and all others' human fallibility. It was playfully adventuresome, patient of ignorance; yeasty with levity, salty with wit, and finally radiant with promise and joy.[17] As Robert Jenson put it, "since Barth's confidence in humanity was confidence in *Christ's* humanity and only thereupon in ours, it could be . . . relaxed, tolerant, self-critical, and disillu-sioned; i.e., humorous—all qualities most desperately needed by the church and most lacking in other theology."[18]

The shape of Barth's university seminars was indicative of the dialogic attitude he brought to his study. The room would be full with thirty or forty students wedged in on all sides of a table-top arrangement in the shape of a long-legged *pi*. The pro-fessor would place himself up front at the closed end flanked or faced by three or four from the group who had been assigned

---

[17] Accordingly, my public lecture at Wilson College, March 23 2010, was entitled, "*If God is for Real: Karl Barth's Life of Playful Humor and Radiant Joy.*"

[18] Robert W. Jenson "In Memoriam Karl Barth," Gettysburg: Lu-theran Theological Seminary: *Summer Bulletin*, 1969, p. 9ff. Jenson vividly describes an ambivalence he felt as a Lutheran confronting Barth's forth-right, direct exchange with students.

the highly pressurized task of representing the class for the day. These representatives would do their semester's best to epitomize and explain the meaning and intent of the day's reading and then pose their most probing questions to it (e.g., what would we ask the author if we had him here?) Primed by Barth's interchange with these specially prepared representatives, open questioning and discussion would follow. This all made for penetrating, challenging sessions.

It quickly became evident that Barth expected a scholar to suspend initial negative reactions or disbelief in order to hear out other thinkers empathetically. One must try standing on the other's own ground, seeing things from the other's particular viewpoint, and be ready to re-conceptualize, temporarily at least, in terms of the other's terminology. It was always a question of going as far as possible in seeking resonance with each new voice. In short, the Christian scholar should try to reflect the Lord's grace intellectually.[19]

For example, when Barth gave his seminar on Paul Tillich, who, though a longtime friend, had become notorious as a theological opponent, students came primed for bear and expecting the air to crackle with polemic fireworks. They were taken aback by how from Day One the Professor resisted all

---

[19] In contrast, Ted Gill describes how German students are often conditioned to "guilliotine" intellectual opponents.

27

their initial disagreements and objections: "Let's wait and see how far we can understand him—in his own terms and from his perspective." How can we grasp him *"in optimum-* (or at least *in meliorem-) partem."*[20] It was only in the last session or two of the entire semester that he relented to entertain negative assessments and reactions. It became clear that he was in the habit himself of giving the greatest respect to the differing perspective of any committed human mind. It was as if he expected a positive gift from every encounter and thanked God for lively opponents.

I began to appreciate how this was in fact a key to Barth's own stance in interacting with other thinkers in general. Here was the reason one can learn so much from and about the most diverse figures he discusses—even when he comes, finally, to disagree with some on basic principles. It shows how he managed to marshal such an astounding, sympathetic understanding, warmth and humor toward minds as contradictory as those of Schleiermacher, Feuerbach, Ritschl, Bultmann and Tillich, glad, finally, for each of them. I don't know whether I

---

[20] I.e., "in the best possible light, or at least a better one." See Barth's own statement of intent in his "Introductory Report" to Sandy McKelway's Dissertation on Tillich: p. 14. Barth's surprising openness to those at odds with his theology was visible in his full support of this doctoral dissertation on Tillich's systematic theology, which was endorsed finally by Tillich himself. See Alexander J. McKelway, *The Systematic Theology of Paul Tillich* (Richmond, VA: John Knox Press, 1964).

28

managed to match his habit of mind in my own later life as professor, but it certainly has been a lasting influence.

He even persuaded the Tübingen Professor, Joseph Ratzinger, who has since become Pope Benedict XVI, to participate as a kind of capstone in one of his last seminars (1966-67), which studied the recent Vatican Council. It was Barth's fervent hope that the revealed Word, better heard in both the Roman and Protestant branches of the Church, might draw them toward each other in response to their common Lord.[21]

DOCTOR ECCLESIAE—

A LIGHTHEARTED INTELLIGENCE

Although the university had become his milieu, the Church was clearly more important to Barth than the academic process. This was suggested by his relaxed attitude toward academic strictures. Part of the lore among American students was the story of how one of them was desperately stumped during his final *rigorosum* exam by a hairsplitting question from one of the assembled professors—a question demanding a straight yes or

---

[21] See further in Busch, *Karl Barth*, especially p. 485. Stuart McLean in his book, *Humanity in the Thought of Karl Barth*, notes that Barth's attitude here actually affected the Roman Church and that his "imprint on Vatican II is unmistakable, especially his insights regarding the authority of scripture, the doctrine of justification and the church as community." (Edinburgh, T & T Clark, 1981, p. 4.)

no answer—when he suddenly became aware that Karl Barth's finger was tracing the correct answer, visible to all, on the tabletop.

Barth tried to distance himself from academic idols, yet he remained a scholar's scholar in the continental mold. Students were to read as widely as possible in the original languages with infinite patience for derivations and critical distinctions. The almost waspish way he once pounced on a misspelled Latin term in Tillich's text startled me. Yet Barth always related to us as a supportive teacher, rather than a dogmatic critic.

Students of the Protestant Reformation know that Martin Luther could not have spearheaded that movement had he not found validation in his vocation as a *"doctor ecclesiae,"* an ordained *teacher of the Church.*[22] For he believed himself commissioned to wear his doctor's hat—scripture- and Spirit-led—with his title as *doctor in Biblia,* over against popes, councils and the vast weight of popular practice. It was in this spirit that Luther said he was ready to give the doctor's hat to anyone capable of rightly correlating law and gospel. There can be no doubt that Karl Barth felt the same singular calling; and it was no accident that his nearly ten-thousand-page major work was

---

[22] See Jaroslav Pelikan, *Luther the Expositor* . . . in Companion Volume to *Luther's Works,* St. Louis: Concordia, 1959, p. 46f.

offered as *"Church Dogmatik";* that is, as a quest for a foundational *teaching* in and for the Church. The theologian has no business being in the secular state university, unless that institution itself respects academic freedom for believers' minds to explore, expose and proclaim their faith.

The nature of Christian faith itself, then, evokes a mood and manner in Church teaching that are quite opposite to what one might at first glance suppose. Being for the Church does not mean to serve and reinforce an authoritarian or hierarchical institution that isolates and vaunts itself over the surrounding world. Barth was a Calvinist here, if anywhere. The Church is not a separate kingdom, not an escape capsule out of the stressful world. Neither is it an external tumor-growth on the periphery of society, nor a gigantic amoeba whose mission is to ingest ever more of those around into itself. The New Testament images still hold: Christians' intelligence is to be like *light* (a hope that permeates across any distance), like *yeast* (a joyful levity that with its interpenetrating mycosis uplifts the whole of life), and like *salt* (a witty humor, that savors and flavors everything). Since Christian teaching functions toward liberation, it must not impose itself apodictically or become dogmatic in spirit. It may take us by surprise, but Karl Barth did not think of himself as a dogmatic person.

Barth's own personal levity, wit and prodigality embodied his grasp of how the Church's "beautiful science" both explores and exposes its calling. Theology exists, not as an end in itself, but in and for God's entire beloved creation—for everybody. The renaissance doctor's beret, that we took away from Basel to wear instead of a gold-tasseled mortarboard, has always reminded me of what a special role it is, to be a *doctor ecclesiae*—the calling to be a teacher in and for a Church that is always flawed, always called to change, yet justified, (*simul iustus et peccator, semper reformandum*) as it exists not for itself, but to be a presence, claiming God's saving grace for his entire world.

Barth saw no place for the kind of anti-intellectualism that has taken hold in some romantic minds. Already in his early lectures on "The Christian Life," he had expressed his views here in no uncertain terms.[23] The μετάνοια that is a Christians' key response (misleadingly translated "repentance") is properly understood not so much as remorse as a *re-orientation of the mind* to grace: "Effect must be given in our thought to the knowledge—which puts our will [and so, our thankfully responding behavior] in motion." The holism that is our response begins in thought, which both sparks affect and motivates ac-

---

[23] See Engl. tr., p. 60f.

tion. Barth's concern for attentive, open reading included a concern that we, as far as possible, grasp texts in their original language with exegetical analysis of vocabulary as well as investigation of their historical background and impact. I recall again his response to my first admittedly one-sided Calvin criticism: "Herr Anderson, you are systematizing what is wrong with Calvin. Now go read *everything* he ever wrote."

THE TEACHER AS WRITER

We've seen how as teaching pastor, Barth did not want anyone to think of his published work as another *Summa Theologica;* for the theologian is at best a *homo viator,* a pilgrim. That is, theology should express someone who is *under way* and result in a creatively new proclamation of the gospel. Yet questions of sequence and order were continually on Barth's mind—not only of the irreversible order intrinsic to Christian faith (see Chapter 7), but the constant creative question, how best to introduce each theological theme and whether to defer dealing with it. One heard him musing, "now where should we bring this under?" And that remained more a question of theological dynamics than style.

In his later years Barth enjoyed the luxury of a close relation with the Zollikon Press in Zürich, so he could feel toward it much as a person might regard her own website today. Once when my own treatment of the philosophical background of Calvin's ethic had grown out of bounds, he remarked matter-of-factly, "You can simply cut it in two—publish both parts separately." I did not, but this apparently was Barth's own attitude toward publication. He did, however, have a sense for waiting until the current discussion was ripe, and he voiced concern, when he felt one of his students had published something prematurely.

In a sense Barth's greatest strengths became literary liabilities, especially for those steeped in the English essay tradition, where pithy, impressionistic brevity is valued for its own sake. His Germanic penchant for examining everything in great detail from all sides can overwhelm even the most positively inclined readers. The *Church Dogmatics* is so daunting that it is seldom simply read for the organized sweep of his thought, but is more often mined here and there as a rich lode for topical research. (Actually, such prospecting works pretty well, since with each new topic he tended to loop back to square one in revelation.) But a vast, multi-volume work once carried a much greater *pondus* in Europe by virtue of its exhaustive treatment than it could enjoy today, especially in the English-speaking world.

Once at a conference, I mentioned to Karl's son, Marcus Barth, a notable New Testament scholar in his own right, that his father's *Dogmatics* would have a greater readership if its wealth of topics were packaged as separately-titled short books, rather than being buried in the heavy tomes that are often fated to huddle unopened on dusty reference shelves. Perhaps some clever publisher will do just that, as Barth's lasting significance as a discussion partner is rediscovered by new generations.[24]

BARTH'S COUNTERPART AND ADJUTANT

Barth could never have created the *Church Dogmatics* unaided. His close associate, Charlotte von Kirschbaum, was usually at his side, and the partnership that existed between them was immediately apparent to any observer. Despite her tightly wound German hairdo, she exuded gentle warmth as soft as her rosy complexion and shared his obvious openness toward all comers. At Barth's lectures she would pull a manuscript copy from her briefcase and carefully note any audience-inspired changes for him to work into this next section of the unfolding *Church Dogmatics*.

In that pre-computer age, it was she who prepared all his manuscripts for publication; and, as I mentioned, she managed his correspondence and schedule, zealously guarding his time.

---

[24] T & T Clark, in their most recently advertised edition of the *Church Dogmatics* (which I have not yet seen), apparently are taking steps in this direction.

But she had gradually become a theologian in her own right as well and, as his constant research assistant and discussion partner, was a virtual alter ego. Her close participation in all his work had led to a living arrangement whereby she was always on call, just down the hall.

So she was much more than a stenographer-secretary and should be given much fuller credit than a woman in her position was granted at the time.[25] It is doubtful that *The Church Dogmatics* could have come into being without this woman's full-time collaboration. Barth confessed as much (a bit late perhaps, and to his already-engaged readers) in his foreword to the later volumes.[26] That the publications of the day did not place her name where it might appropriately have appeared, as collaborating co-author, is a historical and cultural flaw that should be corrected at least in our minds.

The creative collaboration between these two impressed me greatly. As an American, I had never seen anything quite like the scholarly coexistence it signaled, but it seems to have been unique on the Swiss scene, as well. These intellectual partners' entire lives were poured out into a single great work of

---

[25] For her own view of women's potential role in theology see *The Question of Woman: The Collected Writings of Charlotte von Kirschbaum*, tr. John Shepherd (Grand Rapids: Eerdmans, 1996).

[26] See CD III/3: xiif. (a volume in which Barth deals with the relationship of man and woman (S. 344ff. and IV/4: viii).

scholarship. Here was an example of a possible symbiotic relationship of man and woman—where she functioned as a willing intellectual partner. This, of course, was long before the sharp criticism such an arrangement would evoke from some in the women's movement. Charlotte von Kirschbaum certainly didn't feel she was living "in the shadow" of Karl Barth.[27] For her, I think, it was more that she discovered her calling to service, and found self-fulfillment working *in the light* of his undeniable creativity.[28] The theological task to which they felt called was greater than both of them. And, as said, their whole lives were poured out and absorbed into it.

Fraülein von Kirschbaum's position cannot be fully appreciated, however, without reference to how a major general's importance is shared by his staff officers, especially by the chosen personal adjutant, without whom he could scarcely function. The adjutant, who is always at the general's right hand, following him from place to place, has both high rank and status by virtue of this special role. This officer is in charge of official correspondence and personnel records, prepares orders, and often speaks for the general. Such a close collaboration is

---

[27] See Renate Köbler's *In the Shadow of Karl Barth: Charlotte von Kirschbaum* (Louisville: Westminster/John Knox Press, 1989).

[28] Though we can only be grateful for the light shed by Renate Köbler's little book, Charlotte von Kirschbaum herself, I suspect, would have felt misinterpreted and probably belittled by its trade-oriented title.

viewed as anything but abject servitude, but is a high-ranking officer's respected role.[29]

Has anyone pointed out the inner, psychological significance of the fact that Charlotte von Kirschbaum actually was the daughter of an important German major general and had grown up taking for granted the practical need and honor associated with such an adjutant's work?[30]

A German student once told me that his own life would be fulfilled if he could only manage to add a single sentence or two to the world's theological literature. Charlotte, in her role as Barth's adjutant (or to use her favored expression—"his counterpart")[31] was contributing in a major way to Christian thought and theological literature. While doing so, she became an early harbinger of the women's movement and made explicit contributions to that movement with writings and lectures of her own. In a real sense their collaboration was as important to her as it was to him; for as a woman she *manned* the role of adjutant, functioned as an equal, and found sufficient courage to ignore

---

[29] It is significant that Barth's son-in-law, Max Zellweger, who knew them as well as anyone, can refer to Charlotte von Kirschbaum as Barth's "co-worker," and not just as secretary or assistant. *My Father-In-Law* (Allison Park, PA: Pickwick, 1986).

[30] Charlotte was daughter of a Baroness, von Bruck, and Major General, Maximilian von Kirschbaum, who was killed in action while she was in her teens (1916).

[31] Renate Köbler, *op. cit.* See e.g., p.110.

the voices of petty gossip that tattled on about the closeness of their relationship.

Karl Barth cited her work as a theologian in her own right when the subject of "true woman's" status and role came up in the *Church Dogmatics*.[32] Again, it needs to be stressed that in pre-computer days, before the advent of desktop editing, this woman's assistance was providential. Karl Barth could not have accomplished his work without von Kirschbaum's full collaboration.

Beyond question, there was a great bond of love between these two—you sensed it in their conversation and the very way she said his name. But to observe this in no way minimizes the prior covenant of love that bound Karl and his matronly wife, Nelly, the erstwhile violinist and mother of five, who would quietly slip into the background when the scholars were engaged with professional guests.

Obviously, we cannot penetrate their unusual household and it is no one's business to try, but I never had occasion to doubt that the loving respect among *all* these persons was so great that they structured mature and appropriate boundaries between themselves that honored the familial bond Karl and Nelly shared with each other. The serious literary work that the

---

[32] E.g., See KD III/4, S. 192f., references von Kirschbaum's book, *Die wirkliche Frau.*

three of them were bringing to life was far too important for them to pay much attention to those Basel gossips who, we hear, were scandalized at their close household arrangement. Bourgeois culture had no scruple against live-in servants, such as housemaids, governesses, cooks, or nurses, where "inferiors" were concerned. But the gossip in the air was probably occasioned not so much by the proximity of a female secretary, as by the fact that Charlotte acted as Karl's intellectual counterpart and peer.

THE BASEL UNIVERSITY CONTEXT:
CONTRASTS AND TENSIONS

Before we leave our experience of Barth's immediate academic context, perhaps we should add something about the Swiss University itself. Located at the corner of a small park near an ancient city gate, the S*palentor,* the main university building was, built four-square in the hard-edged functional modern style of the late 1930s. The classrooms and lecture halls, bright, but barren with their chalkboards always freshly washed and shining—were spread along marble corridors, softened only a bit by planters with bright coleus. These thrived in the light of an outer hallway's bank of windows that confronted you, just across the street, with a concrete and glass beehive teeming with Basel commerce.

The Basel classroom was a rather formal affair. Students would greet the professor's on-the-dot arrival by rapping their knuckles on the desk. The same sign was used to cheer or chide the professor underway. (This was tame compared to the crescendo of invisible foot-stamping which had startled me at first in Scotland.)

A stark simplicity marked the University's organization. There was an Office of the *Pedell,* a kind of glorified registrar, who handled the organizational nuts and bolts and records of the larger University and a business office, the *Quästor*; and there was, of course, an ancient and growing library. But the University's powers were evidently distributed among the diverse faculties which operated with great autonomy, each with its own *Dekan* (dean), chosen on a rotating basis from among its ranks. Individual scholars treasured their academic freedom, but the Basel City Council retained a voice in naming them, and this gave that process a political edge that made it susceptible to the sort of reactionary changes of mood that many felt occasioned the call of a much more sociologically oriented professor as Karl Barth's successor.

Not all American theology students at Basel were there to study with Barth. Sam Calian (who later became president of Pittsburgh Seminary), for example, was in Eastern Orthodox studies; and Lutheran scholar, Joe Burgess was doing New Testament research while his future wife, Faith, was pursuing Church History. One sensed a certain defensiveness in some students in reaction to Barth's disproportionate prominence.

Certain professors, too, demonstrated a need to compete with him in a way that both students and colleagues found embarrassing. When an extended illness was going to prevent Barth himself from administering my final *rigorosum* exam, Max Geiger, the church historian, sought me out with great concern, to explain that the rest of the faculty found themselves obliged to ask the other professor in systematic theology to officiate. Geiger obviously feared that this colleague's objectivity would be impaired; for his open rivalry with Barth was of scandalous proportions. This did make difficulties for me, since the professor in question insisted that I jump through some hoops of his own design. But it worked out; and when he eventually voted to pass me with high marks, an almost audible sigh of relief ran through the Faculty.

Of course the entire system contrasted with most of the American colleges we knew. Since the European university did no coddling, choice of courses and readings was left to your own responsibility. You verified your participation as a student with a little brochure, your *Studienbuch*, which the professor signed at the semester's outset and end to attest to your attendance. Beyond that, all the regular lectures and seminars were assumed to be on the cutting edge of their fields—a privilege for you, as graduate students to attend of your own volition. Evaluation of your accomplishment was deferred until your degree exam. For committed, self-directed persons such freedom meant a wealth of opportunity, and most Americans welcomed the contrast to their earlier schooling as a refreshing intellectual stimulus.

Everything progressed at your own pace. To be sure, there was enough slack to hang yourself academically should motivation flag. But the challenge was life-absorbing and bracing. You faced up to your own weaknesses, sought help and reinforcement wherever you could find them, and tried to avoid the pitfalls. Those of us who were not married would eye with a certain envy the marital support of those who were. But we scarcely appreciated, I fear, the kind of sacrifices they and their families were making to be there.

When your dissertation was finally completed and approved, you scheduled your oral *rigorosum,* the degree examination, to be administered by a committee including professors from adjacent fields. Utter simplicity with a pinch of Old World pomp reigned at your completion of that ordeal . . . You were no sooner finished, than the evaluating Committee huddled in the same room, while you waited, breathless, outside. Then the *Pedell* of the University appeared as if by magic, decked out in

43

a cutaway and huge Napoleonic hat, and bearing the heavy silver staff of the University. As a successful candidate you were instructed to place your right hand on the head of the staff and answer to the vows put in Latin, "S*pondeo, Spondeo*," pledging to uphold the ancient standards and honor of the University." And that was it.

Your five or six years were complete. You emerged quite dizzy from the examination room, to be greeted in the open hallway by the hurrahs of a small cluster of friends (and, for some, the intense relief and jubilant embrace of spouse and children)—a newly minted *Doctor, magna cum laude.*

Chapter 2

The Mind of Faith
Barth's Quest for Rational Intelligibility

THE GERMAN TRAGEDY—A NATURAL MIND

The sheer mass of Karl Barth's outpouring is almost inconceivable by any standard. His *Church Dogmatics* runs to fourteen large tomes and his other publications number in the hundreds, so his collected works will comprise close to fifty volumes. With that in mind, we must know that anything we might venture to say in summary of such a comprehensive mind's vast enterprise is apt to become so limited and one-sided as to be misleading. Indeed, when I began my studies, much of our writing about Barth had been just that: caricature to the point of distortion. For from the first, Americans had talked much more about Barth than they had actually plunged into his mass of writings. Often he was known only in terms of his one-sided early expositions of Romans (1919 and 1922). In seminary

45

during the 1950s we frequently heard Barth's name, but I don't recall that his books were ever much assigned. Writing at the time of Barth's 70th birthday, Norman F. Langford observed that Barth was "a theologian who in a curious way" was "both famous and little known" in America—"even in professional circles more talked about than read."[1] The man himself used to quip that the angels would greet little old Karl Barth with laughter when he would come trundling into heaven someday pushing a cart piled high with his heavy tomes. In those clarified surroundings all his writings would tumble out on the floor as so much waste paper.

What on earth could have motivated this affable, fun-loving man to submit himself so compulsively to such an enormous disciplined labor?

It should not be forgotten that Barth's lifework was driven by the specter of the horrors that he had seen unleashed in Germany, first under Kaiser Wilhelm in World War I and then through the Nazi movement. A toxic fungus had grown in the shadows of a Nature-based folk religion and insinuated itself into the German Church. His compulsion to refurbish Church teaching flowed out of his consternation at the flaccidity of the humanistic liberalism in which he and his generation's theolo-

---

[1] *Presbyterian Life*, Dec 8, 1956.

gians had been steeped. For liberal theology had proved unable to stem the tide of Germany's militaristic folk worship even in the minds of this theology's greatest proponents among his early teachers.

Those who knew Barth became increasingly aware of an inner compulsion here. His labor of many years on a vast, comprehensive discourse for the churches was fueled by his dismay at the theological sponginess that had been implicated in Christians' failure to present a clear front against the racist nationalism of Nazi Germany.[2] It is broadly recognized that the entire *Church Dogmatics* became in fact a protracted effort to free Church teaching from the toils of natural theology.[3] Close observation of the German Church tragedy was behind this virtual obsession. He had become acutely aware of how the Nazis' appeal to folk-feeling and nationalistic pride was at root a form of natural theology.[4] "A worse disturbance to theological reconstruction can hardly be imagined [than that parading as the total authority of natural reason] the basis and justification of which

---

[2] CD II/1, p.172-178 (English translation).

[3] In the various natural theologies, ordinary experiences are misconstrued to betoken God or ultimate values. See E. Busch, *The Great Passion*, p. 67ff. for a most cogent summary of Barth's concern here.

[4] Compare E. Busch, *The Great Passion*, p. 32f. See also Stanley Hauerwas, *Against the Nations*, p. 65 *et passim*.

47

are supposed to have been discovered in the idea of race."[5]

Barth felt similar roots could be discerned behind the lure to power, the historicism and militarism idolized in Marxist ideology, as well as behind the postwar "way-of-life" materialism embraced by many in the West. When an American student asked whether he saw natural theology as a continuing threat to the present-day Church, Barth answered:

> The world is full of natural theology. In Marxist Communism there's a great amount of natural theology. It has a great deal of theology of history (and man is capable of interpreting history like that—with a dogma of evolution).

> There's an American natural theology: nice principles that are generally admitted; e.g., freedom through right and the collaboration of everyone—freedom to progress. (And perhaps that does mean progress through liberty and has a *certain* relation to Jesus Christ.) But does Jesus Christ become simply a great hero for progress and freedom in the American Church? (In American metaphysics there is a realm for the "reli-

---

[5] CD I/2, p. 663 and context.

gious life," [and "spirituality,"]*[6] etc.) Is the Declaration of Independence a religious doctrine? (It was rationalism in an "Age of Enlightenment" which was an *age of natural theology*.)

The Germans—were a terrific [case in point]. My fight began in the 1930s with the fight against Hitler, because he was supported in many areas by Christians in *a cult of natural theology*: "Blood, land and country!" Soon we had it—now, as a new revelation from God, after the bad times following the First World War. So it began as a very pious attitude that impressed even foreigners. There was mysticism: with Hitler's picture and flag on the altar in certain churches. That national flag [was displayed in] many of the churches. [You see it in America too.] A flag in the church points to a natural theology. Also in Roman Catholic teaching, a natural theology separates God as Redeemer from God as Creator.

The mercy of God is very strong and

---

[6] *Note, square brackets indicate where my written notes have been epitomized or Barth's meaning filled in from memory. The other frequent parentheses are quoted as his own.

deep; and [it reaches even] into the realms of natural theology—even into Hitler's Germany and Marxist Russia. But we're not fighting against windmills, but a real threat to Church and humanity. Look what happens when men are following such other goals. It begins with great hopes, ideas and illusions of all kinds, and ends with shooting.

The Church must have its own line and not be tying itself up to all sorts of natural theology. The dangers are great; but God is greater than the dangers everywhere.[7]

Barth, then, was motivated by his observation that forms of natural theology are implicated at the roots of virtually all warfare, as the ambiguities of human experience allow people to commit themselves to conflicting ideologies, values and ways of life. We often heard him restate his observation that any form of natural theology will inevitably thrust its way toward monopoly and idolatry. He had seen all too clearly how even modest concessions to such "natural" speculation would open a Pandora's box and let various common assumptions

---

[7] Karl Barth in his English Colloquium, Jan. 27, 1959.

worm their way toward dominance over faith. Theology must struggle to disentangle itself from every such tacit accommodation and cling to its ethical commitment to all mankind, as that is engendered by Christ's revelation of a grace that transcends all ordinary experience.

So Barth's life story unfolded as the drama of an intellectual who felt called to throw himself into the breach: his well-known reaction against his liberal teachers' support of the Kaiser's militarism, his later refusal to begin his classes in Bonn with the "*Heil Hitler*" salute, his expulsion from his professorate for refusing to take an unqualified oath to the *Führer*, his key authorship of the Barmen Declaration to bolster the Confessing Church,[8] his military service in defense of Swiss free-

---

[8] At the Barmen meeting of Protestant leaders who refused allegiance to the Nazis' puppet *Deutsche Christen Kirche* at the end of May 1934, Barth almost single-handedly drafted the confessional statement grounding their opposition to nature-based totalitarianism, nationalism and racism. This "Theological Declaration of Barmen" has since been adopted as one of the confessional standards of the Presbyterian Church (U. S. A.). But it has been widely observed (most notably by Dietrich Bonhoeffer) that Barmen, shares guilt with the entire leadership of the day in failing to counter anti-Semitism specifically or strongly enough to prevent the natural theological folk-belief from bludgeoning its way to monopoly and giving rise to the nationwide pogrom that exploded upon Germany a few years later in the brutal *Kristallnacht* of 1938. See Gary Dorrien's balanced assessment here. (*The Barthian Revolt in Modern Theology*, p. 143f.). Also Eric Metaxas, *Bonhoeffer: Pastor, Martyr, Prophet, Spy* . . . (Nashville *et al*: Thomas Nelson 2010.) pp.187, 220ff.

The Barth we knew certainly expressed remorse here. But his mature expressions of solidarity with modern Jewry became far more than a

51

dom, and his unswerving lifelong labor to recall the Church to
its own dogmatic foundations—even his warning against a

---

matter of a tardy opposition to chauvinism and to the injustice of racial intolerance per se. I know of no theologian who made more of the fact that we, as Christians, are ourselves in actuality adoptive Jews—one-sided in our emphasis, perhaps, and in that sense heretical Jews—but Jews nevertheless, members of God's one covenant. He felt that if the churches of Germany had rightly internalized and expressed that fact, history would have been different. [Compare E. Busch, *The Great Passion*, p. 96ff.] This was far more than recognition of our Christian origins; for it was Barth's conviction that the Jewish community continues to be an authentic prophetic witness with vital, providential significance as God's chosen people. See further Eberhard Busch, *Unter dem Bogen des einen Bundes: Karl Barth und die Juden 1933-1945* (Neukirchen-Vluyn: Neukirchener, 1996).

It should be noted, that while the Barmen Declaration didn't mention the oppression of Jews by name, it didn't directly name any of the other flagrant civil rights abuses of the Nazi regime either. Rather, despite the threat of reprisal, it dared to go for the jugular vein of the authority behind them all. No governments or authorities above God. No usurpation of the Church as a co-opted wing of government. This testified to the idolatry of natural-theological folk-chauvinism and settled on the clearest point of confessional concord that might bring the various evangelical churches together (despite their divergence on internal issues) and stiffen their wobbling resistance to Hitler's puppet *Deutsche Christen Kirche*.

That Barth intended Barmen as an audacious alarm bell against the burgeoning anti-Semitism is manifest in the first four issues of *Theologische Existenz Heute!* (1933). In the first, speaking church-politically, he sounds "an unqualified and unreserved 'No' to the spirit and language of this teaching." Anyone holding it is "either a seducer [*ver-führer*] or seduced. . . . The Community of those belonging to the Church is not to be determined through blood and not through race, but through the Holy Spirit and through baptism. When the Evangelical Church shuts out Jewish Christians or treats them as second-class Christians, it has ceased to be a Christian Church" (*Heft* I, SS. 23-25). Barth is clear that the notorious Aryan Paragraph [which had excluded non-Aryans and their spouses from Church employ] and the antisemetic trashing of the Old Testament were not the Confessing Church's *only* objections here, for the underlying evil was an alien "gnosis" which had been masquerading in Christian garb and usurping Christ's church (*Heft 4, Lutherfeier 1933*, S. 20f.).

52

return to the "flesh-pots" of Western consumerism—all were part of his defense against Nature-based ideologies and values. And all were in courageous disregard for how powerfully widespread speculations may have lodged themselves in the popular mind or been hallowed in a national consciousness or way of life.[9]

THE ANSELMIC PERSPECTIVE:

FIDES QUAERENS INTELLECTUM

Both the basis for any knowledge of God and an appropriate stance for our sound meditation upon it had been clarified by a famous scholastic theologian nearly a thousand years ago. Barth came upon this preface to Christian rationality in the book called "Prologue" [*Proslogion*] by the twelfth century thinker, Anselm of Canterbury,[10] who is, perhaps, better known for his classic, *Cur Deus Homo* [*Why God Became Man*]. Barth often

---

[9] It may well be that Brunner's sanguine regard for natural orders (ostensibly based upon an innate human sense of justice [*iustitia originalis*]) as supplemental source for theology and ethics—a view that Reinhold Niebuhr also championed against Barth—reflected the fact that neither had shared Barth's experience. In Nazi Germany he had seen firsthand, how generally acclaimed natural values will inevitably shoulder their way to idolatrous monopoly. (Compare, Niebuhr, *The Nature and Destiny of Man,* Vol. 2, p. 64.)

[10] Whether Anselm had understood himself in the way Barth took him here has been questioned. Even Karl's own philosophy-professor-brother, Heinrich, was not so sure the twelfth century thinker would have agreed. At any rate, Karl Barth was struck by insights here that grounded his own faith's search for intelligence.

referred to his own small 1931 book on Anselm, *Fides quaerens intellectum*, as the most seminal among his own writings and, therefore, the most important.[11] For this book had blazed the trail for his own theological endeavor. In a semester-long 1959 seminar (shortly after a new edition of this work had appeared), he explored Anselm's thought with us as the background for his own theological epistemology.

Barth's *Fides quaerens intellectum* is relentlessly Germanic in style, written with a densely concentrated academic earnestness. So, although the insights he garnered in writing were cardinal for him, this book has yet to receive the wider audience it deserves. Its message awaits someone to present it in a popularized form. This is not the place for that, but this slender volume did give us conceptual keys to Barth's entire undertaking.

It might strike us as arcane that Barth would trace his theological stance to taproots in the teaching of a twelfth century Scholastic; but he repeatedly referred to Anselm of Canterbury's *Proslogion* in this way.[12] For he regarded exploration

---

[11] *Fides quaerens intellectum: Anselms Beweis der Existenz Gottes im Zusammenhang seines theologischen Programms* (2nd ed., Zollikon: Evangelischer Verlag, 1958) [English translation: *Anselm: Fides quaerens intellectum* (Richmond, VA:, John Knox Press, 1960)].

[12] To those of us participating in Barth's Anselm seminar it was clear that this was his feeling. See further, KD II/1, S. 101, for how Barth

here to have been the source of insights that took on the utmost importance, not only in clarifying his theological/philosophical foundations, but in suggesting the attitude and mode for the rest of his work—an approach native to Christian faith itself.

How did this medieval work become his theological Magna Charta? A synopsis of Barth's comments from an English Colloquium in early December 1960 shows the way he would refer to his Anselm exploration as opening the door to a theological pathway that could accommodate his own growing christocentric apperception without constricting it to a presumptuous, pre-set "scientific method." A student mentioned that we had heard this Anselm book represented an important turning in Barth's own development, when he not only had been freed from Existentialism, but also felt himself spurred toward a new christological concentration;[13] so the student wanted to know how taking Anselm as a noetic basis had opened the door for him. In response, Barth told how he had discovered a *faith-intrinsic approach* or *stance* here.

---

borrowed his epistemology from what he saw to be Anselm's basis for doing theology.

[13] von Balthasar, for example, had said that this was basic to the substantial change, visible in CD II/2, as a move from dialectic to analogy. Despite its christocentric ground and focus, the entire structure of the *Church Dogmatics* maintains a wider, trinitarian perspective. Although the Church's witness to Jesus Christ had become normative for Barth, he stoutly resisted the tag of *christomonism* that some, such as Heinrich Vogel, thought to pin on him [i.e. reductionistic concentration on Christ].

It was only opening *the way* to Christological concentration. (Anselm was not that.) What impressed me there was the *theological* concentration: a going from the heights to depths and not the other way around. And I learned that theology must be done so.

In the context of Anselm's *Cur Deus Homo*, you "prove"*[14] the context of christology without beginning with Christ, but within the whole [faith] tradition—where certain elements are directed in a way which cannot be overlooked as incarnation. If we understand these elements, we understand *how* incarnation was necessary. This is the same as his so-called "proof"* of God's existence [in his *Proslogion*]. His method is the *method of Faith*. It "proves"* elements out of the biblical or ecclesiastical content.

I had but to apply Anselmian method to my own theology, which had been [leaning] more toward christological concentration. [So

---

[14] *Anselm's Latin term here is *"demonstrare,"* which, as Barth was at pains to stress, connoted "to show forth" or "make visible and clear"—not to demonstrate a *proof,* as it has been almost universally misunderstood in the modern Q.E.D. sense.

the development was] more in methodology, rather than in content. In the place of Anselm's Catholic tradition as basis, put in place Christ etc. Move [out] from faith alone in *analogia fidei*. If we speak of faith, we implicitly speak of Christ, and vice versa. This is the germ of christology (in speaking of faith).[15]

Faith in itself has the quality of a miraculous gift. For, although this condition of the mind may be well-*occasioned* by objectively claimed, unique events, it is assimilated into our minds without a shred of proof. Therefore, "the purpose of theology can not be to lead people to faith or to free faith from doubt."[16] It would seem that only the inner nudge of God's own Spirit can draw new faith out of the objective hopes we find before us.[17] Our proclamation of his gospel may be the occasion for others' faith, but never a means to lever them into it.

The uniquely hopeful events that trigger faith response purport to come from outside the box of normal human experience. Nevertheless, the believing mind never ceases to be a rational entity that must operate with the tools of language and

---

[15] English Colloquium, Dec. 5, 1960.

[16] *Fides quaerens intellectum*, S. 16.

[17] The Reformers termed this believed source for rational conviction "the inner testimony of the Holy Spirit." See e.g., Calvin's *Institutes* I/vii, § 4&5 on "*le témoignage interior du Saint Esprit.*"

logic—tools which have been formed and funded by ordinary experience. Of necessity, therefore, faith must seek its own distinct mind—an expanded rationality that answers to the new, otherwise unknown parameters of what has been revealed. Faith must seek its *own* intelligence.

FAITH SEEKING ITS OWN MIND—
GREATER THAN WE CAN THINK

How do you pursue a fully rational, scholarly study into the contents of faith without giving human philosophy or gnostic speculations from general experience a separate footing alongside Christ's revelation (as Aquinas and the pre-Reformation Church had become all too prone to do)? If, as Anselm saw so clearly, God can be truly known only by God, then some sort of analogy is necessary if we are to have any perception of him.[18] How do we avoid presumptively projecting vivid self-experience? The greatest and best that we can muster or conceive of as the greatest similitude [or perhaps, *mutatis mutandis,* as the greatest spiritual *contrast* to ourselves], as far as we actually know, may be totally irrelevant or alien to the divine reality. "Insofar as *we* are the subject of our words and thoughts, they [quite possibly] may not bear any similarity to God."

---

[18] See KD II/1, S. 202-5 [CD II/1, p. 181-3].

Anselm saw clearly that when we speak of God, we should always be fully aware that we are referring to the One, *greater than which* (or *better than which*) we cannot think. Our prior categorical notions of the spiritual, the pious, the great, and the good, are irrelevant here and can only lead astray and become idols. Given all the evils and ambiguities of human experience, the myriad of gnostic speculations that reflect them become a contradictory hodgepodge and eventually cancel each other out.

Barth summarized it for us this way:

We are never free here simply to choose one entity from a series. The one holy God can not be known as one instance from a series. For this knowledge is bound to its object in a peculiar way.

1) This, his *self-revelation*, distinguishes it from unreal and false gods. His self-revelation is the presupposition and basis of any knowledge here—rendered distinct [from all else] through his own self-restraint. So we never can come to it as an act of our own autonomous decision. [Our knowledge of God] must come from God's own Action.

2) God in Revelation remains Object, be-

fore man as subject. The distinction between knower and Known is to be kept distinct.

3) Man's knowledge of God is knowledge in and of faith. Faith confirms that knowledge of God is bound to God, as Object, through his Word. (This is not knowledge in a narrow intellectualistic sense, but a special knowledge, fundamentally different from all other forms. It is *mediated knowledge.*)[19]

The bewildering medieval jumble of accretions, that became so scandalous to the Reformers, had entered the Church through a speculative process whereby people had drawn their own natural-seeming analogies for God (or presumably contrasting silhouettes) from Nature or from their own natural feelings. Should one not expect to find the Creator's fingerprints there in analogy to our ordinary experience in an *analogia entis*?[20]

---

[19] English Colloquium, Nov. 25, 1958, discussing KD II/1, §25.

[20] For *analogia entis* as a problem [i.e., thinking theologically in analogy to the way we find things around us to be], see CD II/1, pp. 79-84. Vatican I claimed the possibility of knowing God from created reality in general, as well as from his special revelation (Session III, Cap. 2 Canon I: DS 3004, 3026). Colm O'Grady gives cogent treatment to this issue from a liberal Roman Catholic perspective: See especially p. 27f. in *A Survey of the Theology of Karl Barth* (New York: Corpus, 1968).

What would be slighted there, of course, would be scripture's insistence on *holiness*; i.e., how a gracious God may, in fact, take meticulous care to remain *separate* in order to preserve communal living room for his creatures and to avoid turning them into abject puppets or forcing himself upon them. (In the freedom of his power, he need not impatiently dominate their minds, as mysticism would have it, nor revoke their separateness, as every form of natural theology would imply.) You could never know you wanted or needed God had he not first veiled his powerful self from you, but instead, had made himself part of the furniture of your world, as an inevitable, tyrannical force.

In biblical tradition, then, the first provision of an unfathomably gracious Power's concern for relationship has shown itself to be his scrupulously guarded absence—the unrelieved separateness, described as holiness. It needs to be appreciated as a first act of grace that ordinary experience has been left intrinsically ambiguous and prone to contradictory interpretations, so that where any ultimate Truth is concerned, God is veiled from mortals by the great Unknowns and does not lord it over them in some compelling way.[21]

---

[21] Reflect on Mark 9:33-37; 10:42-45 in this light: "He who would be great must be servant of all." God's Messiah, ready to give his life "for the many," would rather die than lord it over them as the pagans' authorities

61

In fact, temporal powers are allowed such prominence (and death such an appearance of finality) in ordinary experience that Nature-based beliefs always tend to claim ascendancy over other truth claims. Like a refrain came Barth's repeated warning: If you admit any self-evident appearing natural quality alongside Christ's revelation of grace, it will inevitably push toward *monopoly*. The deathly powers of this world will appear to overwhelm and bulldoze aside the gentler claims of grace. Or, equally self-alienating, we will seek escape by indulging in some gnostic speculation (which most often has meant downgrading and despising the whole physical side of God's good creation in favor of a vaunted "spirituality").

Anselm simply clarified what Christians can mean when they utter the word, God. The key idea runs roughly this way: since God is not part of ordinary experience, you cannot appeal to any of your common notions of greatness or goodness or wisdom or whatever—not when you speak about the one who is the subject of our faith.[22] So Anselm would insist, when I, as a Christian, speak of God, I am talking about belief in one who is and will remain in fact *greater than I can think.*" My experi-

---

do. God's intent here is clearly suggested in that his Messiah lets himself be crucified.

[22] This insight, of course, has a prophetic and apostolic basis. "My thoughts are not your thoughts, neither are my ways your ways, says the Lord (Is. 5:8f.). They are "inscrutable" (Rom. 11:33f.).

ence-based ideas and images simply do not contain him in any sense. Neither do analogies from my own inner being apply where God-talk is concerned. Our concepts can in no sense delimit the holy God, for the Creator is greater than anything we can think to conceive of him. (The word *concept* means container; and his Truth would burst our limited concepts every time.)

Anselm sharpens this definition of what Christian believers mean in speaking of God by setting up an illustrative dialogue with a stubborn opponent, one Gaunilo, who argues on the basis of his noble-sounding gross misunderstanding: "God corresponds to the **greatest *I can think***."

"No, no," Anselm would counter. "We cannot predefine here. God is not merely *the greatest*. He is everlastingly **greater than**. I cannot presume a correspondence."

According to Barth, Anselm used the word *demonstrare* here in the Latin sense of "to show forth" what faith means in speaking of God. It is a common anachronism wrongly to suppose that as a Scholastic, he thought thereby to "prove" ontologically the actual existence of God in the modern scientific sense (as if to contain him in my limited concept of existence and transmute faith into *my highest* notion of inescapably compelling knowledge). Nothing could be further from Anselm's understanding. A primary meaning of the incarnation, from crib

63

to cross and beyond, is that God, whose love is greater than any we can imagine, will *not* compel us.

If I am to speak meaningfully about God, then, I am limited to what (if anything) he has made knowable and suggested of himself in human terms. Here my putative highest or best and most compelling ideas can't lay claim to ultimate truth. In fact, they are almost sure to fall short, flounder and mislead where God is concerned.

From this grounding a stance and way for theological thinking follows; and that is what Barth took away from Anselm:[23] (1) You need not, indeed must not, try to prove what we should mean or are invited to believe about the living "God" on the basis of ordinary outer experience or experiment. And by the same token, (2) you cannot, indeed must not, argue either for or against what he may be, based on your inner feelings or common sense. The holy God is not obliged to conform himself—indeed, pointedly avoids conforming himself—either to our outer empirical scientific proof, or to those inner feelings, imaginings or mystical events that we sometimes puff up as religious surrogates. Where God is concerned there can be no

---

[23] It has been tempting to speak simply of "Barth's theological *method*" here. But that is really a bit presumptive and not true to his intent. For he is stressing that since our thought *follows* our theological subject, the sovereign, living Word, we are never in a position to presuppose or harden our own conceptual or *methodological* prolegomena.

analogia entis, no reliable analogy from our experience or be-ing—whether from ordinary world experience, from common religious experience or from our innermost human feelings, be they ever-so "spiritual."

This is not to say that God may not freely comprehend any of these things or use them in imponderable ways that inspire our reflection and gratitude at each turning. But being greater than them all, he is not delimited by them or even reliably indicated by the sentiments they evoke (as Schleiermacher or Paul Tillich would have it).

Christ-centered, our God-given intelligence should seek the coherent web of meaning implicit in the various aspects of revelation, where we have been led to believe God gives himself to be known in human terms.[24] But it would be foolhardy impertinence to pretend that container concepts or categories of our own, which we've gathered far and wide in speculating about our broader experience, even begin to comprehend God. The same goes for our own prior ideas about spirituality or how *non-human* we have presumed any god must be. It also goes for

---

[24] "It is God's innermost being that he makes evident in Jesus Christ. God, the Father, is Father to Jesus Christ. And God the Holy Spirit is the Spirit of Jesus Christ. So there can be no question about God's existence that would not be to be answered through his self-determination in his word and work, no confession of faith that must not mean only him—first and last." *Die Christliche Lehre nach dem Heidelberger Katechismus* (Munich: Chr. Kaiser *Verlag*) S. 51.

our notions of being itself, of goodness, fairness and justice, or our common experience of love, purity or other values. To found or fund our theological reflections with any of these things, even for well-intentioned apologetic or polemic purposes, misses the mark and slides us toward the idolatrous.

In more technical terms, we must observe that Barth claimed no hermeneutic or prior principle of interpretation to muffle our surprise when we, in the humility of true discovery, find ourselves overtaken by the biblical text. For its subject rules with humanity in contrast to all our experience of indifferent forces in nature and with warmth in contrast to cool abstractions from common experience. So with simple scientific objectivity one may be liberated from any presuppositions about God and man, however "self-evident" they may seem—even those presuppositions that would *necessitate* God to subject himself to the laws of his own creation. In all humility before this object, who we believe to be the subject of our very existence, all presuppositions may slough away.

This does not mean Barth's God-thought is anti-rational or dismissive of human intelligence. Quite the opposite turns out to be true. It does, however, orient our thoughts as to where we may begin and warn where we *may not base* thought about God or the other great unknowns. As Barth had become increasingly aware, the negative here, against speculative analogies, was to be understood only as the obverse side of a *positive* revelation. For, as it turns out, what you actually find yourself given in your relationship to Christ is far more surprising, delightful and rationally coherent than all your prior superlatives.

For as our theological Subject unfolds, it is freer, more personal, promising, hopeful and beautiful[25] by far than you ever could have deduced from your ordinary death-bound experience or even could have dared to dream up in your boldest speculations. Where one must say "no," it is in defense of a massively greater and more joyful "yes," affirming the totality of human life and culture, as one finds it stoutly embraced by grace. So any negative is to be sounded only in defense of this resounding positive.

FAITH HAS ITS REASON:
THE HUMANITY OF GOD IN CHRIST

Attuned to the Reformers' recovery of New Testament bases and apostolic witnesses to the living Word, the later Barth's increasingly explicit emphasis on the believed humanity of God was what most distinguished the mature theologian of our experience from his earlier reputation in America. We heard a number of visitors ask why he had changed his mind. But although

---

[25] See e.g., *Fides quaerens intellectum* ..., S. 14.

he knew he had changed in many ways, he insisted it was not here. The humanity of God visible in the incarnation is what has always given an objective and normative content to our adventure with God. [26]

Belief in God's permanent embrace of *full humanity* found its visible expression in Barth himself. His own joyful mien radiated the life-affirming delight he was heartened to take in the world around him. A comment he made about his Reformed forebear, John Calvin is indicative here:

> It is when we look at Jesus Christ that we know decisively that God's deity does not exclude, but includes His *humanity*. Would that Calvin had energetically pushed ahead on this point in his christology, his doctrine of God, his teaching about predestination and logically also in his ethics! His Geneva would then not have been such a gloomy affair. His letters would then not have contained so much bitterness. . . . How

---

[26] Indeed, Barth had long seen the entirety of Christian ethics as unfolding from, and its freedom as answering to, faith's knowledge of the prior humanity of God. See e.g., *Christliche Ethik, 1946:* "Christian ethics cannot be understood if this story is omitted" [i.e., the "history between God and Man" visible in Jesus' humanity and his call to the freedom of discipleship]. (In K. Barth, *God Here and Now,* p. 108). For a fuller development of this aspect of Barth's thought see Stuart A. McLean's *Humanity in the Thought of Karl Barth* (Edinburgh: T & T Clark, 1981).

could God's deity exclude His humanity, since it is God's freedom for love and thus His capacity to be not only in the heights but also in the depths, not only great but also small, not only in and for Himself but also with another distinct from Him, and to offer Himself to him? It is His act. [It is His initiative.]. . . . His deity *encloses humanity in itself.* . . . God does not exist without man.

If Jesus Christ is the Word of Truth, the "mirror of the fatherly heart of God,". . . then the truth of God is . . . his loving-kindness and nothing else.[27]

Barth told us that he never much liked Question 21 of the *Heidelberg Catechism,*[28] where it says faith is not essentially a knowledge, but is *also a feeling* of trust *"which the Holy Spirit creates in me."* To confuse faith with feeling, he said, was

---

[27] *The Humanity of God*, p. 49-52.

[28] The 1563 work represents Reformed belief, largely attuned to Calvin's thought mediated to the German world through Caspar Olevianus and melded to some extent with that of Luther's disciple, Melanchthon, through the latter's student, Zacharias Ursinus, a co-author. One of our most congenial confessional symbols, the *Heidelberg Catechism,* organizes the entire subsequent Christian life as gifted by the Holy Spirit, under the single rubric of "gratitude."

in danger of sidestepping the crucial role of Christ, who should be definitive for our human *knowledge* of God (even as he enables our faith through his Spirit's inner nudging).[29] Barth sensed Melanchthon's voice behind *Heidelberg* at this point, obscuring the clarity of Calvin, who regarded Christ himself as sole norm. Calvin rightly "insists faith is knowledge. For Calvin, a pure knowledge implies also a trust in God, but it also is *obedience* according to [the rest of] *The Heidelberg Catechism*"—*an* objective personal knowledge—more than mere feeling, though appropriate feelings inevitably do follow.[30]

FAITH'S INTELLIGENCE:
RATIONAL UNITY IN DIVERSITY

The intimate faith relationship unfolds as a renewed intelligence. Surprisingly perhaps, as we shall see, Barth's avoidance of any anthropologically-based theology resulted in a higher elevation of mankind than we could dare imagine from experience. Likewise, his avoidance of natural theology only enhanced his concern for nature in all its wondrous abundance. (He can easily be misconstrued here.) For God's holistic cove-

---

[29] N.B., this is the point that the Western Church had defended by its classic *filioque* clause.

[30] English Colloquium, Nov. 25, 1958. Here Barth was in part countering the Catholic notion of *fides implecita* (faith as mere assent).

nant with the creature should ground the highest possible appreciation for the God-given world as womb-of-all-life and evoke a stoutly elaborated theology about nature—a regard for both its unity and its awe-inspiring diversity.[31]

Again, just as it turns out that Christian faith, not grounded on Nature, has issued in the highest valuation of nature, it is a faith not grounded in natural reason that evokes the highest respect for our God-given intelligence. For Barth's final

---

[31] The famed Gifford Lectures in Scotland are endowed to treat on Natural Theology. (I first became aware of them when as a student there, I heard Arnold Toynbee hold forth on how organisms' sense of self-at-the-center-of-the-universe is a lie, and, as such, translates into a universal—call it a natural theological fallacy, an original sin). Karl Barth had in 1937 rather boldly twisted the endowed topic back upon itself, taking the famed platform as an occasion to develop his theological rejection of all natural theology (with tongue in cheek offering himself as a useful foil for any who would still speculate regarding ultimate truths on the basis of natural experience).

Stanley Hauerwas in 2001, moving forward with Barth's earlier lead, again took the Gifford honor as occasion for an audacious turning by rehabilitating the old terminology. He simply adopted the term "*theological metaphysics*" (which may strike some as an oxymoron) to describe what I am here calling Barth's *theology of nature*, as the only reliable surrogate for the kind of metaphysics which has been so widely discounted by positivistic philosophers and scientists today (see e.g., p. 184). [He also refers to this as Barth's "overcoming of metaphysics," viz. p. 189.] For the purposes of the lectureship's endowed theme, Hauerwas shrewdly re-baptized Barth's faith-founded and funded grasp of nature as something we are free to re-label, "natural theology," while aware that we are using the adjective in an entirely new sense (see 159f. and context). Indeed, why not? Couldn't this recycled familiar term well be used, as he pleasantly suggests, to name "how Christian convictions work to describe all that is, as God's good creation" (p. 142; see further *in loc.*). Seen in this light, "Karl Barth is the great 'natural theologian' of the Gifford Lectures, because he rightly understood that natural theology is impossible abstracted from a full doctrine of God" (p. 9f.).

ground, the revealed Word or λογος comprehends the logic behind the entire creation. He would say "If we speak of faith, we implicitly speak of Christ, and vice versa." There is the germ of christology in speaking of faith. The resurrection of Christ, then, is "axiomatic" for the whole "science of Evangelical Theology." At root here was an intentional childlike simplicity, which for Barth was anything but naïve.

Yet Barth would defend himself against a caricature of his concentration upon Christ as having reduced God himself to his revelation, as if this knowledge exhausts all that God is or can be.[32] Barth also wanted to guard against thinking of the Christ-motivated life in terms of an abstract intellectual program or method.[33] Our thinking should be guided in conversation with the living Christ himself, who is not to be reduced to an abstract principle or constricted by a set method. Not wanting to be misunderstood here, Barth could even mention on oc-

---

[32] Heinrich Vogel, Paul Althaus and Reinhold Niebuhr had early lodged this complaint. See Henri Blocher, "Karl Barth's Christocentric Method," in Gibson and Strange, eds., *Engaging with Barth . . .* (New York & London: T & T Clark, 2008), p. 26ff. Compare A. Come, *Barth's Dogmatics . . . ,* p. 134.

[33] Barth saw most theological errors as resulting from abstraction. Rationalistic systems result when we abstract a theology of man prior to or apart from the man, Jesus Christ; while vague mysticisms result when we abstract a pneumatology from the character of the man, Jesus, and speculate about "an anonymous 'Spirit.'" (Compare Barth's summary notes on the Apostles' Creed in *The Faith of the Church,* especially p. 54.)

casion that he did not much "like the word, 'christology.'"[34] Knowledge of a living person is slighted by any abstraction. Objectively "to know," in the biblical sense, extends into the deepest dynamic personal intimacy. Jesus himself was no Christomonist though the vast diversity of creation does relate to him as its inner, human logic or *logos*. The character of Barth's theology as it reflects that personal relationship, then, is the subject of our next chapter.

---

[34] Cited by E. Busch, *Karl Barth*, p. 41. John Godsey quotes Barth as having said, "The Holy Spirit does not like a 'system'—not even a christological one." (*Karl Barth's Table Talk*), p. 24.

Chapter 3

The Beautiful Craft of Theology:
Showing Faith's Inner Coherence

BARTH'S STANCE: INCARNATIONAL THEOLOGY
IN PNEUMATIC RESPONSE

For the Barth we knew, the remedy for conflicting natural theologies entailed attentive hearing and free responsiveness to the
living Christ, who revealed himself to and through the apostles.[1]
Apparently this was a very personal and living thing for Barth,
the man. He once confessed to us,

> Every morning I feel a beginner to this
> kind of theology—every day anew, I must make
> the jump to say this kind of theology in an un-

---

[1] Catholic scholar Colm O'Grady does well to point out how Barth
has moved "from a theology of mediation [relating to God as if he were our
own inner subject] to a theology of response, flowing out of the revelation in
Christ of his living presence as accompanying Spirit." See *An Introduction to
the Theology of Karl Barth* . . . (New York: Corpus, 1970), p. 23f.

common way. God has opened his heart to us. There is no other kind of God behind God. (That latter was Calvin's view; and for Calvin it is within that unknown that predestination takes place. He can't quite think of Christ as revealing God fully.)[2]

At theology's core must be belief in the living Christ, whose Spirit will continue to act with a personal integrity that coheres with the Jesus of apostolic memory. If, as God's living Word, Jesus manifested the logic of Creation, then we find it is God's self-defining, free election to be *for* all his creatures (as Christ showed himself to be). This free choice or election of God must be at the very beginning and core of faith's intelligence. Here is manifest both his everlasting "yes" to all persons in grace and the obverse, grace-supporting "no," whereby he will deliver us, finally, from all that has been ungracious and ingrate in our lives.

To think theologically, then, means quite pointedly to remain inside the sphere of apostolic Christ-centered faith. It never means trying to judge faith claims regarding the empiri-

---

[2] English Colloquium, Jan. 13, 1959. For current discussion of Barth vs. Calvin's view of election see David Gibson's 2009 study, *Reading the Decree*.

cally Unknown God on the basis of ordinary scientific, historical or sociological data. (This much resonance with Kierkegaard, Barth retained; although paradox itself, once acknowledged, may be left behind.)[3] The basis and stance that he carves out should distinguish theology and give it independence from every other intellectual discipline or field of study, for it has its unique subject in the revelation that has been redefined and brought to its focus in Jesus Christ.[4]

It is inescapable that, as a self-declared *Church* theologian, Barth's basic stance was grounded in a Jesus-responsive piety which is the foundation for his vast, intellectually disciplined enterprise. Indeed, in his last years Barth showed a softening toward Christians of a more emotive, pietistic stripe,

---

[3] Kierkegaard's recognition of the radical disjunction between our knowledge and the Unknown, along with the *possibly* infinite qualitative distinction between time and eternity that it entails, is overcome by a claim based on what he calls the "Absolute Paradox"; i.e., the possibility that the Unknown can make itself known in human terms and thereby occasion rational belief. The mature Barth, too, comes ever more to emphasize how we can be given belief that the absolute otherness of God may be trans-pierced by God himself through the storied objectivity of the incarnation whereby our faith is claimed. Through the gospel we have been given occasion to believe that by God's own initiative the curtain of separation is rent; so Barth's language regarding the "Wholly Other" is pushed into the background, supplanted by faith's regard for the hopeful claim of God's own self-analogic humanity in Christ.

[4] The early Barth ended a 1929 lecture with the words "Theology will really be *theology*—of Word, election, faith—when from beginning to end it is christology." See *"Shicksal und Idée"* [tr. "Fate and Idea in Theology"], *"Theologische Frage und Antworten"* in Rumscheidt, *The Way of Theology,* p. 60.

such as Zinzendorf.[5] This fact, which may serve as his legitimization within certain faith communities, strikes others as maddeningly naïve and cloying (with its sweet and almost maudlin Jesus imagery). So it inevitably has evoked derision among some, who assume our minds must be boxed in by a purely empirical or "professionally scientific" frame of reference.

"Christ-responsive," one must say, then, in describing Barth's theology—but I've seen him discomfited by and ready to dispose of every one of the other labels commonly used to pigeonhole him: christomonist; anti-rational or irrationalist; Neo-Orthodox; dialectic theologian; theologian of crisis; theologian of paradox; Neo-Protestant; Biblicist; or universalist. He would accept none of these tags. For him, as a theologian, Christ-centeredness called for open conversation in all directions as well as the freedom to find ourselves in disagreement.

Professor Barth, since you give centrality to the incarnate Word, why not begin your theology with the doctrine of the incarnation and christology, rather than with the classic doctrines of God and creation, as you have done?

---

[5] N.B., E. Busch, *Karl Barth*, p. 447.

To this question, he stoked his briar a moment and then said, "*Ja.* Why not? Why don't *you* try doing that? It could be interesting." Of course, he added that you would have to keep in mind the Torah's drama of the holy God, who is distinct from nature, and of the prophets' expectations. Otherwise, the possibility of messianic incarnation would dangle in thin air with no historical frame of reference.

Barth's maxim that sequential "order is everything" in theology[6] did not mean that you shouldn't re-examine the whole from different points of view (as indeed the biblical authors themselves already had done). Instead it meant that our subject, the gracious God himself, always takes priority. He has acted and spoken, and from first to last engages us to be attentive and listen.

In a Colloquium Grover Foley asked Barth which theologians he had found to have been the "most christocentric," like himself: "The Reformers? Schleiermacher? Zinzendorf?"

Barth's response was telling:

> Luther, Calvin and the Reformers were
> also christocentric. For Calvin the center was not
> the doctrine of election, but the togetherness of
> God and man and the Holy Spirit that implants

---

[6] See in Chapter 7.

us in Christ.

Luther can make a certain overestimate of faith—as if faith is itself God. (And certain existentialists today can claim to be good Lutherans here.) But for Luther himself, faith is *always* "in Christ." I have understood a concept in Luther and Calvin which was outlined by neither Luther nor Calvin.

A heretic, Marcion, was christocentric, too, in a definite way. But I'd prefer a heretic who was christocentric to a pope who is not. (Adolf von Harnack revived something of Marcion for us.)

Zinzendorf? I don't like his sentimentality. He was not a theologian, perhaps, but a great man. He spoke in a baroque way. We'll have a good talk about him in heaven.

Schleiermacher? Schleiermacher was a convinced *Schleiermachianer.* In [his view of] Christ, all which is to be done and told is concentrated [in one's self—] one's own feeling. But all of his philosophical elements notwithstanding, he was *trying*, in his own manner, to build up Jesus Christ alone (i.e., Jesus Christ is the background of the *religious feeling of a religious man*).

Wilhelm Hermann, a disciple of Ritschl, was my most esteemed teacher as a student. I went to the University of Marburg [where he taught] as if to the source of Truth. My way to him was Immanuel Kant and practical reason. I had filled myself with Kant and was sure theology should build on practical reason. Hermann built his ethic on Kant and his categorical imperative. He used the imperative as law. And then he came to Jesus Christ, as an extraordinary human life that convinces us that the law is valid; but at the same time [we] can experience forgiveness within the same experience. And all had to be built up on that.

If you should ask me where I come from: Jesus Christ is the center of Truth. I have learned what that meant.[7]

---

[7] English Colloquium, Dec. 5, 1960.

ANALOGIA FIDEI AND

RELATIONAL COHERENCE

Barth's concern to rid theology of attempted proofs of God and of experience-based analogy (*analogia entis*) is well-known;[8] but he was even more concerned that Church teaching be vastly more than naysaying to natural tendencies. Theological craft must mobilize positive reflection upon the special personal relationship it has been given with the one whose self-bestowing love and ongoing resurrection-life is believed to be God's Word for us.

We are called to speak and act in analogy to that believed relationship and continue in common cause with the others living in its light. So, as we have seen, the theologian's question becomes what current strategies are appropriate to explore and communicate in *analogia fidei et relationis* [by means of analogy from faith itself or from its relationship] in lieu of a wayward *analogia entis* [i.e., as opposed to an analogy of or from ordinary being].

A turning point in the theology of the young Barth has been characterized by some as a move from dialectic method in

---

[8] What Barth was opposing here could well be understood as a modern resurgence of gnosticism, which in its myriad of speculative "spiritual" guises has dogged Christianity as its most virulent heresy from the beginning—so prevalent, in fact, that it has been described aptly as a major World Religion. (See Gilles Quispel's *Gnosis als Welt Religion.*)

theology to a more positive exploration of the giftedness of a living relationship within God's own being and between him and his human creatures—a re-centering upon the *analogia fidei*, which contains within itself an *analogia relationis*. This shift has been exaggerated as if it represented a sharp change of mind or transformation where Barth's emerging epistemology is concerned. But he did not acknowledge a radical mind-change. In any case, the increasingly dynamic dialogic nature of his theology both *vis à vis* its storied subject and its ongoing conversation partners becomes its vital drama.

I repeat, *dialogic* is a better term than *dialectic* to characterize this trait, since we here have to do with the dynamic drama of storied interpersonal exchange, rather than the mechanics of antithesis and synthesis. First, there is a living intercourse with God as Person, and then we become with others his theologizing partners.[9] Barth would tell us quite forcefully that he disliked the term "dialectic." In the context under discussion he said he would prefer "story."

We have said that he was much influenced by Kierkegaard underway.[10] It would be interesting to know whether he

---

[9] Indeed Reinhold Niebuhr repeatedly reproached Barth for not being dialectic enough; which for Niebuhr meant being unwilling to begin God-talk with human cultural realities. (See Gordon Harland, *the Thought of Reinhold Niebuhr* (New York: Oxford, 1960), pp. 38-42.

[10] Paradox persists, to be sure, but it has been filled in by what

was thinking in terms of that passage in the *Philosophical Fragments,* where Kierkegaard reflects on what a small amount of experience would actually be necessary to occasion the full sweep of revelation-based teaching. For as Adolf von Harnack, the liberal dogma history giant who was the young Barth's teacher, had been quick to point out regarding his former Swiss student's first publications, it was their return to the claim of *positive revelation* that made Barth part company with the theology his liberal teachers had tried to inculcate as "scientific."

Harnack's main complaint was that what Barth appealed to as "revelation" was in his view far too loose and vague.[11] But in his subsequent thought Barth was to become ever more pointedly christocentric —a tightening focus that came to its sharpest expression in the summarizing essay he published during my time at Basel, *The Humanity of God.*[12]

Where the origins of such faith were concerned, Kierkegaard had insisted that the whole inner coherence of what is

---

Kierkegaard called *the Absolute Paradox* [see p.77]. As faith has been given to believe, God in his own inner reality has been free to maintain a rationality in his Creation, a *logos,* which is to be shared as the fundamental logic for bering human.

[11] See the first of Harnack's "Fifteen Questions to Those Among the Theologians Who Are Contemptuous of the Scientific Theology," in *The Beginnings of Dialectic Theology,* James M. Robinson, ed., (Richmond,VA: John Knox Press, Vol. I, 1968, p. 165).

[12] English translation, Richmond, VA: John Knox, 1966; from a lecture delivered already in September 1956 to Swiss pastors at Aarau.

given us to be believed could well rest on the most slender factual basis, which need be no more than the existence of a persistent rumor (i.e., something "*sagenhaft*"—told as having actually happened, but beyond historical verification). This comes into sharp focus where Kierkegaard answers Enlightenment skepticism by stressing how very little historically documented "fact" would be necessary to occasion and shape a fully rational, but incarnation-funded faith. The disciples around Jesus "at first hand" were really no closer to the actual giftedness of such a new condition of mind, than any of us, who, as "disciples at second hand," may have heard only the rumor of his life. (As a matter of fact, the sweaty presence of the Man might even have been a worse block for those first disciples, than the idea of God's humanity is for us.) Belief never has been, nor will be, based on compelling common experience.

CHRISTOCENTRIC REFLECTION—
A NOETIC NECESSITY

Kierkegaard insists that the slender historical claim "that the God has existed in human form is the essence of the matter," and a body of further actual historical data "is not even as important as [it would be] if we had to do with a human being, instead of with the God" who takes pains to be human.

If the contemporary generation had left nothing behind them but these words: "We have believed that in such and such a year God appeared among us in the humble figure of a servant, that he lived and taught in our community, and finally died," it would be more than enough. This little advertisement, this *nota bene* on a page of universal history, would be Sufficient to afford occasion for a successor [quite rationally to believe], and the most voluminous account can in all eternity do nothing more.[13]

While the *analogia relationis* (or *analogia fidei, revelationis*) has been widely recognized as a hinge for Barth, basic to faith's own quest for intelligence, the closely related way forward which Barth found here deserves more attention. For as Kierkegaard was saying, the entire, many-faceted contents of faith are already implicated—and may be unfolded, as having been already implicit in the sparest incarnation claim (along with ethical impetus for an appropriate way of life).

Here is where Anselm figured in. We saw how basic for Anselm was his insistence that when we speak of God, we are

---

[13] S. Kierkegaard, *Philosophical Fragments or a Fragment of Philosophy* (Princeton: Princeton University Press, 1936), p. 87.

speaking of something that is, in fact, greater (and better) than anything in our experience, or anything "we could think." This awareness immediately warned against the appeal to general experience or even so-called religious experience as a pre-condition or defining parameter for what may be believed. The God of belief has presented self as being self-defining; so faith must acknowledge him to be greater than any prior or competing category of experience.

This rational faith militates against the kind of rationalizations that liberal theologians deemed "scientific." For empirically compelling fact is the very thing a Gaunilo-type Anselm opponent would put forward today as the greatest surety he could think or imagine. But Anselm would surely have answered again, "No! Greater! Immeasurably greater than you can think or imagine!"

Anselm saw that theology, the rational self-understanding of faith, need not, and finally must not be lured into testing itself against the vagaries and ambiguities of either natural history or general human experience. That is, it must oppose our almost universal natural tendencies toward styling our grasp of ultimate reality to mirror some aspect of general experience (including what is popularly called spiritual, mystical or religious experience). In Barth's terms, a theological thinker never need—indeed never may—base his or her teaching outside the sphere of God's self-revelation that is foundational to Christ-funded faith.

Yet, though given his self-limitation, and despite the appearance of Absolute Paradox, nothing prevents God, the Unknown, from maintaining humanity within himself for our sake (should God choose to remain knowable). God may have the power to retain even within his own eternal subsistence, the most wonderfully knowable human dimension. "[God's] self-limitation is real, yes," Barth would tell us, "but at no place is he so fully God as in Christ. That's where *we* learn what it really means to be Lord and God."

As we have stressed already, if Barth came to say "no" to amorphous, nature-based theologies, it was in order to say "yes" to the particular, concrete knowledge of both God and Man claimed for us as God's own living Word. Here God is more knowable, with more definiteness than nature could ever suggest, and astonishingly perhaps, there is far greater impetus and freedom "in Christ" regarding what Man may be and become.

Barth describes this elemental awareness in his Anselm book in terms of an original, inner rationality of God.[14] This

---

[14] In *Fides quaerens intellectum* Barth described at length, how God's own *prevenient rationality* with its intrinsic *ontological necessity* becomes incarnate and is proffered to us, as the *noetic necessity* that may

ontological logic of God is proffered as *logos*, the divine-human basis for human faith's own rationality. Because this prior humane rationality is God's own, it has already a prior, intrinsic structure and order native to God's transcendent being. When communicated to our human sphere of empirical time, this prior dynamic structure stands as a given necessity (including an essential inner freedom) that gives definite shape to our responsive human knowing and teaching of our faith. In Barth's view all we can know about God must follow freely from this gifted prior divine necessity.

Faith seeking intelligence, then, finds itself becoming aware of its correspondence to this prior eternal necessity which Barth's Anselm book sees as God's dynamic initiative acting in an ordered downward (or outward) movement as in the chart on the next page.[15]

THE GRACE-GROUNDED, FAITH-BOUNDED WAY

To do theology alongside Barth, then, meant to participate in his openness toward one's living subject and sources rather than to conform to any prescribed method. In fact, far too

---

become the objective substance of dogma.

[15] In his book, *Fides quarens intellectum,* Barth stresses the distinction Anselm makes between the Latin ablative case and the accusative (object case). (S. 42 ff.) See diagram of faith's theological source.

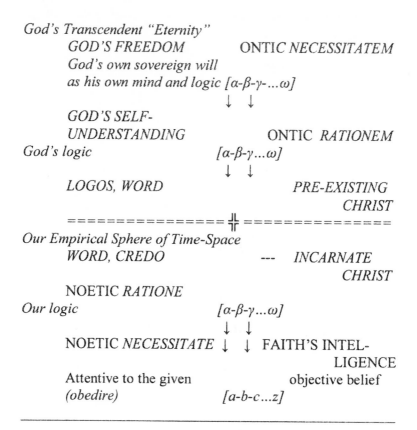

God's Transcendent "Eternity"
    GOD'S FREEDOM   ONTIC *NECESSITATEM*
    God's own sovereign will
    as his own mind and logic [α-β-γ-...ω]
                ↓ ↓

    GOD'S SELF-
    UNDERSTANDING   ONTIC *RATIONEM*
God's logic   *[α-β-γ...ω]*
                ↓ ↓

    LOGOS, WORD   *PRE-EXISTING*
                       CHRIST
===============✝===============
Our Empirical Sphere of Time-Space
    WORD, CREDO   --- *INCARNATE*
                       CHRIST

    NOETIC *RATIONE*
Our logic   *[α-β-γ...ω]*
                ↓ ↓
    NOETIC *NECESSITATE* ↓ ↓ FAITH'S INTEL-
                       LIGENCE
    Attentive to the given   objective belief
    (obedire)   *[a-b-c...z]*

much has been made of Karl Barth's "methodology."[1] For he resisted giving priority to any pre-set method that we might import from our manipulation of material in other areas, as if to impose our own criteria upon God's sovereign action or to suggest his living Word is under our control. If faith means a new and living sovereign relationship, it will always have to wait to see what thought and expression forms unfold here and now within that relationship. Of course this means our habitual or would-be methods are to be resisted whenever any of them claims ascendancy where God is concerned. Any such method, if superimposed on our subject from outside the realm of faith, would imply a kind of natural theology, the very thing Barth most strenuously resisted his entire life.[16]

Methodology, then, is not to be a prolegomenon preceding Christ-attentive theology. The ways our minds take here must follow from confrontation with the living subject and object of life itself. Anything akin to a theological method should flow from the priority of God's own humane wisdom—ontological in the freedom of his eternal grace, with the form of thought itself liberated to show forth the free, inner relationship that is received with belief in Christ as God's Word.

---

[16] If the research methods that usually reign must be suspended where faith regarding the otherwise Unknown is concerned, then the reliability and appropriateness of our usual scientific methods, such as inductive verification by repeatable empirical testing, would be the first to be surrendered here (along with application of prior qualitative and quantitative criteria, prior analysis of contemporary relevance, sociological function, social usefulness, consensus, or any other "imported" method, such as demythologization, desacralization, or the deductive observation of man's spiritual nature or ethnographic religious patterns). Such things may well be illuminated and rendered more intelligible by an overlay of Christ-founded faith. But faith itself funds our intelligence, quite independent of such methodologies.

But what, then, should guide theological epistemology and faith's own way of thought? To have claimed a more definite incarnation focus leaves us still with the problem of the rather fuzzy image of the historical Jesus that presents itself to the scientific mind. Barth, like Kierkegaard in the above quotation, seemed quite satisfied that after textual-critical analysis has done its utmost (even if, as Rudolf Bultmann would rather baldly state, we cannot authenticate a single thing about Jesus with absolute certainty), there are, nevertheless, definite historical claims before us that warrant a fully examined faith. If God is actually behind these faith claims, he has gone to great lengths to keep them from tyrannizing us or taking our minds by force.

Horizontal coherence remains an inner-scriptural norm for Barth. If we seek our faith's own intelligence, we will give precedence to clearly cohering texts and to inter-related articles of belief over those that are less clear. Such coherently integrated meanings of Christ-mediated faith may be explored in great depth—witness the confidence behind Barth's many thousand pages of writings.

The significant meaning-test for him became the challenge to explore the inner logic that binds together the different aspects of incarnation-based faith and to display the *"spider web" of their inter-connectedness.*[17] As Stanley Hauerwas observes, "the way he does theology is an ongoing attempt to show the interconnections between the various aspects of the Christian faith."[18]

There is nothing provable at root here, nothing to be polemically or apologetically enhanced. Once the inner relationships are exposed between the different tenets of faith, the self-authenticating attractiveness of what has been passed along by believers to be intelligently believed may be left quite confidently to the Holy Spirit. Whether or not Barth shared Kierkegaard's view regarding the sufficiency of a very minimal historical kernel, he certainly had confidence that we have far more than enough to found and fund the received articles of faith. Theology's task is to show how these emanate from that historical kernel and relate intelligibly to each other. So much the better, if that kernel is supplemented with a whole basket-full of teachings and works of Jesus! Everything is to be tested for coherence. The Spirit that particular faith claims seem to express is thus to be tested to see whether it is "of" the graciously

---

[17] Robert W. Jenson uses this apt expression to describe Barth's way of unfolding faith. "Karl Barth" in *the Modern Theologians: An Introduction to Christian Theology in the Twentieth Century*, Vol. I, David F. Ford, ed., (Oxford & Cambridge: Blackwell, 1989), pp. 33 & 35.

[18] *With the Grain of the Universe* (p. 156).

liberating God.[19]

The pathway Barth saw himself entering upon is really quite straightforward (though this may be obscured by the prolix shrubbery of his explorations). The theologian is simply to select one or another aspect of the received apostolic faith, and temporarily set it aside—hold it in abeyance for a time—in order to expose how our God-given intelligence will arrive at it again, as a complement to the other tenets of faith. Thus the Church teacher is called to show forth (*"demonstrare,"* as Anselm would put it)[20] the inner-confessional "noetic necessity" for one tenet of Christian belief after another.

Such "demonstration" never seeks its grounding in general experience outside of faith's sphere, never tries to compel anyone Q.E.D, but rather deals from first to last with the promise that unfolds within the historical hope and belief that the otherwise Unknown God has truly expressed himself through Christ, in sharply objective contrast to the death-bound banalities and power-thrusts of everyday experience.

---

[19] I Jn. 4:1; I Thess. 5:21.

[20] One must again stress that the sense of *"demonstrare"* that Barth reads from Anselm's traditionally tagged "ontological proof" of God, while "showing forth" faith's rational inner coherence, has nothing in common with the modern concept of empirical, scientific demonstration or proof and was not originally intended in our sense to prove the actual "existence of God." We are left mercifully free of such logical necessity. But given good grounds to hope, we find our rational blocks dwindling as the force of passionate faith takes root in our minds.

Of course, our theological intelligence is not only called to contemplate and show forth coherence; we are also given a way of testing the appropriateness of any purported faith claim. Does it meaningfully key into the others? This way of exploring inner-faith coherence, not only demonstrates faith's rationality and its distinctness from all the man-centered religions, but it also offers criteria for purging inappropriate "spiritual" speculations from the Christian churches' thought and traditions as well.

So a web of coherence is to be "demonstrated" (i.e. exhibited), not by empirical proofs from our larger experience, but by exposing meaningful interrelationships with the incarnate Word—the saga-founded and apostle-funded kerygma. It remains the occasion for this new Spirit-attested *condition*, this reason-implicating *passion* called "faith." The later, mature Barth we knew tended to leave other aspects of Kierkegaard's paradox behind, but the historical saga as kernel of revelation is far larger and more objective for him than it would need to be in order to occasion a full-fledged faith.

Positive revelation claims became ever more insistent, more christocentric and christomorphic for the later Barth. The altar painting by Grünewald[21] that hung over his desk really was

---

[21] From the Isenheim altar in nearby Colmar, France.

emblematic of his whole theological enterprise, with its portrayal of John the Baptist pointing to the figure of Jesus hanging on the cross. Christ, epitomized as representing God's all-power in suffering servitude is the sign that has appeared insistently in our common past. That sign is all-important, though Barth maintained his "stringent insistence that God's representative Messiah is made known only in sign."[22] To be sure, the christocentric focus on the crucified Lord is to be regarded through the resurrection optic that Barth saw as "axiomatic."

The best crucifix, by Grünewald, is frightful: with John to the side pointing [toward Christ]. Who, except God himself, can really say who this figure is! Hiddenness is there. Directly behind this [i.e., on the outer panel of the great altarpiece] is not the resurrection scene [which is portrayed on a side wing], but the Christmas story and the Old Testament temple facing toward this middle with an angel choir in the foreground. Mary is there also on the right with child—a fantastic child—who is looking back and upwards into the mountain heights. And there God the Father is indicated, looking

---

[22] Gary Dorrien, *The Barthian Revolt in Modern Theology* (Louisville: Westminster/John Knox, 2000, p. 183).

downwards. The whole Old Testament is suggested with a modest fantasy. An entire theology
is back of it: the openly revealed mystery of the
Cross.[23]

In our *Kleiner Kreis* Barth told of a discussion with a
noted scientist who asked him if there was in theology a single
axiom to which all else has its reference, such as he sought in
his mathematical system.

"Yes," Barth answered, "that Jesus Christ rose from the
dead."

Surprised at this from a world-class scholar, the scientist
asked, "How do you mean that? Literally? With a physical body
and all?"

"Yes, quite literally."

Then the other's face lit up. "Ah, now I understand: it
breaks all the laws of physics and chemistry and contradicts all
our empirical philosophy; but now I understand."

"We were worlds apart still," Barth reflected, "but he finally understood what we are about."

So, Barth's christology did find its focus in the cross and
resurrection claim. Yet in his view, it is when Christian theo-

---

[23] Barth in *Sozietät* discussion, May 8, 1964. See my Prologue regarding his use of masculine designations for God.

logy sees to this objective center of its own discipline that it evokes the most understanding and respect from the other disciplines.

THEOLOGY'S WAY IN ACTION—COMPLEX
UNITY AND COHERENT DIVERSITY

If there is an article of faith which one would question, understand better, or even test for its authenticity, one should, as said, set it aside, as it were, hold it in abeyance for the time being (*vorübergehend*) in order to approach it from the perspective of other affirmations of faith and thus make clearly visible how it follows, of necessity, in rational consequence in coherence from them.[24]

Let us take as our own random example the rather obscure early creedal claim regarding Christ's descending into hell to bring his grace to the worst offenders.[25] and apply Barth's way of testing coherence. First, set it aside; hold it in abeyance; then approach its issue regarding the fate of unbelieving persons "who have died in their sins" in terms of a cluster of other articles of biblical faith.

---

[24] Barth speaks here of discerning *"eine Vernüftigkeit im Zusammenhang"* [a reasonableness in their interconnectedness].
[25] I Peter 3:18f.

For our example, God is fully himself, present even to Sheol (Ps.139).[26] Jesus came to "seek and save those who are lost"[27] and "in order that the whole cosmos might be saved."[28] "All have sinned," all are broken, "there is no distinction."[29] He called for love even toward enemies "consigned all people to disobedience in order that he might show mercy to all."[30] God's Messiah took the initiative to heal all kinds of brokenness in all comers—to heal even death itself.

Our healing, then, is his decision and re-creation, not our own achievement, but a relationship he has miraculously re-stored.[31] By the same token, the man who asks how he can invest his own power—what he can do, *in order to save him-self*—goes away from Jesus disappointed. "Impossible for a man!" Jesus declares ("but all things are possible for God.")[32]

---

[26] The last part of this Psalm which glories in hatred towards God's enemies, meanwhile, would perhaps not carry the same coherent force—much less the homesick vindictiveness of Psalm 137:9 that gloats over the thought of dashing out the brains of enemies' babies.

[27] Lk. 19:10, Titus 3:5 *et al.*

[28] Jn. 3:17 *et al.*

[29] Rom. 3:22f.

[30] Rom. 11:32.

[31] This key kerygmatic theme, which runs through the entire earliest Gospel, Mark, was the subject of my extended analysis in a paper I delivered at the 2007 meeting of the Society of Christian Ethics: "'At God's Right Hand,' A Healer Re-Defines Justice (the Crucial Role of Psalm 110 in the Earliest Christians' Move Towards Restorative Justice)."

[32] Mk. 10:27.

Further, as the lifelong healer, who heals not only human ailments but the physical storm and finally death itself in Mark—this Christ, who championed unlimited forgiveness and bestowed it even on those who nailed him to the cross, is to be our only judge. As such, he is "at the right hand of the Father," as the human representation of God's own healing intent.[33] God is constant, always to be trusted: always like himself. So forever maintaining that healing character, "*he [i.e., none other than Christ, the healer]* will come again to judge the quick and the dead."[34] (Healing re-creation will be the last word in judgment.)

From the aggregate of these biblical faith claims, does there not follow, a necessity to understand that God's own unqualified grace—as visible in Christ's healings and promise of re-creation—extends also toward any who have "died in their sins"? His grace extends even to those who according to the ancient story (envisioned here as the worst-case scenario) were so evil they evoked the deluge. Even such as they, are not out of reach of God's Christ-shaped re-creative power: the unlimited initiative of God's all-healing grace. If this is so in this most extreme of cases, how much more will it be true for ordinary

---

[33] Mk. 14:61f., *et al.*

[34] A plethora of N.T. texts are thus summarized by the Apostles' Creed.

people such as we.[35]

Thus, as our example works out, we have arrived back at the meaning and validity of the descent-into-hell motif through sounding out faith's inner coherence. Prodded by the Spirit, perhaps, we will have become clearer about its implications for us through holding it in abeyance for a time and "testing the spirit" wherein we can recognize its significance as true.

By the same token, common distortions of this descent image may be exposed. How, for example, could it possibly mean that those who have died in their sins can and must purge and "give form to their faith" to achieve finally a life perfection?[36] Rather, those who are truly lost, victims of their own ingrained evil choosing (what Eastern thinkers would call their destructive *karma*), were from the first the ones Jesus came to seek and save. Isn't it to be hoped that they too are embraced by sovereign grace that freely gifts the miracle of restored relationship? How, then, could medieval notions of score-sheet retributive justice or a long, punitive temporal purgatory begin to cohere?

---

[35] Here is to be recognized a favorite form of rabbinic argument, following a "voice" that moves from "heavy to light," or vice-versa. E.g. "If God so clothes the lilies, . . . how much more . . . you."

[36] Thus the Council of Trent, *Session 6*, on justification of faith.

As in our example, the showing forth of *inner* coherence is the only proofing or demonstration that faith seeking intelligence can make for itself. Theology is tasked to show how any matter of faith follows out of the larger faith perspective and how it all "hangs together." The moment theology pretends to prop up faith by reference to the external realm of empirical experience (as if some parallel in nature could give clear evidence), it has, in fact, appealed to a lie. Such a lie is fated to be exposed by unbelievers themselves. Thereby both the objective reality of faith and the complete freedom of its salvation claims will have been tragically confused and our Lord misrepresented.

Having said all this, we must nevertheless dispel the rumor that Barth would think theology's own language must be limited to the Bible text's usage.[37] Our terminology as theologians is meant to be incarnate in the common language of our day, and will inevitably adapt elements of the culture and familiar thought forms of the moment. As we have stressed, revelation has been both directed toward and funded by the person of Christ, but its expression forms remain free and fluid, though they are not to be fused or confused with any metaphysical speculation.

---

[37] See e.g., Langdon Gilkey, *Naming the Whirlwind: the Renewal of God Language*, p. 14ff.

To summarize then, in Barth's view Anselm's so-called "proof" was neither more nor less than this: "to show forth" the inner relatedness between any one aspect of faith and all the rest that has been received and shared as worthy of belief. The inner necessity faith sets out to elucidate corresponds analogically to its one necessary subject (which God has made his own inner necessity as the living One who bestows himself to mankind). Our rationality is to correspond to God's own prior inner objectivity—his own reason, which he has given as the basis for faith's logic and truth. Our thought here is to take form within the sphere of the assurance we are given, which first hopes and then believes that the confessions of faith may, in large, be true. None of Anselm's writing, Barth would stress, was apodictic or apologetic in the technical sense. God does not enslave us or take our minds by a *tour de force*. Barth said he would embrace the theological stance, brought home to him during his Anselm study, whether or not his was a correct reading of the saint.

Christian theology's recognition of *unity in diversity* and its converse freedom for diversity in unity have their analogical basis already in the trinitarian relationship within God's own Self. But this kind of relationship reverberates throughout God's work. His Essence and Act are correlates not to be separrated in our witness to him. His integral simplicity and ordered coherence are never to be abstracted from the complexity of his creativity. An important corollary of this is Barth's insistence that our lives' complex ethical expressions are to remain an expression of our one, simple, permanent relationship to God, to be confessed as his one, simultaneous grasp of our whole life drama in all of its diversity. So our way of life and ethics are never to be "explained" apart from it.[38]

---

[38] This means a single train of events, in a special segment of human history, Christ's self-revelation, along with our acts of discovery expressing dependence on him (i.e., the extension of our prayer communion into action) have everlasting permanence for God. Our integral life, as revealed in Christ, should begin to resonate through everything we do. For we may believe our whole life drama is embraced in God's simultaneity (see Chapter 10).

Chapter 4

Dialogue in the Vertical

Barth's uncanny capacity as a Christian scholar to defer judgment and insist on listening openly at each new juncture marked not only his teaching style, as we have seen, but his exegesis of the biblical sources, and finally his way with every mind he met. As I was to discover, this expectant deference was the inner substance behind the appeal for "obedient" response that had become so prominent, not only in his interaction with the scriptures, but also in his dealings with the witness of later thinkers, and in his approach to Christians' way of life in general.[1] A Reformed theologian is never working alone; and Barth's way with dogma was grounded in person-to-person

---

[1] For example, despite his tensions with Schleiermacher, Barth respected him as a theologian in that he "takes on the problem of theology where it must be if it is to be taken on at all, with thorough attention [*grundsätzlichen Besinnung*] in connection with the biblical norm, on one side, and with the Church's past on the other, in the contemporary presentation of the Church regarding what may, can and must be taught" (*Die protestantische Theologie im 19. Jarhhundert*, S. 384).

counterpoint—the untrammeled expression of shared belief in the living Word of God. The Spirit of the Person we meet there, the Holy Spirit, may be relied upon to begin winning our trust and to motivate in us new reflections and grace-shaped actions—all as a free rejoinder. As Robert McAfee Brown succinctly put it, "For Barth, it seems to me, theology is no more and no less than an act of gratitude."[2] *Actions de grace*, as in idiomatic French, express prayerful thanks. Here one sees how Christian ethics always unfolds from theology. For by Barth's definition, "that action of man's is good in which man is thankful for God's grace" or "which corresponds to it." And evil at root is defined quite simply as that which for whatever cause is unthankful. "Nothing else."[3]

DOGMA IN "OBEDIENCE"?—
SPIRIT-LED HEARING

Barth was one of the most liberated and liberating thinkers of his generation. Yet insistent calls to *obedience* figure prominently—all too prominently, perhaps—across his discourse.

---

[2] "Good News from Karl Barth" in *How Karl Barth Changed My Mind* (Grand Rapids: Eerdmans, 1986, p. 97). In this Barth was in direct line with the Reformed Heidelberg Catechism, which follows Calvin in explicitly treating the whole of Christians' life and thought as properly expression media for gratitude and, as such, further extensions, in effect, of prayer.
[3] *God Here and Now*, p.89.

Often he speaks of "obedience," where we might well expect him to be describing Christians' freedom as an unfettered renewal. We might object and ask, "Don't we meet God as the loving One who saves us from our failure before his law and exercises authority obliquely by *liberating* us into grace-sealed covenanted community?"[4] The prominence Barth gave coercive-sounding calls to obedience could easily occasion a misreading of his intent. I found this to be one of the points where he is most easily misconstrued by Anglo-American readers.[5]

---

[4] I was, of course, arguing that Jesus' affirmation of God's law in scriptures (e.g., Matt. 5:17-20) was understood in Reformation thought as having mainly a diagnostic, *elenchticus* or preparatory function toward our grace-based reorientation (i.e., repentance). Hearing God's command may turn us toward his grace, by actively showing us his will; but though it is useful to us *"in renatus"* in this way [i.e., toward Christians' renewal], it remains quite incapable of healing us by motivating or restoring us, who, already enmeshed in the toils of human evil, are inwardly out of phase with the entire spirit of the Law (Jas. 2:19). Restored wholeness of life, then, may be had only as the re-creative act of God, which, to be sure, begins to motivate a change of heart and "actions of grace"; but these are never to be vaunted as independent human accomplishments.

[5] Typical of this misunderstanding, R. H. Roberts of Durham University caricatures Barth's dogmatic stance as authoritarian and apodictic. Since Barth's *"method"* derives "all theological explanations from the posited 'reality' of revelation," Roberts wrongly concludes that this reality *"demands conformity and submission rather than critical investigation."* [Italics mine.] (R. H. Roberts in Sykes, *Karl Barth,* p. 89). Bruce McCormack came closer to the mark, when he declared Barth's *Dogmatics* "non-dogmatic" and observed that "in a cultural moment of 'post-modernism,' it is the open-endedness of Barth's theology that makes it attractive" (Basel lecture, April 12, 2002).

As a child of the American West, I felt Barth's continual call to "obedience" smacked of abject submission to authority and mechanical conformity (just as his title word, "dogmatic," could suggest a shuttered, authoritarian mindset). What had happened to his freedom in Christ?

As it turned out, being obedient in response to the revealed Christ had for Barth a tone quite opposite to what my California ears were predisposed to hear. I still bore the scars of various forms of judgmental legalism, and had begun to find my remedy in St. Paul's Christian freedom. So I reacted strongly against the predominant role Barth, like Calvin, kept claiming for Christians' obedience. For as we had always used the term, "obedience" connoted an abject subservience. As if you were now being coerced to override your inner truth, split and alienate your inner self in order to comply with an adamant other.

A "WORD-STUDY FOR AMERICANS"

During one Colloquium I took the professor to task: Wouldn't his emphasis on obedience imply we must repress the truth of who we are and act hypocritically, as we are ordered around by a domineering autocrat? How could that describe a loving impulse appropriate to the gospel? If we're driven by command, isn't that quite opposite to being drawn by the Spirit into a willing consonance with God's Grace?

On Obedience
in Bach

Gehorchen (obedire ti dat—)
derives from the root
meaning hören, to hear,
to listen, ——— thus
" to have been rendered
wholeheartedly attentive —
inwardly attuned to
another person. Through
a free love-motivated
"holistic abandon"

After his next *Dogmatics* lecture, Barth with a shy smile handed me a palm-sized slip of paper. In his tightly crabbed hand it was headed, "Word-Study for Americans." It outlined how the German verb, *gehorchen*, parallel to its Latin equivalent, *obedire*, derives from the root meaning, *hören*, to hear, or even more positively, to listen. His point: the theological term "obedience" at root, means to have been rendered wholeheartedly attentive—i.e., inwardly attuned to another person—through a free, love-motivated holistic abandon. So this is something quite opposite from going against one's emerging inclination or desire. You can no more be *ge-hor-sam* by an act of self-repressive will, than you can attach new ears to your head.

As a heartfelt, personal response to Christ, Barth's "obedience" was intended as something quite opposite to the reluctant, duty-bound subservience we were prone to associate with the term. From first to last any true obedience is—and can only be—itself a gift, a freedom.[6] "We are unworthy servants"

---

[6] Compare, Eberhard Busch, *The Great Passion*, p. 119: "This obedience toward God is also freedom." As is often the case, Busch, Barth's last assistant, is clearer than most as to Barth's intent. He cites KD IV/1, S. 257. Also IV/1, S. 108 [= p.101]: "Freedom means being in a spontaneous and, therefore, willing agreement with the sovereign freedom of God" (which is itself expressed as a liberating decision or decision to liberate). Busch develops this theme as an ethic of concrete relationships (p.169), where I would describe it similarly, as an ethic of pneumatic response to or "in" Christ.

when "we have only done what was our duty."[7] But if, being ourselves, we find we've become deeply attentive to the Lord, we may believe his own initiative to be behind it; he will have already[8] touched us inwardly with his grace.[9]

An objection parallel to my own initial reaction here can be seen in Stanley Hauerwas's reading of Barth's frequent stress on obedience as "response or failure of response to individual *commands*." Hauerwas takes this to run contrary to the dynamic life trajectory that he usually prefers to describe under the rubric of character or habitual virtue. So he feels that *character* would have been more appropriate than *obedience* as a "correlative" to

---

Here Barth would make no prior attempt with E. Brunner to decipher "orders of nature" from our ambiguous general experience.

[7] Lk. 17:10. As we will further note below, this slighting remark was Jesus' only recorded reference to the Stoic virtue, *duty*. So much for the notion of a Christian duty ethic!

[8] Note: the masculine pronouns and fatherhood image for God are used advisedly throughout. See Prologue note.

[9] Already in a 1929 lecture Barth's concept of obedience was turning in this direction: "theology is justified only by obedience. For even obedience can be obedience only when it understands itself as faith—as the human affirmation of God's free, unearned, and uncompelled grace" (in Rumscheidt, *The Way of Theology*, p. 60). Typically, in CD II/1 Barth observes that in all the relevant New Testament passages, "it is a question of child-like seeing and *free obedience* and hence the *obedience of faith.*" True, love's freedom does evoke fear, but its own kind of fear (not anxiety [*Angst*] but a kind of fear and trembling [*Furcht* or *Ehrfurcht*]). Considering faith's object, then, "how can it fail to be a question of *obedience*? How can there be love without [this kind of awesome] fear? And as *love in fear*, how can it fail to be *obedience*?" CD II/1, p. 37). To fear God's *judgment*, however, "'is a pagan, not a Christian idea" (italics mine; see *The Faith of the Church*, p. 118 to Geneva Catechism, Q. 86 f.).

110

Barth's own underlying image of life as a journey. Despite his early dependence on Barth, he had good reason to object that Barth's christology finally *"forces"* Barth "to conceive of existence in a way that qualifies *his constant use of the language of command"* (italics mine).[10]

But, as I was beginning to learn, Barth's "obedience," despite its prophetic tone, was not intended to settle into the language of command. Barth did not want to be understood as demanding mechanical submission to external authority. As it is likely that we will read him so, Hauerwas's observation is most appropriate. And as it turns out, despite this problem with Barth's coercive-sounding command language, Hauerwas comes quite close to his underlying concerns here.

For in Barth's own understanding we have not even begun to be obedient until we find ourselves both inwardly and outwardly freely attuned to and motivated by our partner's heart's desire. As said, such attunement is always, and can only be, a gift. You cannot simply conjure it up in yourself at command, no matter who the authority. For Barth it is always to be re-discovered in immediate person-to-Person response, here and now.

---

[10] Stanley Hauerwas, *Reader* (Durham, NC: Duke University, 2001), p. 85. See also *in loc.* p. 59, 63, & 87.

Christians' life, then, is never to be left *solely* to habitual duty, virtuous character formation or pre-set social structures, however real and important these things may be. Images of life as our journey (or even more problematic, notions of our Christian growth) are not to be separated from the living dynamic of current person-to-person intercourse. If we do so, we slight the Reformation's rediscovery of Christians' freedom in the Spirit of Christ.

By the same token, since we meet a passionate and compassionate Lord, actions that are not motivated in part by our present passion and compassion or are not expressive of our whole person have not begun to be appropriate to his grace. Love coldly understood as "good action" apart from affect is simply not humanly good—and certainly is not the love Christ evokes and commands. From Barth's perspective, then, the so-called New Morality or Situation Ethics, which made a point of setting Christian love apart from spontaneous affection with the slogan "Love is not liking." had rationalized and trivialized it beyond recognition.[11]

---

[11] This type of Neo-Kantian ethic that was popularized in the 1960s under the misnomer of "new morality" by Joseph Fletcher, Bishop John A.T. Robinson and others might have seemed adequate to Barth when he was very young and still trying to apply Kant's moral philosophy. But as a New Testament scholar, he came to realize that Christ's passionately expressed love command is not to be discounted simply because our deepest feelings remain

Since as fallible creatures we have only begun positively to listen and since, as said, our deepest feelings escape rational control, Christ's holistic love remains largely something to pray for. Prayer, not self-repression, then, becomes the inner, *sine qua non* for our obedience, as Barth would use the term. Space for our full freedom in obedience is staked out in God's own prior freedom as liberator.[12] His authority enacted as justice (along with his wrath and any punishing sanctions) we discover to be expressive of, and coherent with, the priority of grace-framed freedom.

The little "word-study for Americans" spoke volumes about Barth's theological intent. It showed that in his mouth the call to "obedience" meant something quite opposite to the connotations it had suggested to me. But his note also showed how, as a traditional European thinker, Barth was dogged by a scho-

---

beyond our rational control. Action that is not impassioned and in part motivated by God-given feeling for another person is, in Christ's terms, quite subhuman. Yet prayer for the warmth we lack jump-starts the relationship.

[12] Compare Eberhard Busch, *Karl Barth,* p. 418. For Barth's own close discussion of God's authority and Christians' freedom see CD I/1, pp. 663-669. Our native notions either of idealized authority or of human freedom can lead the Church astray. For we are to be attentive, instead, to the *liberating intent* of God's entire action towards us. Paradoxically, this is the *ultimate authority* of the universe, which becomes fully visible only in Christ and is recognizable in his Spirit's leading. As a matter of living communion, this relationship may not be reduced to dialectic between our prior concepts of authority-in-the-abstract and our-freedom-in-general or to some compromise setting on a gradient scale between them. God's personal authority is unqualified. The freedom he extends is imperative.

lastic need to keep intact our lines of linguistic derivation. And, of course, a question follows: given our more fluid language context, should we Americans undertake a will-o'-the-wisp effort to let remote root meanings determine our use of such a common term as obedience? I think not.

Yet, as I was to discover, this expectant deference was the inner substance behind the appeal for "obedience" that had become so prominent, not only in his interaction with the scriptures, but also in his dealings with the witness of later thinkers, and in his approach to Christians' way of life in general.

In any case, this remains a key point where clarification of Barth is called for, if his driving force is to be understood in the English-speaking world. *Obedience*, as he insistently stressed the term, describes attentive hearing as a genuine freedom, a Spirit-gifted joyful attunement that comes with hearing the gospel. The "obedience" he spoke of so often is possible only as this complete freedom. A halfhearted, grudging concession or outward conformity has nothing to do with it, but is in effect its opposite. We are fated to misunderstand Barth totally, unless we grasp this. Faith's "obedience," which is a leitmotif for his theology, rings differently in Anglo-American ears. The abstract obedience of following orders, doing one's duty, developing virtuous character habits or even of assuming "free-will responsibility," does not begin to translate his intent. He would indeed mention our *responsibility* sometimes,[13] but then protest that it "is too weak" a word.[14]

It becomes clear that for Barth acting in a free counterpoint to grace may carry one beyond any formal dictates (whether of natural orders, legal casuistry, habitual duty, virtuous character, or even Christ-shaped models) when we consider that he believed the attempt to assassinate Hitler could well have been a free act of genuine obedience for those involved.[15] Yet to American ears Barth's talk of "free obedience"[16] continues to sound like an oxymoron.

It seems that through interaction with his American students Barth did become increasingly aware that his prevalent stress on *obedience* could occasion a misunderstanding (as if he had been moving in the direction of abject legalism). His growing concern to avoid this pitfall was evidenced when, in planning his sole American tour, he chose to represent his entire enterprise as a *"theology of freedom."*[17]

---

[13] See Eberhard Busch, *The Great Passion*, p. 164ff. for a poised summary of Barth's usage here.

[14] English Colloquium discussion, Dec. 18, 1961.

[15] Eberhard Busch cites CD III/4, S. 513 = p. 449 (*The Great Passion*, p. 169).

[16] *Ibid.*, p. 79f.

[17] Clifford Green's 1991 selection of Barth's works under title of *Karl Barth, Theologian of Freedom* is most appropriate here. Green's cogent introduction to this book ranks alongside Eberhard Busch's, *The Great Passion*, as one of the best entrees to Barth's theology available. See Barth's

Saint Paul really meant it when he told the Galatians, "For freedom Christ has set us free; stand fast therefore." [18] The apostle certainly would have included himself among those who have no right to impose any slavish "yoke" of legalism. This means that when he sometimes wished they might "be as he was,"[19] Paul was not imposing himself as a behavioral pattern, but concerned for them to enjoy the kind of freedom for which he was notorious and was being hounded to death by pharasaic legalists.

In the same way, Barth really meant it when he spoke out for Christian freedom. It was no hyperbole. He really meant that we may be and are to be ourselves—who we find we truly are in frank correspondence with the living Christ and as permanent agents of his Covenant community. This does not mean toeing the line in imitation of some restyled law or norm for "Christian behavior," but really to find ourselves, as Paul discovered himself to be, truly free in Christ. In a strict sense this does not even mean dutifully to ape Jesus, much less Saint Paul—and certainly not Karl Barth. Rather it is true liberation: freedom to express yourself uniquely; that is, as the one you find yourself to be right now, in relation to Jesus Christ within

Foreword to the American edition of *Evangelical Theology*, p. xif.
    [18] Gal. 5:1.
    [19] E.g., Gal. 4:12; I Cor. 4:16f.; 10:33f.

his company of saints. The ethical question for Christians, then, is always what *we will do* today, creatively responding along with those around in company with him. As Barth liked to put it: "You are allowed to be free; now be it; do it."[20] That has become our solemn moral imperative.

This has been so often under-appreciated as the ethical command and imperative, at the very heart of Christians' paraenetic urging, that we must keep reminding ourselves. Many of our most ingrained pieties fall short. To bow my head, fold my hands and mutter, "Not my will, but thine be done" is strictly, speaking, not obedient to this imperative. Even the recently popularized teenage slogan, "What would Jesus do?" is too weak, unless we're thinking of Jesus' own freedom for creative action in grace.

What will *we* do—ourselves—our unique response?

That's the concern.

Originally ourselves?

In a prayerful relationship. . . Yes indeed!

Creatively?

That is to be hoped. What we will do just now, at this time, as perhaps at no other, being truly ourselves from the heart—prodded by Christ's Spirit, certainly, while recalling his

---

[20] English Colloquium, Feb. 24, 1959.

117

word and sharing his spirit alongside these other people, here and now, in his community of grace.

ATTENTIVE OPENNESS AND
SPONTANEOUS INTERACTION

As in Calvin's thought, the force of direct person-to-person response pushes any abstract notion of autonomous free will to the side. To be sure, the whole person is *free* to be herself; but the clenched-teeth self-mastery commonly associated with notions of free will is simply not to be the efficient cause where Christ-attentive action is concerned.[21] So free will theories are marginalized.

Despite his rejection of any theology grounded in nature or empirical observation, Barth's attentive stance is analogous in one important respect to the methodology of natural science. Physical science is tentative, open, subservient to new empirical discovery regarding its subject/object in nature. Theology, likewise, should be committed to readjust itself ever again, in conformity to its discrete Subject: the historically-revealed living

---

[21] As John Macmurray used to point out, Early Christianity stressed direct person-response more than self-mastery or character formation. Jesus is remembered to have mentioned the virtuous Stoic ideal, "duty," only once, and that quite dismissively (Lk. 17:9). The emerging church, however, could easily slide into a Stoic attitude and preach fixed duties in an inconsistent, domineering way (for example see I Tim. 4:15f.).

Word. Church theology should always be free to reform itself—
semper reformandum.

Attentive hearing should draw a theologian into multi-
dimensional dialogues with diverse voices of faith. As said,
Barth's sense of a common calling within the context of grace
clearly became an impetus for conversation with other thinkers,
both vertically, spanning history, and horizontally, across the
modern scene.[22] Yet although attentive engagement with others
became an ultra-serious concern, hearing them out never kept
him from raising his own voice finally, for change. Hopefully,
in all this, one will be attuned critically to the living accompaniment of the one who is remembered as promising, "Lo I am
with you always."

Theology—both in its intellectual expression and in the
ethical life it engenders—is to be conversationally engaged with
its living subject. It is, in fact, always to become a kind of prayer (as Calvin had long since urged for the totality of life's expressions). I would stress again that only in reference to such
ongoing dialogic engagement might it be appropriate to continue referring to Barth as a *dialectic* theologian (a common tag

---

[22] Compare E. Busch, The *Great Passion*, p. 40f. In the course of
my Calvin study Barth insisted that full preliminary attention be given to
other earnest voices on every theme. Theology is never to become a mono-
logue.

which, because of its philosophical baggage, he finally came to avoid).[23]

Barth's stance, then, included listening to, and conversing with others. In shared resonance with the self-revealing Word: one's own openness was to entail tripartite conversation, first with scripture, then with the historical Church, and finally, with contemporary scholarly intelligence. We will look further into the dynamics of these three interactions in this and the following chapter.

OPENNESS TO THE CANON AS A WHOLE: BIBLICAL COHERENCE

Karl Barth's open hearing was directed before all to the canon. Yet he was often criticized for handling Bible texts in a way that was just as attentive to their face meaning as to their historical- and textual-critical analysis. He took such objections seriously, but responded with some dismay; for he felt he always had been ready to give careful prior attention to the findings of such analysis.[24]

---

[23] For Barth's early (1920) use of "dialectic" to describe the "inassimilable opposites," which often confront ordinary experience in revelation see in H. Martin Rumscheidt, *The Way of Theology,* p. 13.

[24] It's worth noting here that two of Barth's own sons felt encouraged to become textual scholars.

A Church theologian's relation to the biblical exegete was analogous for him to a medical internist's relation to his pharmacologist. Theirs are distinct roles. But it is not only the original meanings and intent of a text that are important to the theologian. The later interpretations and uses given to it are also grist for his mill. So the theologian's further hypotheses regarding meaning are to take their place right alongside those of the historical/textual critic. Critical analysis cannot exhaust or predetermine the significance a text has had, or should have, for us. Here we find resonance with some of the themes of a postmodern hermeneutic which Barth anticipated from his Christological frame of reference, where God's self-revelation and the living testimony of his Spirit may be in play.

Barth's unapologetically christocentric earpiece for discerning an unfolding "main line" of divine revelation assumes that whenever the gracious God speaks, it will always fit in as part of the same message. His actions, it is to be believed, will be coherent, though in ways that may still escape us.

Barth's readiness to regard the Hebrew Scripture as funneling into New Testament fulfillment and his view that an unfolding main line extends across the whole Bible has bothered some Old Testament exegetes. But on the other hand, when American fundamentalists or evangelicals, such as Billy Graham, having heard that he had a constructive view of scripture,

121

visited Basel looking to buttress their own movement, they were disappointed. For Barth was taken aback by their level of indifference toward the centuries of historical-critical textual analysis of which he felt Christian theologians should be respectful beneficiaries. He was astonished by the strangely wooden perspective of conservatives who had never faced up to the complexity of what "according to the Scripture" (*schriftgemässe*) must mean.

Being "biblical" for him had little in common with those who blithely defend themselves against the diversity of meanings that is embraced by the Scripture itself and violate it by trying to shoehorn everything into a univocal harmony. For Barth, to be biblical means for us to be as attentive to a plurality of Christ-responsive interpretations as the canon-forming community showed itself to have been from the first. At one point he exclaimed, "The Bible itself has a hundred theologies."[25]

ATTENTIVE TO PROPHETIC WITNESS

Barth, with his scientifically informed exegesis, said that the obscure passages of the Scripture are to be explained relative to the more clear ones. We should keep in view general lines, as these develop through *both* the Old and New Testaments, point-

---

[25] English Colloquium, Jan. 27, 1959.

ing to the gospel of a living Word.[26] Yet Barth would shake his head in affectionate dismay over Wilhelm Vischer,[27] who, carried away by sentimental enthusiasm, had tried to read back into every story of the Old Testament symbolic meanings for what comes clear only in Jesus' incarnation.

When a student asked Barth about his own hermeneutic principle for the Old Testament—whether he could approach it in a textual-critical fashion, he said,

> I try to discern the main lines of what is being said concerning God and man. You can make a fruitful use of the criticism. I always speak of the "sagas" of the Old Testament. That is biblical criticism. (There is a Babylonian influence on the text in the Psalms, etc.) My method is a critical one. I have always tried to show the meaning, not only out of the text, but also out of the context of the book, of the chapter—of the whole Bible. The principle of context is an im-

---

[26] English Colloquium, June 26, 1961. One of the greatest distortions of Barth's thought has been the tendency to read "*the Word,*" which for him is theology's foundation, as signifying *the Scriptures* themselves. In his view, however, the Bible presents us instead with variously inspired witnesses to Christ, who alone was and is the living, human-scaled, Word of God. To be sure, Reformed symbols, such as the Westminster Catechism, had long fuzzed this distinction (see e.g., Q. 88-90).

[27] See Vischer's *Bedeutung des Alten Testaments für das christliche Leben* (Zollikon-Zürich: Evangelischer Verlag, 1947).

portant hermeneutic principle.[28]

In order to understand Barth here as English-speaking readers, we must give special attention to a distinction—crucial for him—between two terms that are both casually translated by the single English word "history." For Barth consistently referred to biblical *Geschichte* in strong contrast to bare *Historia.*

Historia is a mere record or sequential chronicle of happenings. But *Geschichte* for him refers to interconnected events, which are not just related in cause-and-effect data sequences, but also as purposeful narrative clusters invested with lasting meaning. *Geschichte*, as Barth often used the term to describe biblical narrative, already had firmly in view the emphasis upon *"story"* (as opposed to bare historical data) that has since come into vogue in America. *Geschichte* narrates the believed personal drama between God and the storied persons he is creating. Of course, as Barth sees it, theirs is not just any story (where one imaginative tale might be as good as another). It is a living drama that is plotted within God's own time-full creativity— precisely *his* story. Theology's reference to *Heilsgeschichte* (the story of salvation), as opposed to bare historical data, is often coupled, for Barth, with his introduction of the category of *saga*

---

[28] English Colloquium, Jan. 27, 1959.

124

to characterize much of biblical narrative (as distinct both from mere recorded event, on the one hand, and from myth, on the other).

GESCHICHTE AND THE WARRANT OF SAGA

Barth's constructive appeal to the "Word of God" has sometimes been thought to involve an uncritical use of texts that most scholars dismiss as mythological. Here it is well to take stock of his use of "saga" as a separate category in assessing the significance of biblical narratives. Sagas portray events as having happened, that yet lie beyond the bounds of verifiable history and elude critical control.[29] Narratives such as those regarding the creation and fall, Abraham and Isaac, YHWH's self-communication to Moses or to Elijah on Mount Carmel, were in his eyes the Bible-people's treasured *sagas* and are to be interpreted and valued as such. Those who approach such texts with a presupposition of verbal inspiration or literal infallibility could only find themselves out of phase with Barth. Yet he too gave the canon primacy in faith and practice.

For sagas present us with claims regarding crucial, significant transformative-event. They are distinct from both myths and chronicled history in that they have been retold in the belief

---

[29] See CD III,1, pp. 81-85.

that the events described not only *actually happened,* but that their significance depends upon that fact—even though any possibility of verification and dating remain beyond our reach. Sagas are told in the belief that the treasured events they describe actually changed, "once and for all" the course and meaning of history.

A myth, by contrast, is told on quite the opposite assumption, that the value or insight it celebrates is a seemingly self-evident general truth, quite apart from whatever stories celebrate it. Though speculative in nature, myths represent common assumptions, taken to be truer than true, so to speak. It is patent that the values, life cycles, etc. symbolized by the myth, are seen to mirror (*speculare*) general experience-based notions regarding the way things always are (and would be, quite apart from their mythic symbolization).[30]

In other words, sagas refer to particular happenings that are believed to have shaped *Geschichte* (in the German sense of unfolding meaningful, storied event). Though they are not to be

---

[30] There is nothing really new in the way Barth embraced the possibility of revelatory saga, as opposed to myths that derive from the human propensity for blanketing over the Unknown with speculation. As I have mentioned, such speculation mirrors aspects of general experience and projects a macrocosm that reflects or silhouettes the microcosm of our self-experience. Such gnosticism in a myriad of forms has dogged the Christian Church from its earliest times and presents perennial challenges to theology. I Tim. 1:4 and 4:7 document typical confrontations.

confused with verifiable history, they affect our grasp of truth by describing how a believed key event signaled or brought about real change. As opposed to the cyclic or timeless, generalities that evoke myth-making, saga is retold with conviction that some *actual happening* changed what is to be known about the course and meaning of life.

This in itself set Barth's interpretation at odds with that of his early compeer Rudolf Bultmann, who called modern readers to "demythologize"; that is, to disregard obsolete mythic or supernatural elements that appear in the textual vehicles of faith.[31] Saga, however, describes a kind of de-mythologization that took place at the first stages of revelation history, as non-provable claims to *key events actually having happened* were passed along.

ATTENTIVE TO APOSTOLIC WITNESS:
THE EARLY CHRISTIAN SAGAS

Christians' openness to the past means, above all, attentive hearing of the Apostles' witness to the incarnate Christ as fulfillment and defining focus of scriptural expectations. Bultmann might leave theology wringing its hands over his accurate observation that there is not a single Jesus testimony that can be

---

[31] See e.g., *Jesus Christ and Mythology* (New York: Scribners, 1958), notably p. 67.

handled as verifiable fact. (Bultmann would suggest that this problem of historicity might be bypassed only by taking our own present existential faith decision as self-sufficient, unfazed by historical doubts).

Here we would expect Barth to apply his Old Testament understanding of "saga" again to such elements of the New Testament gospel narrative as incarnation, miraculous healings and resurrection. Some have held that he would not want to describe the essentials of the Jesus narrative as *sagenhaft* in character. But we have noticed that on occasion, he quite explicitly did do just that, while still maintaining their factual quality for faith. [32]

The gospel claims warrant attentive listening for their positive story. "Ask yourself," Barth would say,

> The Christian always is described as a pilgrim
> [with] something out front as a goal. Christ is the
> goal (see Paul in Philippians 3—a sportsman

---

[32] See e.g., KD IV/1, S. 370f. I have observed a misunderstanding of Barth's recognition that the resurrection is not within verifiable *Historia*, as somehow impinging on its believed factuality. That, of course, has failed to grasp the German concept of meaningful *Geschictlichkeit*, and Barth's recognition of saga as believed actual event, which the translation "legendary" may fail to communicate. Again, Barth would not have agreed with Moltmann who avoids the historical problem of Jesus' resurrection by relegating it to God's eternity, whereas apostolic faith claims its saga character as actual event in time. (See *The Way of Jesus Christ: Christology in Messianic Dimensions* (Minneapolis: Fortress Press, 1993, p. 231 *et passim.*)

running toward a goal. But he is sure of it.) So
leave behind whatever we have been underway.
In full reality before us is the new being, Christ.
The old man is at your back—not before you.

BARTH'S PAULINE PERSPECTIVE
ON THE TIME OF OUR LIVES

That Barth's doctrine was nurtured before all in dialogue with
the apostolic texts is so obvious that we need not rehearse it
here. However, many fail to grasp the divine simultaneity that
was always in the background for him, as he followed St. Paul.
In the last part of this book we will take a brief look at what it
means for our teaching and ministry to be reflecting on the
difference between divine and human perspectives where the
promises of grace are concerned. Paul tends to shift back and
forth between two perspectives. At one moment we find him
sharing his surprise, that our actual fulfillment *subsists already*
with permanence in God's embrace; but at another moment,
typically, he will have down-shifted to a lower gear, so to
speak, to promise it as still in the future, regarded from our
time-bound human viewpoint.[33]

---

[33] See in Chapter 10.

Since Time itself is God's creature, the abiding substance of all temporal event, past and future—including what is promised in the gospel (our salvation assurance, our justification, our new life unfolding as new creation, etc.) must be seen in a startling non-natural, and counter-intuitive, perspective. All of it subsists as already present, permanent and guarded for us, in God's awesome simultaneous grasp. All of that, which must be proclaimed as our future, subsists already as actual for him. This, even though it persists for us only as eschatological promise—"already, but not yet."[34]

Discourse responsive to the New Testament, inevitably becomes christocentric, while its take on both our human promise and present ethic becomes Christ-shaped. That is to say, our perspective becomes essentially trinitarian: it discovers a human grasp of how God relates to God's self, to us, and to his entire creation—all uniquely in Jesus Christ. If the Father decides and the Spirit acts with loyal consistency, he is in himself and always will be the same One for us he has shown himself to be in Jesus Christ. Where else can we look without endless speculation flooding in to splotch across our view?

---

[34] This perspective was implicit to Luther's recognition that despite our continuing sinfulness, we can see ourselves in faith as already permanently justified—*simul iustus et peccator.*

Barth's New Testament dialogue issued in a startling reversal of field for much American theology, which during the mid-century was often caught up in self-centered questions: "What in the Christian tradition is *relevant to us*? How can it contribute to *our own* growth?"—whereas Barth, like Luther, Calvin and Wesley in studying Romans, had found himself accosted by the one who asks, "What in you and your culture and traditions is relevant to my grace for all in Christ? What in your fitful growth and evolutionary process has abiding worth in our Time-transcending Covenant Community?"

ATTENTIVE TO THE
CHURCH'S VOICE IN HISTORY

Theology has a living, moving Person as subject. This means, as Barth often said, one must begin a new dynamic flight as one takes off again at square one with each new topic in a theology that follows the Christ-responsive apperceptions of faith. Under way one finds oneself not just conversing with the apostles, but listening to others' later witness as well. Barth's respect for past thinkers and his readiness to hear them out were palpable. I think of those World War II devices for early aircraft warning. They enhanced civil defense by literally turning wide-open listening funnels first in one direction, then in another. Barth wanted to be attentive and open to Christians' intelligence through the ages. Listening positively meant serious engagement with a much broader range of Church thinkers than most of us knew.

I have mentioned how Barth insisted with me that the younger theologian needs a historical buttonhook. "Try to read everything written" on the topic in question. Then perhaps as a mature scholar "you might someday be ready to write your own" account of doctrine. This is the standard he held up both for his own studies and those of his students.

The way Barth had fended off my initial peeves and problems with Calvin was indicative of his own way in research. He, of course, had had his own lover's quarrels with Calvin. But as scholar, you were to work yourself into the research subject's mentality just as positively as you could. As we saw in his Seminar, this meant you should suspend your negative reactions and judgments as long as possible. His goal was first to understand concepts within others' frames of reference—to begin to apperceive meanings through others' eyes—and only then, cautiously to frame one's own positive or questioning responses.

For most of us American Protestants, theology had been epitomized with the Reformers. But Barth also would regularly engage seventeenth and eighteenth century thinkers as serious *Gespräch* partners—scholastic, biblistic and pietistic voices—to

132

listen and be questioned by them. "Work through Heppe," he'd advise.[35] One of the things that made some Americans flinch and feel that Barth was self-willed and out of touch may have been his insistence on hearing out such a broad array of witnesses. But his openness and ability to focus on others' history actually bolstered his ability to find his own way and lead, rather than simply fall in with the *Zeitgeist* of his peers.

Bible studies in our churches are often short-circuited by asking, from first to last, how a text grabs us; whereas the perspectives of other times might go far to soften the hard edges of all we have begun to take for granted and dampen the membranes of our thought, so to speak, to make them more permeable. So we might do well to ask, as Barth did, why a text or doctrine was important to believers of other eras before we indulge in the self-centered question, what the Spirit would say therein to us.

As one whose serious theological conversation had been mainly limited to the Bible and the Reformers, I soon discovered with Barth how useful it can be to read also in the Fathers and across the sweep of Post-Reformation theologies if we are to grasp our contemporary situation in the Church.[36] For exam-

---

[35] Heinrich Heppe, *Reformed Dogmatics Set Out and Illustrated from the Sources* (London: George Allen & Unwin, 1950).

[36] For example, to be digested were the emerging Protestant creeds,

ple, something like the American split between the liberals and the John Machen-type fundamentalists is put in perspective when we discover that the notion of verbal inspiration did not even come in question before the historically late writings of seventeenth century Scholastics, such as John Koch (Coccejus) of Bremen.

Or again, it may be healthy to discover that the problem of suffering, which seems to have burst in upon the evangelical scholar Bart Ehrman, as a recent, faith-shattering shock, would never have taken earlier Reformed thinkers by surprise. Rather, it had always been one of the realistic starting blocks that gave their faith its traction. What looms so large as a modern block to faith for Ehrman,[37] they long since found to be transcended by Spirit-gifted hope.[38] Apparently he ends where they had begun.

Heinrich Heppe's compilation of Reformed Scholastics' texts, Hans Emil Weber's *Reformation, Orthodoxie und Rationalismus,* and perhaps Barth's own book on the background and theology of the nineteenth century.

[37] A prolific author of scholarly New Testament textbooks, Bart D. Ehrman recently made a media event of how his own earlier evangelical beliefs have been overwhelmed by what appears to have been his midlife awakening to the theodicy problem. (Viz. his Feb. 19, 2008 Public Radio discussion of his book, *God's Problem.*) Tellingly, he admitted still praying sometimes to the God in whom he says he can no longer rationally believe.

[38] In Reformed thought Barth found the ability to leave the excruciating experiences of life and death behind as evanescent evil that is already eliminated from God's past perfect—a "nothingness," finally, as Barth came to term it. See Petruschka Schaafsma's careful study of Barth's demystification of evil as life-negating nothingness or "*das Nichtige*": *Reconsidering Evil—Confronting Reflection with Confessions* (Leuven: Peeters, 2006), pp. 193ff.

Thus Barth's vertical attentiveness included a concern that as far as possible we grasp later Church writers (and not only the biblical texts) in their original language with exegetical concern for their terminology and historical background. I was to "go back and read everything Calvin ever wrote" in French and Latin. For Calvin too, was like ourselves, a *homo viator,* a pilgrim underway, living into a drama of exploration, who was only gradually discovering further implications of God's free grace for his own time and place.

In retrospect, it strikes me as indicative of Barth's respect for original texts that during my years of Calvin study, he never even hinted that I might take my bearings from his own early response to Calvin in the provocative lectures he had published in 1922. As a teacher Barth was interested in my interaction and objective response to the Reformer, and avoided intervening to color my response. He never even suggested that I could or should cite his own early writing on the subject of Calvin's ethics.

The larger Basel faculty expected one to be conversant with the entire scope of Church history. (One had to digest Karl Heussi's compendium from cover to cover.) But Barth encouraged his students to become especially familiar with the post-Reformation chapters of Reformed theology, which meant studying the twists and turns of seventeenth century Protestant Neo-

135

Scholastic and Aristotelian revivals. His affirmation of the unity of the covenant stretched backward and forward across the entire history and future of the Church.

Through all of this, the subject and object of each generation's responsive attentiveness has been the vital and personal Living Word, who is confronted through hearing others' faith, as such faith has been first recorded in and later occasioned for us through the Scripture. Since a fresh response to this gracious One is liberating, Barth has always been most adventuresome in his biblical interpretation and invites us to be so bold as well. He would always ask what a text might mean in inner coherence with the living Word. Yet a theologian, given his or her wider contextualization, is to evoke questions beyond those of the biblical scholar and need not limit reflections to what a passage originally meant. Theologians in seeking to understand[39] may freely take the typology of grace beyond the texts' original context to venture into further dialogue, hopefully still in company with the one who is their theological Subject.[40]

---

[39] Viz. the *fides quaerens intelligere* theme from Anselm.

[40] Barth has been construed in the direction of a biblistic fundamentalism by some Americans who misunderstand his interaction with the *living "Word"* as speaking of the "Bible" per se. Thus in a lecture at Virginia's Union Seminary after his return from Basel, John N. Thomas said that according to Barth, "the Bible should not be approached with any *Vorkentniss"* (i.e., with no preconceptions). Does that mean you should discard your geological or paleontological evolutionary view of nature in favor of Gene-

The whole ensemble of Barth's characteristic themes displays this kind of adventuresome following. You find prominent examples of such creative exegesis already in his provocative interpretations of the Genesis saga, with creation as a benefit and a template for woman's equality and rights, and with the exclusion from the Tree of Life interpreted as a kindness, and with the Noah story, seen as promise, and so on. You meet such audacious interpretation again and again, across his works, such as in his striking concept of *das Nichtige* (which refuses to afford any ultimate substance to evil alongside God). You can see it in his societal grasp of the Trinity, in his view of the simultaneousness of God's Time, in his recognition of a unitary covenant embracing both Judaism and Christianity, in his hope for the election of all in Christ, in his insistence that Jesus of Nazareth is the only sacrament[41] and in his constant appeal to faith's relationship-based analogy, to name but a few.

Next, let us follow how, according to Barth, this adventuresome freedom a theologian may enjoy in pneumatic response extends out into interrelationships in the present community of scholarship and beyond.

---

sis? That is not Barth. But Thomas misreads this as an "attack on reason" and then marvels that a man who "so brilliantly attacks reason should so brilliantly use reason on every page of the attack" (Union Seminary, VA, tape collection).

[41] I. e., as Augustine defined sacrament (an outward and visible sign of God's hidden, inner Truth).

Chapter 5

Interactive Dialogue: Horizontal

Openness Today

BARTH'S WAY WITH OTHERS' VOICES

Another aspect of Barth's creative listening, then, was his insistence that one do a good job of attending to other voices across the horizontal field of current scholarship. One of the striking things for us about the mind behind the monumental *Church Dogmatics* was how un-dogmatic Barth could be in conversation.[1] For him theology is always underway, mobile, as it follows, reflective of its vitally present living subject, sharing in attentive dialogue along with others around.

---

[1] There is an amusing father-in-law's letter in which Barth in introducing himself to his daughter's new husband, Max Zellweger, a chemist, assured him that despite his own academic title, he was in all honesty not really a dogmatic soul: "I indeed teach and write 'dogmatics' (as long as God has patience with me), but I am basically not a dogmatic person. I go from one day to the next and always try to learn something new, so that no one needs fear my meanings—least of all you."

139

Before framing your position or teaching on any theme, you need to be able to grasp and epitomize other serious voices of belief in our times. Grace-based attentiveness also means to be in conversation across cultural and denominational lines. And for that you need to become familiar, as best you can, with diverse thought-worlds and current events; so theologians were not Barth's only discussion partners.

"A good dogmatic," he would tell us, "is a Christian philosophy" and "we must study philosophy earnestly," if for no other reason, "in order that we not confuse theology and philosophy."[2] Post-modern appreciation of how the "world is flat" for important current conversation would not have startled him. The horizontal openness of his theology was visible in his office, where the daily paper often was spread across his desk to be comprehended from a faith perspective. Even recent sporting events could find their way into his lectures. He would quip to interviewing reporters that theirs is the most important calling in the world (save that of a theologian, of course)! He claimed a universe-wide ecumenical scope for theology, however much his own perceptions remained those of a Western European. I've mentioned already his remarkable interest in the American Church, the American Civil War and our conception of "the

---

[2] English Colloquium, Jan. 22, 1964.

American way of life."

We are always, as Luther would say, under *Anfechtung.* That means we are challenged continually to readjust our own responsive thought and expression. And a vital thrust of the Holy Spirit's present impetus is often mediated by others, who are themselves becoming more or less attentive to Jesus Christ (who, even as our ultimate judge, said, "Do not think I will categorize you").[3]

So obedience, as Barth conceived it, opens out to include attentiveness to other thinkers, who are also called to attunement from their various angles of address. My San Francisco teacher and Basel colleague, Arnold Come, put this strongly: "Barth seems to have honestly, sensitively, deeply opened his very life and being to diverse streams of Christian thought and non-Christian philosophy, and *in him* they have found their irrefragable unity."[4]

As we've noted, in sharp contrast to Barth's surprising patience with all sorts of intellectual pilgrims and theologies of every kind, was the dismay he expressed toward the self-styled Barthians who were beginning to think of his always open-ended and searching work as a rigid system.[5] It strikes me as

---

[3] John 5: 45; 12:47.
[4] *An Introduction to Barth's "Dogmatics" for Preachers*, p. 66.
[5] "My theology is not written in heaven, but in Basel; not by an an-

ironic that his insistent openness itself has offended some American theologians, as a kind of self-willed fixity.[6]

BASEL DIALOGUES

Barth's dialogic intent was visible in his cordial demeanor toward the most diverse guests. He would welcome those of widely divergent positions as dialogue partners and try to ease his way into their shoes, as if he wanted to contextualize and grasp their thoughts as vividly as they did. Visitors of all stripes joined us during my stay: Amos Wilder from Harvard; Arnold Come and Benjamin Reist from San Francisco; Dietrich Ritschl, home from Pittsburgh; Adolpho Ham from Cuba, and many others, including Hans Küng, who was to become instrumental in bringing the future pope, Joseph Ratzinger, to Tübingen.[7] (In fact, Ratzinger himself visited Barth and contributed as a guest to his seminar on the Trent and the Vatican Councils.)[8]

As mentioned in Chapter 4, American evangelicals, having heard of Karl Barth's positive approach to revelation, would come to Basel expecting to find an ally. But Barth found some

---

gel, but by a man" (John D. Godsey, *Karl Barth's Table Talk*, p. 24).

[6] Compare John B. Cobb Jr.'s "Critical Appraisal" in McKim, *op. cit.*, p. 174f.

[7] Küng, who was deeply influenced by Karl Barth, apparently would live to regret his support of Ratzinger when he found his own orthodoxy questioned and his license to teach Roman Catholic candidates withdrawn.

[8] E. Busch, *Karl Barth*, pp. 482-5.

of the things the fundamentalists among them took for granted to be strange. The word "evangelical" on the continent retained its ancient grace-centered force; so it must have saddened Barth to observe how American groups believing and often behaving in ways he found at odds with gracious "good news" had usurped the "evangel" tag.

As we noted regarding Barth's classroom, it was characteristic of him to go just as far with any theological "conversation partner" as he could: Tillich, Schleiermacher, and Feuerbach. Self-irony far outweighed defensiveness in Barth's attitude and counsel. Don't begin by insulating yourself polemically from the force and inner coherence of some thoughtful mind's insights just because you intuit final disagreement may be in store. You should digest and follow the other's conceptualizations and terminology as fairly as possible. Try sincerely to suspend disagreement and doubts. Respect the awesome stature of any other human mind and strive to grasp its integrity. Reserve your still-unanswered questions and reluctant criticisms until the very end of the process. Try to grasp with sanctified imagination what the world looks like through the other's eyes. Stand, at least for the time being, where she or he stands. If you are working in company with the incarnational Spirit of Christ, you will avoid sliding into a defensive or a polemic position.[9] Reflect the golden rule in thinking.

I found myself influenced by this approach later in my own nearly half century of teaching; though I did not succeed with his consistency. I have to remind myself we studied with the sagacious, much mellowed aging scholar who at an earlier time had emblazoned "NEIN!" in blaring typeface across the cover of his blast against a colleague. For Barth's positive spirit struck us in everything he did. I suspect that earlier students experienced a greater "ambiguity in his tolerance"[10] than those of us who knew the professor in his 70s.

Where the younger Barth had thrived on controversy, I have to stress again that the seasoned teacher we knew often warned against polemic either as mood or method in theology. He counseled against defensiveness as a temptation that could only provoke opposition, increased distortion and obfuscation. A Hegelian evocation of juxtaposed opposites is not the avenue to higher truth. The Word is not better heard through conflict.

---

[9] Barth's stance in listening to others, as we have described it, was clearly already taking form in his early work as an academic scholar. For a beautiful reflection see the Introduction to his 1922 lectures on *The Theology of John Calvin*: We should read, he says, "with a certain free and understanding humor, presuming that the author is probably always right in some sense even when wrong, so that our only task is to see how far this is always so . . . See further *in loc.*, p. 6.

[10] See e.g., Dietrich Ritschl in Donald K. McKim ed., *op cit.*, pp. 88-90.

(After all, selective one-sidedness is the real root meaning of that ugly word, "heresy.") The Prince of Peace is not well-represented by warring opposites. Neither is fierce debate practical, since extreme positions developing on either side of an argument simply compound error and generate more heat than light. Here our hardball political pundits and even Public Television's sober-sided "News Hour" could learn something from the mature Karl Barth.

Nevertheless, to the end he kept a leathery insistence on expressing a forceful "no" when needed to clarify the greater "yes" of grace against the nothingness that has no final power to undermine it.[11] So his call to engage in chastening dialogue meant finally to stand fast in one's full stature and freely represent a Christ-responsive conceptualization of one's own. By the same token, a theologian has no business enlarging upon doubt or projecting it into the foreground, as if doubt could be a springboard to belief. Where doubt still reigns, faith can take hold at any moment. So we should proclaim grace in the hope that new faith will be given. For the simple gospel claim is not only contagious, it has God's sovereign initiative behind it. Christian faith is a positive experiential actuality, though its

---

[11] See Schaafsma, Petruschka, *Reconsidering Evil,* p. 193ff. for a most recent summation of Barth's view of evil as *"das Nichtige"* or life-negating nothingness.

contents are not to be construed as provable general knowledge.

SAYING YES TO LIFE
AND NO TO NOTHINGNESS

So the common academic regard for an open frame of mind was reinforced for Barth by mutual respect within the body of Christ. But as we see, this does not mean that we should not eventually gain a vantage point whence, with fear and trembling perhaps, we may feel called to take a positive stand for the "yes" of God's grace by voicing a robust "no" in its defense. For our primary responsiveness is to faith's living subject/object, Jesus Christ as ultimate core Wisdom, Word and Norm. Yes!

Since our responses to others are to be free in grace, there comes a point sometimes—at least a penultimate point— when despite having heard well, we should freely agree to disagree, for the time being, without breaking our covenanted interrelationship within the Body of Christ. But Barth's notorious ability to say "no," as he often told us had always been *intended* as the obverse side of a sovereign yes. A decade earlier in *Christian Century* articles[12] he already described how he had had to learn that it is far more important to say yes than to say

---

[12] Mar. 9 & 16, 1949 (pp. 298-300 & 333f.).

no, and that where God is concerned, positive grace precedes and encompasses his judging. This can scarcely be stressed enough. In Barth's mature view (as in Paul's) justice itself has been completely redefined by grace. (See Chapter 10.) So if we speak of God's justice it must refer to his uniquely promising, up-building, and restorative way and should never be confused with a score sheet equity or vindictive spirit of retribution.[13]

FREEDOM TO DISAGREE
IN THE SPHERE OF GRACE

Openness to hear with attentive respect, then, in no way diminishes one's confident freedom to differ, challenge or carry further what one hears from other people. As said, attentiveness to others includes the freedom to find one's own mind in the exchange and for the time being, perhaps, to agree to disagree. It is indicative of Barth's concern for faith-bounded theology that he found a far greater problem with Rudolf Bultmann (who, in his view, displayed a gnostic mindset in allowing empirical norms to impinge upon the sphere of faith) than with such a frank skeptic as Ludwig Feuerbach who simply clarified how

---

[13] See further below. The basis of Barth's strong criticism of our often brutal criminal "justice" system is striking here. The ancient *lex talionis* is to be understood as having put a rational brake on violent retaliation, but not as a divine sanction for punitive retribution.

things look in the absence of faith.

When it came down to the wire, Barth would stoutly defend his considered opinions, though he hoped to avoid reactionary polemic, hyperbole, and *ad personam* arguments. An example for me of how he could defend his ground even at the margins, was his resistant reaction to the manuscript that Prof. Arnold Come had put together intended as a quite positive introduction to Barth's works for preachers.[14] I knew Arnold well and had scurried around to rent a house for him and his wife for their sabbatical stay in Basel, where he hoped to find his work warmly endorsed.

Come intended his book to be positive and laudatory, but knowing Barth was allergic to sycophants, who were beginning to venerate his growing *Dogmatics* as a kind of authoritative *Summa,* and wanting to avoid the stigma of being a Barthian, he had been frank in expressing his typically American reaction to "the length, the wordiness, and repetitiousness" of Barth's massive work,[15] and he, in effect, seemed to encourage preachers to take Barth's theology with a grain of salt while exploiting his works largely as a Bible-study resource.

---

[14] *An Introduction to Barth's "Dogmatics" for Preachers,* Philadelphia: Westminster Press, 1963.
[15] p. 131.

In a chapter whimsically entitled "How to Avoid Becoming a Barthian," Come gave short summaries of critical reservations that might be held against Barth, in effect faulting him for those "average readers," who might misread him. Barth's christomonism, for example, could all too easily be thought to absorb and denigrate humanity; and despite his modest self-view, he had managed to leave the "overpowering impression of having said the whole word and the last word on every subject." And wasn't his "wide and radical biblical interpretation overloaded with revelational presuppositions?" Hadn't he exaggerated the problem of *analogia entis* and introduced themes that "if taken by themselves could easily suggest a kind of gnosticism" from on high or "monistic idealism"—a "faith rationalism"?[16] Come felt Barth had failed to cover himself against such misinterpretation, even though his whole life had been explicitly directed against gnostic speculation.

As an American, Come assumed (and wrote) that Barth, being known for his openness, would, "take [his] critique with great good cheer."[17] He was deeply disappointed and stung when Barth did not simply take his well-meant criticism with a gentle shrug. For Barth, feeling misconstrued, was less than delighted and took strong issue with the book. He obviously felt

---

[16] See especially pp. 140 and 149.
[17] *In op. cit.*, p. 132.

Come's grains of salt had disfavored his entire *Dogmatics.*

A MEDIEVAL VIEW OF DISPUTATION?

There was certainly a cultural difference at play. European scholars, more than their American counterparts, retained glimmerings of the medieval tradition that truth can and should be arrived at through unyielding formal debate. This assumption increased the difficulty of continuing an amiable relationship when discussion turned up irreconcilable differences. So in Germanic academic circles, openness and self-irony were more easily prized in theory than practiced in ongoing face-to-face confrontations. Should disagreement persist, personal rapprochement became difficult. Despite Barth's concern for attentive openness, he retained a strain of this Old World notion that rational discussion will lead earnest minds to truth.

In our experience, as Americans we did not feel quite so ready to let personal relationships depend, finally, on a meeting of minds. It may be that, conditioned by our pluralistic experience, we are forced to value even superficial friendships and cultivate them, where we know there will be no ultimate agreement. To do so has become a survival skill in our multi-cultural society. An acquaintance in Denmark once described his feeling that trying to have more than one or two true, lifelong personal friends would be a breech of loyalty, perhaps even more suspect than marital infidelity. Such rare close friendships, he felt, render one vulnerable and are to be kept under tight wraps. Such inability to maintain multiple friendships on other levels than intellectual harmony struck us as dysfunctional.

We had to ask ourselves whether our own ever-tolerant American individualism and good-buddy familiarity might simply cloak superficiality; but still we were taken aback by how, despite their commitment to covenanted community, our European peers would seek a meeting of minds by withdrawing into their respective studies to confront one another's ideas in print, rather than really putting up with each other in person. So we nourished the conceit that we had something to teach our more reserved European peers about easy relationships.

When we discovered that Karl Barth and Emil Brunner had avoided face-to-face contact for years following their dispute over natural orders in theological ethics, it struck us as a loss. These Swiss compeers had once conversed earnestly with each other; but after their debate had ground to an impasse, all exchange had stopped.[18] We found this freeze in personal relationship especially ironic in someone like Barth, whose theology was so devoted to "obedient" attentiveness between Chris-

---

[18] Interestingly, Barth managed a friendlier personal openness toward Tillich, where a much wider philosophical distance separated them. ("I like him as a man.")

tians.

John Hesselink, who, as a missionary teacher in Japan had become acquainted with Emil Brunner during the latter's stay there, made it his mission to bring the two of them amicably together. We have photos John took of Barth and Brunner facing one another as warily as a couple of alert gamecocks during the visit he finally engineered in November 1960.[19] Both men did show a desire to restore a personal bridge across their intellectual impasse; and John calls to my attention that "Barth's last letter to Brunner, which the latter received the day before his death is probably the most tender, moving letter Barth wrote to anyone."

OPENNESS TO NATURE?

As suggested above, Barth's horizontal openness included appreciation and concern for the larger, non-human creation. Although theology is written for human beings, its humble awe before the totality, of which our life is but a part, is far from the narrow man-centeredness that later ecologically-minded thinkers have often faulted in traditional theology. Although for Barth's generation, the horrific waste and destruction wreaked upon nature by warfare was far more immediate in people's

---

[19] See Hesselink's own account in Donald McKim's *How Karl Barth Changed My Mind* (1986).

152

minds than was gradual ecological degradation, his thought showed moments of cosmic scope, soaring beyond those human concerns theologians are indeed called to address.

As the power of a fine microscope is best demonstrated by its high-resolution focus on the tiniest objects, God's own grandeur is known in his power to attend intimately to the smallest of his creatures. His eye is on the sparrow.[20] For many that awareness seemed to be snuffed out, when medieval man's place at the center gave way to a heliocentric world-view. If you take the vastness of the solar system as the basis for a natural theology it overwhelms us. How can such tiny creatures have significance, when the earth itself is reduced to a mere speck adrift amid the cosmic reaches and black holes of space?

For Barth, it is the wondrous claim of grace that time-sovereign divine love *simultaneously* grasps every person, indeed every creature, in the universe as an equivalent *center of the whole*. (See further in Chapter 10.) If taken seriously, this counterintuitive claim should evoke a responsive ethic that begins to respect and value every human being—every employee, finally—not just as a "human resource," but as a co-equal partner and center of concern with plenty of room left over to love every part of our natural environment as well.

---

[20] Ps. 84:3; Matt, 10:29ff.

153

OPENNESS TO THE FUTURE?

It must be added that Barth's dialogic openness had a future dimension as well. At one of our *Kleiner Kreis* meetings, he commented regarding Jürgen Moltmann's newly published future-oriented *Theology of Hope* that it was a luxury for him, as a retired theologian, to be able to sit back and listen, without feeling any personal necessity to respond to the younger man. His only hope was that Moltmann would not become one-sided or reductionist with his futuristic theme.

In these conversations Barth was quite clairvoyant, as it has turned out, regarding the immediate future of academic theology. For he said he expected there to be a fateful period of resurgence of man-centered theology reminiscent of Schleiermacher. Though he scarcely could have foreseen to what extent a preoccupation with "human spirituality" would super-saturate activity in the field by century's end.

Barth's theoretical openness toward all sorts of theological pilgrims meant that he was disposed to be open to inevitable correctives and shifts of emphases over against his own thought by future theologians, who would be writing just as freely for their time as he did for ours. He did not feel he had been carving out anything final, though he hoped his work might be given the same attentive regard by future Christians that he had given those of the past.

HEARING OTHERS—BARTH'S LAST WORD

In summary, we have seen that Karl Barth's enormous respect for other minds, past, present and future was palpable—especially his respect for the efforts of critical scholars. He sought to be attuned to Christians' intelligent voices through the ages, and not just those thought to be relevant or popular at present. In the last paragraph he ever wrote, just before he fell asleep on the eve of his death, Barth was urging our "attentive" hearing and free response to ancient believers, as well as modern, across denominational lines. For "God is not the God of the dead but of the living" and "all live in him." So believers of the Old Testament and of our entire past have relevance and a right to be heard today—"not uncritically, not with automatic [submission], but still, attentively. The Church would not be [God's] Church [if, absorbed only in the present,] it would not listen to them." Thus spoke Karl Barth just before he himself was taken off to join his future with God's living people, who bear witness from our past.[21]

---

[21] *Final Testimonies,* Eberhard Busch, ed. (Grand Rapids: Eerdmans, 1977, p. 60).

Chapter 6

Listening In:

The Tone of Barth's Anglo-American Colloquies

HOW BARTH EPITOMIZED HIS VIEWS IN ENGLISH

In the excerpts below I mean to document something of the atmosphere of Barth's biweekly English language Colloquia where he dealt with sections of his *Church Dogmatics*. I have rather freely digested and sometimes paraphrased a selection of the students' questions and challenges to the professor below; but my record of Barth's responses, while somewhat fragmentary, are close to his exact words. The greater simplicity of language that he used, as he strove to explain the essentials of his thinking in the basic English he had taught himself late in life, gave a special significance to these private Colloquia. For this effort often pushed him to epitomize in a fresh, telegraphic way what he meant to be the essential points in his writing.

157

These evening discussions took place—always over a glass of white wine or *Apfelsaft*—at the Bruderholz Restaurant near Barth's home with several dozen in voluntary attendance.

ON NATURAL THEOLOGY

Of these typical Colloquia, chosen almost at random, the first was dealing with a section of *the Dogmatics* where discussion turned on Barth's avoidance of natural theology.[1] His introductory remarks included this comment:

> The triumph of natural theology comes in its encounter with men who [feel themselves to be] "of God." The most dangerous form of natural theology is among Christians who are making the gospel "respectable." [E.g.,] the organizing man—the great "I"—who enjoys being a Christian and for whom the gospel is only a help to him in being a good bourgeois.
>
> "Respectability!"

He then turned to address the student leader's set questions—some queries more substantial than others.

---

[1] Feb. 24, 1959 discussing KD II/1 (§26ff.), S. 141ff. = CD II/1, p. 128ff. on "The Readiness of Man."

[Scholar] Where you are describing how people can acknowledge grace without actually living out of it, but misuse it instead for a kind of self-aggrandizement, I think there is a mistranslation: The English says people can "*appraise* it, perhaps teach it, perhaps defend it" in this self-centered way. But aren't you here saying they actually can come to "**praise**" grace, and not merely evaluate or "appraise" it? (The German word is *preisen*.)[2]

[Karl Barth] Yes, that's right.

[S] But explain yourself here. Can a man have such knowledge of grace, willingness for it, without having grace itself? Can he have faith without its having been given to him by grace? Can he sense his need, without actually participating in grace?

> [KB] We are men who have a knowledge of grace—a willingness. But always, "*we.*" It is man, as such, who has heard the gospel (or even accepted it)—has heard of grace. But as man, he doesn't like it—not out of himself. That is the tragedy of Christianity.

---

[2] Engl. p. 134 = S. 148f.

Nevertheless, we are what we are [including the] bourgeois, who will "deal" with Christ as a means for his own "humble" pride. When we consider what we are (and what I am), we are on the lookout to help Self, even with the gospel. That's our Christian tragedy, our weakness, while we are men in the world. And for those outside the Church it is often more a stumbling block than a help.

[S] But for those who have not really appropriated through faith the knowledge of God in Jesus Christ, what is it that makes them aware of their need? Doesn't the Christian speaking from the pulpit or in personal contacts with "men-as-such" have more to say than simply, "You are unaware of it, but Christ is your savior"?

[KB] If something happens, some other One has taken our place: Jesus Christ has stepped in and used our poor witness. It's not [of] ourselves.

[S] Can't all people be considered both "men-as-such" and men whose lives are "hid with Christ"? You say Christ is the only "true man." Surely you don't mean that people who are not Christians are not even men at all? Can't a natural man, who is still "man-as-such," begin to *know* Christ? After all, Jesus said, "If you had known me, you would have known my Father also (Jn. 14:7).

[KB] The question arising here [was to be]: "What is Natural Theology?"

You have only to look in self. Here is the root: natural theology as companion of a two-sided revelation. It becomes a fact [for us], instead of an enemy—becomes a *praeambula fidei* [precursor of faith]. But because we've allowed it to enter, it becomes "the very thing," [for us] and won't long remain [a mere companion or preamble to faith.] Sin wins its greatest triumph right here.

[S] Would you explain what this difference is that you seem so intent on maintaining, between faith itself and people's experience of it?[3]

[KB] Receiving Grace, having grace, and living in grace are not the same. Faith, as such, [inasmuch as it is *our* faith,] is also a human act. But faith is saving only insofar as it is "in Jesus

_____

[3] CD II/1, p. 141=KD II/1, S.157.

Christ." You ask the difference between Faith itself, and man's experience of faith? There may be an experience of faith which senses it as real. But what we call an experience in psychology is finally *me*—my readiness, my feeling, etc.

Real faith in Jesus Christ, however, has nothing to do with my state of mind; nor is it borne out by experience. It is only real in pointing at Christ. [To be sure,] there is no faith without experience. But experience apart from faith can be equivocal. Experience of faith is not necessarily a negative aspect, but experience also can be merely an experience of *what I am*.

Christianity is not a "religion"—not a kind of religion.[4] Faith is a work of God. I do it, but even insofar as it is an experience, it is a gift and work of God.

[S] In describing your view that knowledge of God can only be a miracle—an actual miracle of grace—you say, man "cannot exist just as well (*ebensogut*) without knowing God. And he cannot know Him just as well without His grace."

---

[4] E.g., Contrast William James' *Varieties of Religious Experience*.

Cannot exist and know as well as what?

[KB] Man, as such, is a justified sinner (with Luther, *simul peccator et iustus*). The same man is sinner (man as such *and* man in Christ). But this is not a relationship of two sides, but of a story that happens: Justice lies before you; and sin will lie behind you. You can't escape this double existence. But it is one of [different] moments and not of two sides (such as [Anders] Nygren's overlapping eons or two stations between which we live).

[Consider how] for Paul (using gnosis as something that concerns the whole man) the relation to Christ always is the deciding moment. He, before and within us: the beginning, the way, goal, light, and truth.

Faith? Accept His "I am." Always find my own I, as a sinful I. My elevation is not mine, but participating in his.

[S] If you say knowledge of God is in essence sheer miracle and gift, aren't you making moral effort unnecessary?

[KB] Think "obedience" here: Then all is clear. There's a pilgrim's progress [within] resurrection finally. Simply live: I am, as I am. Sin always lies behind me and *Heil* [healing-salvation always] before me. "Look homeward Angel"; and don't (like Lot's wife) look behind you.

We're dealing with a history. It happens in moments. At no moment are we in heaven and at no moment in hell, but always in between. It'll always be a "more or less." And that makes life interesting—always changing. But it's not a change in principle, but a living between two eons. We are not carrying the past, present, and future in self, somehow, simultaneously [as God does]. This is not the togetherness of two parts or sides of ourselves, but a reference: the past and the future—a real union between the sinner and the right, in a movement, in a story.

Our continuity—what always remains of us—is Christ. Because we are together with him, there is always continuity. There are catastrophes of all kinds; but believing in him, we believe in a continuity of ourselves in his love. Jesus Christ has taken **our** flesh and borne **our** judgment.

In the mission field or pulpit, announce the gospel as we understand it. Proclaim it as justification and sanctification and law, etc.; but try to do it in such a way that you don't suppress the mystery of the gospel, the mystery of Christ, so that misunderstanding can arise. ("Oh well, now *I choose to love and I choose to obey.*") Don't make it a moral instruction in order to improve my human situation, so that psychological pedagogy and the like (as *my means* of improvement) will seem to be on the same plane.

If it is only a means, then it is not the gospel. Don't *use* it. Make that clear: It's an action of God. Make it clear throughout that God has acted and is important and not you! He[5] is something real and new entering your life! If you preach, try to pray with your listeners. So the gospel is not something *within* them, but *before* them, as the mystery of God's action. Help them and do your best to explain the gospel, so it will not be misunderstood as prey to human pride.

[S (John Hesselink)] Isn't proclamation of gospel primarily an objective proclamation of what God has done?

---

[5] See Prologue regarding the gender specific language for God as Father.

[KB] Yes, but it is *for us* and not far away. We are in the midst of it. It is first an allowance, a freedom, and only then, something to be done—but never the kind of action, where God begins to be a passive observer.

Peter preaches Christ. Then the people ask, "What are we to do?" The answer is simple: Do what is implicated in faith. You are allowed to be *free*. Now be it; do it! Paul's ethics too are bound together: faith-and-life. The notion of incarnation and of reconciliation can't be separated. Its one thing: the incarnate Word to reconcile the world to God.

[S] Is Christ, then, an ontological necessity?
[KB] The real omnipresence of God is the *Sitz-im-Leben*. God's presence is his presence in Christ. All that happened in Creation and long before. Christ is the image. (I am supra-lapsarian.)[6]

---

[6] A "supralapsarian" believes that the drama of salvation was already in God's intent *before the fall* of man—in fact that the entire history of redemption and salvation represents God's permanent relation to his Creation —with Christ as both Alpha and Omega of history.

[S] What, then, is the relation of the Old Testament to this knowledge of God which is "only in Christ"?

[KB] The Old Testament is human witness to a history.[7] The sense of this history was a covenant—a history of covenant between God and his people—in which God covenanted looking upon a future. There's a process of history marching toward this goal. What happened was not the result of this covenant. (Man was unfaithful—not God.) The end[-goal] of the Old Testament is the beginning of a new covenant, fulfilled. Christ is the fulfillment. But the Old Testament points to him—the whole flesh of this people pointing to this flesh.

[S] You refer to *religious movements* as being a means of surprising and overcoming the unsure and not-so-clever natural man, and then again, as being chapters in the history of the Church's proclamation.[8] What do you think of revival movements, such as the American movement of Billy Graham? Do they have a place in the Church?

---

[7] Barth uses "history" here in the sense of German, *Geschichte*; i.e., as a dramatic, meaningfully storied whole.

[8] CD II/1, p. 146 = KD II/1, S. 163 f.

[KB] I can't say they are other than what is said about [all ordinary] experience. Within the larger field of humanity's experience is this experience of religious movements. But history is in the hands of God, and one can give no general answer.

[Considering John Wesley and Billy Graham] there will always be a double aspect. There can be no question but that in their sermons there's a magnificent call to Christ's grace (a positive side). But along with that, there's such an interest in sin and hell. It was thundered out in gay old England: [Scare the people to death.] Make them afraid.

What was that movement? It was *about* Christ, to be sure; but perhaps it was also a historical movement to tell them, be careful of pleasures and the like. The "fist of God" is more on the human side—the side of the little I; but not the big I. There are some [similar] places at the height of Luther: But moralism, chastisement and the like? (It was sometimes the same with Luther.) [But no.]

Billy Graham? I heard him and had the impression of someone who had a pistol: "Go and pray and read the Bible. You *must* do it!"

Impressive. But I prefer Wesley to Billy Graham because I heard more of gospel by Wesley. With Billy Graham, more of law. Billy Graham's a real organization man. Is it more of a religion than Christianity that he does? (I ask—don't judge.)

If I were a minister in a place where Billy Graham came, I would invite him to have a theological chat and ask him questions. The Church has neglected so many opportunities that it may be thankful to have such a man—but perhaps not *too* thankful. One may arouse *moral* feelings which direct men more away from Christ than to him—to the little I, and not the Great I. The Church should listen and learn to make a direct approach—but more with gospel than law.

ON OLD TESTAMENT PROMISE

A second sampling of Barth in his Colloquium discussions centers on a *Church Dogmatics* section on the relations between Old Testament's promise, the New Testament's gospel, and

169

God's election on peoples' behalf—an area where many found Barth's views problematic.[9]

Preliminary conversation turned to a recent article—it may have been in *Christianity Today*—on the theme "from Barth to Bultmann." Barth voiced a level of displeasure unusual for him: "These people who call themselves 'evangelical scholars'—I am tempted to say they are neither evangelical nor scholars. There's a lack of humor—even a lack of brain—in this article."

Since students delighted in correcting significant mistranslations in the English text, the leader for the evening led off with this observation:

[Scholar] There seems to be some confusion between "subject" and "object." For example, in a place where you move from "*Objekt*" to "*Subjekt*" in German, our English translation reads "object" in both places; so it reads, Christ, "the individual who as the original object of the divine election is for all the rest indeed the original *object* of election—He is everything for them and gives them all things. . . ."[10] [The original has '*Subjekt*' here.] Does the difference matter? Don't you want to

[9] English Colloqium, May 29, 1961: a discussion of KD II/2 (§35), "Jesus Christ the Promise and Recipient" [Engl. tr. pp. 306-340].
[10] KD, II/2, S. 314 = CD II/2, p. 310.

stress that Christ is also the original *subject* of God's election of all the rest of mankind?

[KB] Yes, the meaning has been inverted.

[S] [On Israel's relation to Christ] where you're describing the message that the community of the Jewish Scriptures has for everyone,[11] you begin talking about "an elect community" that knows about man's situation "according to the revelation of the crucified Jesus Christ in his resurrection."[12] But this is only true of the Church, isn't it? You don't really want to say that the larger Jewish community has that knowledge do you? Don't you mean to say "Church" and not "Jewish community"?

[KB] For Christian faith, the one alliance or covenant is the same in both economies. The subject was still the Messiah, Christ. The real object of the faith of Israel is the same Christ who is crucified and resurrected from the dead. The Church pre-exists in Israel and Israel post-exists in the Church. There's not a change in the intent of revelation, but only another form of it. The center of all things is the same in both the Old and New Testaments.

---

[11] CD II/2, p. 318f.
[12] CD II/2, p. 320.

171

[S] But how can we say Israel "*knew*" the resurrection of Christ? (Isn't the "knowledge" concept totally out of place here?)

[KB] "Knowledge" here has a double meaning. The word "knew" can refer to direct, abstract knowledge. (One can know something as already objectively here, but not yet present in complete revelation.) Here knowledge is objective possibility—given—but not yet accepted, not recognized. Such knowledge does express revelation present.

But there is a second meaning that is subjective and personal. In the history of Israel, objectively speaking, Christ was *in fact* present.[13] Exodus and the Return from the Babylonian Captivity are two examples of antetypes of resurrection in the New Testament.

[S] But the word "promise" pledges the *future*. So if you want to say that what God has done for the individual in election has already happened, wouldn't it be better to call it a

---

[13] See Chapter 10 on God's simultaneousness.

"proclamation"? Isn't there a radical difference in the new knowledge—the "now" we meet in Romans?

[KB] Ah, but doesn't that *"nun"* [that "now"] include the life of pre-existing in the history of Israel all the same? Can we understand Christ without his body? The first appearance of Christ is in the body of his people. Christ is always together with his people, Israel and the Church. The Church has always seen itself as together with Abraham and the Old Testament. The citats in the New Testament from the Old are not "proofs"; they express the identity of the New Israel with the old one. Abraham in Romans 4 is the great example of faith.

So we have distinct forms of an identical substance of saving truth. We have the great deliverance of Israel as a whole and the image of Jonah and the whale. The New Testament sees them both as looking directly to the resurrection of Jesus—a mirror. He is the lamb in sacrifice "slain from the foundation of the world." The author of Hebrews looks back in terms of Old Testament sacrifice speaking of Israel in a given situation.

[S (John Hesselink)] But Calvin sees the Old Testament speaking of Israel in a definite, given situation, while Christ cannot be separated from his people.

[KB] Ireneus said the Christ [or Messiah] was first born and the head from one end to the other [from creation to the final "recapitulation"]. A disbelieving Jew still remains directly a brother in the flesh. The ontological difference is no different between an unbelieving Jew and his unbelieving elder brother, and an unbelieving Gentile as his younger brother. At the story's end they belong together.

[S] What about Muslims? Don't Turkish students have the Ten Commandments just as we do?

[KB] Even in the Ten Commandments we have the whole gospel. The problem is to explain them in the light of Christ. The history of Israel is the march toward incarnation. Although ambiguous or ambivalent, a real promise is given and understood. The actualization or fulfillment of that promise comes afterwards. But accepting a promise is to be in the presence of its fulfillment. Paul calls it an *epangelia*[14] to Abraham which is accounted to him as justice. There is only one justice: It is present in the form of the promise of a son—looking forward to the one who will come. So for Paul Christ was there in the O.T. where Calvin saw two economies.

[S (Hesselink)] So in relation to the covenants you follow Calvin, who said that the substance of the two covenants is the same? With Colossians 2:17 the shadow in the Old Testament has its substance in the New (like a painter who uses a rough draft): The form is different, but the substance is not?

[KB] If you suppose the Old Testament is giving the real picture, the real *analogia*, the real shadow of Christ, why not put forward the claim of real continuity? There is a real identity here between Jesus, the Christ, and the Christ [Messiah] of the Old Testament, as the fulfillment of Promise, despite its ambiguity. When the Church began to forget the Old Testament during the second and third centuries, it was a great deviation. The Church can't forgo making use of the Old

---

[14] I.e., "a positive announcement" or "promise" (Romans 4:13).

Testament. Without the Old Testament there is no eschatology.

[S] "Promise," however, has future reference; but you say God's permanent decision or election has already happened. Wouldn't "proclamation" really be the better word?

[KB] Christian truth is not a complex of doctrines. (That is "orthodoxy.") The same thing that proclaims a fact today proclaims a promise. You can't "*believe in*" facts as such. Promise is given to this proclamation of claimed facts; so promise itself is a present fact. It can't merely be replaced by orthodoxy. It is not a wooden relationship that obtains between people and God. Even baptism is a way *to accept* a promise—a form of promise which is understood—not an abstract implanting. *Euanggelia* equals *epanggelia.* It is the proclamation of promise. Something is to happen—must happen—between God and us. This is not just asserted, not just a first step [in a process]. The **event of promise is itself, a fact**. This promise, if it is from God's side, [expresses his own inalienable commitment]: "I have done something for you,

for your good use"—the great promise of the life
he gives.

[S] In speaking of the negative side of individualism, you say that man, in taking his individual value as his natural possession, isolates himself from God. Is this just as true for societies where people think value basically resides in the group—Communist societies, for example, where the individual is but a means to the communal end?

[KB] If ours really is his proclamation, great deeds are thereby announced and proclaimed to *all mankind* already in the Old Testament. Remember, the Holy Spirit is not lacking in this Old Testament promise: the Spirit of the Word— the living Word—the gusting wind of the Spirit. We find ourselves seeing and believing; but this can't be done without the Old Testament. There is something to C.H. Dodd's realized eschatology; but we, in our prayer and in our actions, are *also* looking forward to promise.

The following rather typical colloquy took place a month later, on the evening of June 26, 1961 with Barth responding to questions that were prepared and circulated this time by Richard McConnell.[15] The *Church Dogmatics* text under discussion here turned upon the "solidarity" that believers should recognize with all the godless of this world.[16] (This was followed by further questions on the relationship between the Old and New Testaments.)

Barth had re-channeled the Reformed stress on free and sovereign election by insisting that God elects to be himself *for all people* and acts *toward all* with the same healing and saving that we meet in Jesus Christ. God's election to be for mankind in grace, then, is not limited to a privileged few. This, of course, rankles some strict Calvinists, who, were it not for their tradition's notion of "limited atonement," might be more favorably disposed toward Barth's theology.

At the outset Barth asked Mr. McConnell whether he agreed on basic presuppositions (the scope of God's grace in Christ, etc.); for otherwise, an introductory discussion would be necessary before one could go on to the questions at hand. McConnell said he did not agree on Barth's "expectation for the reject."

Barth responded that we are given a starting point for our view of election—"for both types of election." Both the

---

[15] McConnell is a New Testament scholar who was working under Oscar Cullmann on Law and Prophecy in the Gospel of Matthew.

[16] Vol. II/2, § 35 on "The Elect and the Rejected."

election of *all* and the rejection of *all* are laid on the same Christ. If there is a wrath of God, the man who has visibly suffered it is Jesus Christ. He is **both** elected and rejected.

[S] What then of the statements regarding judgment and damnation that come from Christ himself?

[KB] The more obscure passages of Scripture must be explained relative to the clear ones, while looking at the whole general line of the gospel and the work of God [as it develops both] in the Old and New Testaments. Christ, as he himself is burdened by the wrath of God, is at the central point. All these other points must be seen around this center, and never as another center. The message of Scripture is *one thing*; and all parts must be seen in this thing. All parts must be read as relating to this center, and not some other center. [I try to find the harmony of Scripture.] We must listen to the harmony of Scripture and not make a cacophony of Scripture. *My whole theological enterprise is to find out the harmony of Scripture.* One is not obliged to make all parts the center.

179

Then we turned to the questions McConnell had prepared:

[S] Must it be expected that at some time the rejected will join the ranks of the elected because the grace of Christ is *for all* men, and besides, there is only one rejected, i.e., Jesus Christ?

[KB] I didn't make it a "*must!*"

The grace of God and the hope of men are never under a *must*. A hope? We *are allowed to hope*! [That's the better way to express it.] Hope doesn't imply we've caught the good Lord in a "*must.*" The elected ones must expect that the rejected ones will join them. [But that is not to imply a *must* for God.] I want to avoid a theory of God's behavior that says he **has to** do something. But if man is allowed to believe in his own election, then by necessity, he must expect that there will be a way for others. No merits. He himself is a sinner. He can't refuse that others should participate in God's grace. Think of the parable of the freed debtor who refuses to forgive another—the ingrate![17]

---

[17] Lk. 18:10ff.

[S] Then, can one conclude that the distinction is only a matter of time?

[KB] Even here I object to your vocabulary: "Can one *conclude?*" *Conclusion* is from logic (thesis; a statement participating in the thesis; and conclusion). In God's Word there are no "conclusions." The divine logic is not a human logic where thesis and conclusion rule, but rather here we are in the realm of the [personal] freedom of God. I would prefer to say, "Can one hope?" Otherwise the terms here become again too much a question of necessity.

It becomes, rather, a matter of God's time. The distinction between an elect and a reject person is a *way*—a way we are all going. The distinction is a question of where one is upon the way—a difference of a story, a history, and not just of time. Now two persons—one elected and one rejected? There is not identification between them, but a way between them. The two (both the rejecting and accepting one) must be seen as brothers. One represents the beginning of the way, and the other, the end of it.

We are all under promise. We can't put
our finger on such-and-such a man and say "he is
elect," and of another, "he isn't." Think of the
story of David and Saul [cited in the evening's
text]: If anything, David [who is analogous to the
elect in this account] commits sins that are more
lurid than Saul's.

[S (Grover Foley)] This treatment of the story of David
and Saul doesn't seem to appear elsewhere. Is it your idea, or
did you take it from someone else?

[KB] I reflected on the story a long, long time.
Sources? [Barth shrugs laughing, and touches the
back of his head.]

[S] What of Wilhelm Vischer's type of Old Testament
interpretation which finds a rather exaggerated christocentric
interpretation of prophecy etc. and in the Old Testament in
general?[18]

[KB] Insist on the unity in the Old and New Testaments. But the *Old* Testament must be allowed
to speak as such, and not be too quickly ex-

---

[18] See e.g., Vischer, W., *Bedeutung des Alten Testaments für das
christliche Leben* (Zollikon-Zürich: Evangelischer Verlag, 1947).

plained out of the New Testament. Vischer is a virtuoso, a genius, but he goes too far and takes even the book of Esther as a prophecy and proclamation of Christ. He goes too quickly over the details of the text. I find myself disappointed in reading Vischer. He is a glowing light; but I am more pedantic. To read Vischer one must be ready to fly [over the details]. But we are good friends and mean the same thing.

[S] But when do the rejected pass from a personal rejection of Jesus Christ to acceptance of him?

[KB] In Christ we see the "Way" from rejection to election. If someone asks me, "what way?" I can only say, "Jesus Christ is that Way—Christ [not alone but] as head of a community, a nation, a people." We are together participating. We are living in the shadow of the cross. But we are allowed to live in the light of the resurrection.

Faith means to accept this position humbly. God deals with men and not with stone. He proclaims his will that all shall be saved. We have to hear something—this proclamation of his wills that all *shall be* saved.

183

Men are in no way able to frustrate the will of God. In disobedience to him, they are not somehow creating a new reality over—somehow creating a new reality over and against his will.[19]

[S] But what of a liar, one who doesn't accept the truth? [KB] A liar doesn't change the Truth. [His lie does not create a truth over against the Truth to replace it.] The love of God isn't a weak [flaccid] thing. When one is opposed to it, it becomes a burning fire, while yet *remaining* love. All of the burning judgment in the New Testament does not change God [as we meet him in Christ's grace].

OFF-THE-CUFF REFLECTIONS ON TILLICH: GNOSIS VS. THEOLOGY?

Paul Tillich, Barth's earlier colleague and friend, had come to Union Seminary in New York, during the Nazi ascendency in Germany, and his *Systematic Theology* had become prominent in American theological education of the period. Barth's re-

---

[19] Barth's position here is to be related to his view of God's "impossible possibility" and the final impermanence of "*das Nichtige*" (evil, unmasked, finally, as nothingness).

marks about Tillich at some of our English-speaking colloquia were perhaps the pithiest he ever made about the epistemological issues that separated him from this erstwhile German colleague and friend.[20]

Tillich came under discussion at the first English Colloquium I attended (in February 1958).[21] Alexander McKelway was leader for the evening. Sandy, as we called him, had earlier been pastor of the American church in Vienna, and was well under way with a dissertation for Barth on Tillich's theology. Since the text for the evening's discussion was on "the freedom of the Word,"[22] his questions inevitably gravitated to Tillich's ideas about the relation between theology and philosophy.

Later, during the winter semester of the same year, Barth offered a university seminar on Tillich's *Systematic*

---

[20] A version of my recollections here was published in *The Christian Century*, two years after Barth's death, under the title "Barth on Tillich: Neo-gnosticism? Recollections revealing what were behind the tension that developed between these two influential thinkers" (December 9, 1970, p. 1774ff.). This article, used with permission here, was occasioned by a letter from Al Krass, who though occupied as a missionary in Africa, felt the time had come for us to read into the record the revealing comments Barth had made about Tillich at our English Colloquia.

[21] February 18, 1958, Bruderholz Restaurant, Basel.

[22] *Church Dogmatics.* See I/2: pp. 661-697 in particular on the "Freedom in the Church" (§ 21). As McKelway pointed out, "This section of the *Dogmatics* was written in 1938, at a time when the political-philosophical question of the relationship between the authority of the state and the freedom of the individual was peculiarly critical."

Theology, which had become, as he continually was at pains to remind us, "an attempt to understand him." Below you will find the gist of Barth's responses, first to McKelway's questioning, and then his summary comments regarding Tillich at another Colloquium after our seminar's shared "attempt to understand him."

There was nothing in these rather off-the-cuff remarks that Karl Barth could not have said more publicly. But they were unusual, for at this stage of his career he often made it clear that he did not conceive of his role as a polemic one. As we have seen, he maintained that polemics become nonproductive in theology, since they seduce one into overstatement and provoke equally exaggerated reactions. He usually seemed satisfied to state his own findings as clearly as his talents would allow, and leave it to others to make comparisons. This, of course, was the later Barth.

[S (McKelway)] Tillich holds that since symbols, in our experience, have the power to participate in the things they symbolize, "a religious symbol *participates* in the power of the divine toward which it points."[23] You speak of daemonic and magic power as natural to literature [i.e., something Scripture

---

[23] *Systematic Theology* (Chicago: University of Chicago Press, 1951, Vol. I, p. 239).

has in common with other writings[24] Again, you use the concept of analogy between the Christ of faith and God as he is in himself.] Would you [agree with Tillich and] describe this power as symbolic *participation*?

[KB] Participates? A high being in a general relationship to the world (as Tillich)? It's a question of how we, for ourselves, deal with it. Is it by symbols? They are our creation, an act of man. *Participate*? With *this* object?

The Platonic Idea or appearance participates in the reality of the Ideal. Plato calls it "divine." With the symbol he points at the divine Idea. An interesting philosophy—but don't mix it with what I've said on these pages. We can't discuss this as philosophy here. As theologian, I don't speak in general terms. I speak of God and the history that goes on between [God and man]. Participation [here] will always be an event and not a general relation of ideas. First of all, God speaking to us in his freedom and his power in freedom: God's act, not ours.

---

[24] CD I/2, p. 675.

[S] Often you employ the analogy of Christ; that is, you explain theological questions in terms of Jesus Christ, as he is incarnate and as he is a member of the Trinity.[25] (You explain the relationship between *authority* and freedom in terms of the interrelationship between the Son and the Spirit.) On what *basis* do you use this analogy in writing theology? Wouldn't you agree with Tillich that this analogy has its power as symbol? What is the relationship between this philosophy of symbolism and the power of the Word to use and assimilate symbol?

[KB] For Tillich, the whole world is baptized in a sacramental state of things: there's an unending process [coming down] to us from above. I object that this is no such general process. It is [instead] a specific story. I fear Paul Tillich and I cannot be reconciled. No, we are far, far, far away. It's wrong to introduce symbols.

There's no question of our choosing authority. It's not a choice between error and truth. The sinner is wrong in his belief he can *choose* "the good." The choice is not between two possibilities, but between a possibility and impossibility. Any contradiction here is not in revela-

---

[25] See CD I/2, p. 666.

188

tion, but in our understanding of it.

[S] What about the symbols we use in worship?

[KB] We are not free to introduce symbols—candles, flags—in the Church.[26] Every such thing should be criticized as to whether we are asked to do it. We are *allowed* to—but are we asked? A national banner? No! In the Old Testament the *theme* of symbol is not used. Symbols there are used following the command of God and not out of the religious liberty of these good people. The whole Bible does not use the term symbol. A picture or likeness in the Bible is not something coming out of *our idea* of Jesus Christ.

[McKelway] Shouldn't our God-talk maintain a *relevant dialectic with the world*?

[KB] Don't overemphasize what I have said in regard to Luther's position on the Peasants'

---

[26] The display of the swastika flag, Hitler photo, etc. on the German-Christians' altars was still fresh in Barth's mind here. Inevitably he found the presence of national and so-called Christian flags prevalent in American sanctuaries to be saying the wrong thing.

Wars; I don't like it at all. Though I have said the best word that I feel can be said there,[27] I can't approve of what he did and said.

[S] But must we not say that in every situation, and not only that of 1938, the Church must be *relevant* and enter into the dialectic of the world, taking the risk of partisanship and of becoming "spotty" [in its self interest]?[28]

[KB] No, I can't approve of what he [Luther] did and said. You can't make a principle of it: "Let us be spotted!"

The dictionary distinguishes "freedom" from "license." But the Scripture is not an element of power—not in a fundamental way. [And

---

[27] In this *Dogmatics* section on how true freedom is matrixed in divine authority, Barth recalls how secular power-grabs for freedom, such as that of the towns and princes against the Papacy on the one hand, or of the peasants against their feudal lords on the other, could be occasioned by ulterior motives. Self-seeking interests, right and left, occasioned a short-lived common cause with the Reformation, but such opportunistic misreadings of divine authority on the one hand, or its gifted freedom on the other, evoked the Reformers' opposition. Thus Luther's fateful denunciation of the peasants' revolt should not be construed as a reactionary affirmation of established authority, but as his misplaced attempt to keep clear the Spirit-reflective lines of Christians' freedom. (See CD I/2, p. 664f.)

[28] In this context Barth had expressed the need of keeping the Church's message of divine authority as source of our gifted freedom "unspotted"; i.e., unsullied by confusions with similar sounding secular abstractions ["*von der Welt unbefleckt*"] (KD I/2, S.745 = CD I/2, p. 665).

as to] *"free choice"*—a donkey tethered in a field
with two piles of hay—is his choice free? Later
he's led right out of the field.

After a much later Colloquium, Al Krass and I transcribed and edited the following off-the-cuff remarks from
Barth on Tillich's methods. There were some Tillich fans
among the students and friends present; and Barth was ru-
minating over a glass of wine and puffing on his pipe. One
cannot capture on paper the puckishness of his manner or
the humorous intonation which evoked laughter from his
listeners. His words were not waspish or petulant, but were
punctuated by the didactic challenge-with-a-twinkle that
characterized his easy *entre-nous* manner with students.

Although the remarks that follow were voiced in this
relaxed and good-humored way, they certainly represent
Barth's considered position. Confident that he had truly
listened and understood his old friend's intention and terminology, he still felt pushed to the conclusion that he must
disagree. He said he would have preferred to appreciate
Tillich's work as a clever apology for Christian faith spring-
ing from a deep concern to connect with the larger intellectual community. But he finally had to conclude that Tillich
was attempting to graft a Christian superstructure onto an
experiential-philosophical basis foreign to it.

191

Tillich's transplant effort required an intuitive leap from one species of reality to another—from general-experience-based humanistic conceptions of relevance to Christian beliefs—and had never overcome the problem of ambiguity in nature or what one might call natural man's built-in rejection mechanisms. Could such a foundation really support the transplant Tillich tried so enthusiastically to embed there? Or did the whole project risk withering Christian thought by trying to detach it from its living roots and norms in incarnation-based faith?

In the course of discussion an American student pinned Barth down with a point-blank question: "Can Paul Tillich's statement that God is the 'ground-of-being' be understood in any way as an acceptable dogmatic statement?"

"Why not?" Barth responded. "It could be done."

Then he evoked the semester-long seminar we had just shared on Tillich's *Systematic Theology*:

My method in interpreting Tillich in all the sessions of my seminar was to explain Tillich in the best possible way: *in meliorem partem—in optimum partem.* "Be silent," I said to the students, "maybe we can explain him in a reasonable way." The students always said "No, no." And I must confess, in the end I was not right. But I have done my best to explain Tillich. The "ground-of-being" *could* be translated as "Creator of heaven and earth." The "power of being in and about" *could* mean his transcendence. That is acceptable. But Tillich's own explanation makes it impossible to interpret him in this way.

In his *Systematic Theology* I don't find the Creator, the Reconciler and the Redeemer. But I find only this—what is it called in English?—this "method of correlation." [For Tillich there's] no God who is truly above and then, as he who is above, *also* in our being.[29] But always a similarity to us. In reading Tillich I am always a bit suspicious whether his "God" really is God or whether it is—and I wouldn't be un-

---

[29] Tillich's *correlation method,* which is intent on maintaining a dialectic beginning with our prior "ultimate concern" (within our general human experience and situation) seemed to miss the essential in Barth's view, that the Word, in revealing himself in history has made himself the key factor in our actual situation—created a new human reality with which theology and anything like a Christian situation-ethics must begin.

kind—an idol, though a very deeply thought-out one.

In Tillich's theology man is alone. There isn't another who meets him, of whom it might be said: "He stands for me. He is above me; I am below him, I obey him." I can find nothing in Tillich comparable to the biblical story: man as creature meeting God his Creator. So I couldn't say this is an acceptable theological statement. I would like to say it. I like Paul Tillich as a man. I believe that in his own way and in his own manner he is a good Christian. But as a theologian?

No-o-o! I can't even be sure he is a good philosopher. His theology is something of a gnostic system. As such I cannot accept his phrase.

The students pursued the issue further, asking what Barth thought of Tillich's statement that God cannot be understood as the highest being alongside other beings. He shot back:

194

The Creator is [not] alongside the creature as such. But this statement should not be made in such an exclusive way, as Tillich does. Paul Tillich forgot about incarnation. The same God who is "not alongside" is also alongside: that's the point.

His [may be] good philosophy, but not theology. Because, at the same time, his christology in the second volume—ah, that's a weak affair!—is a very docetic christology;[30] because the Word, following Paul Tillich, didn't become flesh. Since he can't understand that, he can say only this negative side of truth. And half-truth is not Truth. It's a pity he can't understand the incarnation. But why not?

His christology has it that Jesus had to die that Christ may live. Jesus had to disappear so that Christ could appear. Hmmm.

---

[30] Docetism [from Greek, δοκεω] was the early one-sided heresy which, following Hellenistic dualistic assumptions, speculated that a High God could not sully itself with material contact, and assumed the revealer could not have been truly human or suffered as a mortal, so must have given an illusion, only *seeming* to be man, while remaining an insubstantial phantom or the like.

Not so! Jesus doesn't disappear. That's docetism. Agreed?

I believe that Tillich is doing his best within his limits. He had very poor teachers in Germany. At a certain point he ceased to go forward and ever since he has been going round and round in his Schelling philosophy.[31] It's not right to exclude him from the Kingdom. [Ours is] a technical difference. He is a stranger to me in theology; I hope to meet him in heaven, together with Schleiermacher and some others, and have a discussion with him for some thousand years— a *peaceful* discussion.

[S] And what of other heretics, like Arius? Would you say the same of them?

[KB] All the "heretics" of the New Testament were *within* the community of saints. I

---

[31] Friedrich Schelling (1775-1854) developed a romantic philosophy of nature. According to his speculations there is a single, actively striving world-will whose temporary inner polarities give rise to disparate things. Yet an underlying unity persists for him even between apparent opposites (such as between thought and substance, subject and object, light and mass, etc.).

consider a "heretic," old or modern, as one who has understood the gospel less well. But at the last judgment, who has had the perfect truth? Let us fight the heretics, yes—but not burn them. Heretics can be fought only with spiritual means, not by punishing them with judgments. We cannot be our own judges. Often you'll find me weeping or smiling with a bit of irony about such people—even with bitterness sometimes. But always in the spirit of "*We* poor Christian saints."

Barth was fond of telling a much cited anecdote that is well worth recalling again here as epitomizing the disagreement that crystallized between these two men despite their warm regard for each other. Tillich, Barth recalled, had dropped by to visit him after a trip to the Holy Land. While reminiscing about this experience, Tillich told him how scandalized he had been at one point:

"And you know, Karl, they showed us a ramshackle old hut in Palestine with a plaque on it that read: '*hoc deus caro genitum est* [or words to that effect]—here God became flesh.' Can you imagine: Hoc, hoc, *hoc*!"

Barth said he couldn't help responding, "But Paul, that's the whole point, isn't it."

"Oh, it's not a question of that particular old house," Barth would clarify in recounting the exchange. "That's rubbish, of course—but of the *hoc*, the *here*—in this world, this history! This was and must remain a scandal for Tillich."

So for Barth, the whole significance is that through a non-compelling, yet memorable event, God actually appeared in our world—became man at a particular, but otherwise unremarkable, time and place. The Christian faith could in a sense be encapsulated in that one word, "*hoc*"—the here-among-us in a concrete human history; i.e., the very thing that had been a scandal for Tillich. Barth couldn't help but see in Tillich's speculations about the existence of an impersonal "God above God" a parallel to the thought of Marcion, the second century Christian Gnostic.

Barth also recounted how Tillich had told him that he liked John Robinson's recent *Honest to God*[32] (a book that Barth considered rather frothy with its puerile critique of a literalistic *God-up-There*). "Tillich said, 'Rob-

---

[32] Remarks to Barth's *Sozietät*, April 30, 1964, re Bishop John A.T. Robinson's *Honest to God* (SCM Press, 1963).

inson cited me so nicely'!" In common with Robinson, "Tillich makes a value, a positive thing, of guilt itself [as part of] the 'ground of being—down there.' He doesn't escape from the abyss [*Grube*], always looking down instead of up and out."

AND AS TO EXISTENTIALISM. . .

In 1964, Barth was wont to say that he foresaw the fate of the existentialist school in theology as a scattering and dissolution into self-contradiction such as befell the "historical Jesus" movement of the nineteenth century. "I don't think the Bultmann school has much future," he said. "Already I'm beginning to see how the young Bultmannians are running here and there into blind alleys."[33]

He said he could not feel as did his Basel colleague, Oscar Cullmann, that it was his task to engage in polemic against the existentialists: He had his own positive work to do.[34] But to the end Barth questioned Bultmann and the other existentialists as to "whether the humanity of Christ is ever taken seriously" (and with it the claim of a humanity for God himself). Did they ever escape a "docetism with a

---

[33] *Ibid.*
[34] Remarks to *Sozietät*, April 30, 1964.

199

mystical flavor" reminiscent of the ancient Gnostics who, with their culture's dualistic prejudice against physical existence, sexuality, worldly attachments and the like, presumed to relegate God's freedom to act to a denatured realm of pure "spirituality"? Was this taking seriously that God, if he is *God*, has been free to enter time and act in history and thus underwrite the value of physical nature and time-spanned aspects of his own creation?

Barth believed that the mystical bent of a neo-gnosticism was already evident in post-war Germany in what he saw as the strange marriage between some young Bultmannians and pietism. He predicted that the whole Bultmann movement would dissolve into a new pietism.[35] Already in the early 1960s, he said, the existential theologians were moving toward that dead end; and he was convinced that their school would soon lose its significance. The later "death of God" impasse and the symptoms of frustration and disillusionment that surfaced among those who had been tripping out with the new brands of do-your-own-thing mysticism may have been blind alleys, such as Barth had in mind.

---

[35] Viz. the subsequent preoccupation of many religious thinkers with the notion of "human spirituality," which has since become the theme of hundreds of books and articles.

The fiery days of the *Letter to the Romans* were long past, however, and the mature Barth, as we've seen, avoided making "a frontal attack." (At least he intended to avoid it.) Further, he indicated that, as he viewed his own position over and against the existential one, he did not by any means feel a total separation. He had begun his theological odyssey fascinated by that prime mover of existentialism, Søren Kierkegaard (although he came to believe that the incarnation claim requires abandonment of Kierkegaard's paradox as a *final principle*). For Barth, God's incarnational event became the crucial existential act[36] for all mankind, the act that stands fast over and against all other human existence and action. As he came to put it: "More and more clearly I've seen that you can't speak of *Sein* [being or essence] without at the same time speaking of *Akt* [action itself] as pure *Sein.*"[37]

Indeed, his concept of the inner-trinitarian relationships within God himself implies this: God's own inner history is a history of *action*—not of pure essence unmoved and unmoving. There is no impersonal God above God

---

[36] I.e., understanding existence to follow action, instead of vice versa.

[37] This relationship had also become a hinge in Bonhoeffer's ethics and was already the theme of his qualifying lecture for joining the faculty at the University of Berlin (1931).

deprived of various orders of time or place or action to call his own. For Barth, God himself can be something of an existentialist—and that, in quite human terms. Essence does not have to precede action where God is concerned; but neither does God's action (such as may be visible in Jesus Christ) ever split itself off from what he is in the depths of his being. Who and what God has been in himself without man is in no way separate from or contrary to who he is for man, as he creates, lives both incarnate and as Spirit, and re-creates on man's behalf. For he is at every point fully himself; and as Calvin often said, he is not to be divided.

In a spring 1961 Colloquium[38] Barth summed up his difference with Bultmann:

> The whole New Testament looks back in retrospect: something certainly happened with Jesus in 30 or 33 A.D.—happened as an event that could be described: "We have seen and have heard and touched" and believed— believed not in resurrection as a concept, but in the resurrected One (both visible and also through the invisible Spirit). This is the necessary foundation for a Christian faith: not faith

---

[38] May 1, 1961.

in a far-away historical person, but dependence on a living person—here and now.

Rudolph Bultmann says resurrection was the creation of faith, which for him is itself a kind of virgin birth, parthenogenesis, a beginning without a beginning. But faith has an object—is itself *a relationship* to God, acting and revealed in Christ. The Creed regarding resurrection makes it plainly clear: here God is in our midst—not just you with your own little faith, but infinitely more. Real faith is a meeting in history.

For Bultmann, however, it is only an inner mystery beginning around a larger mystery—as if faith begins with the [notion of] resurrection within the *kerygma*. But how can the living Christ be *in* the *kerygma* [*inside* the early proclamation, as such]? Faith is not just our *kerygma* historically claimed; but *he* is there: a statement of fact which can't be proved or explained.)

But as Calvin would say, the life of the Church is a succession of resurrections: wherever someone finds self allowed to believe, it is an analogy to the resurrection of Christ. One is lifted, raised up into belief. It is a reality between two partners, and not a reality within oneself alone. What I miss in the theology of Bultmann is an encounter—a historical and *geschictliche* encounter with a Person. This is the *telos*—not the end of the Jewish Law [and Prophets], but their goal.

Chapter 7

Barth's Resonance for an American

This personal retrospective now will take a turn. We are going to be sketching key insights and special teachings from the mature Barth that in the years since Barth's death have shown themselves to carry special significance for our American college classroom, church school and pulpit. As we move forward in that direction some background regarding his relationship to America in general and my own perspective as an ordinary American student is in order.

BARTH AND THE AMERICANS

Karl Barth's own relation to the New World was bumpy. For years his name was revered more in America than he was actually read and understood there. He never found opportunity to travel to the United States until after his semi-retirement from the University in 1962; but he was fascinated by American history and values. As I mentioned previously, at our first interview he said he would like to have a graduate student focus a doctoral study on "the American way of life." His special interest in the Civil War has received a good deal of publicity. He lacked much formal training in English, but for years he had been reading Civil War novels along with detective stories in an effort to learn that language as well as for diversion. "You can't do theology all the time," he would laugh. But this was also out of deep interest, as he often made clear to students from the American South.[1]

I think the peculiar American mix of idealism and materialism puzzled him, as did our complex of sturdy individualism and social consciousness. He had also been quite astounded by the theological extremes represented by those Americans who had made their way to Basel. Some still championed a one-sided social gospel, while others had come on the false assumption that they would find a kindred spirit for their rock-hard biblicism, blithely unaware that he would view any verbal inspiration theory as an aberrant, modern notion.

One day, with great amusement and a grain of muted pride, Barth showed me the spacious new desk Pittsburgh Seminary had given him in exchange for his little old one: "Can you

---

[1] Viz. anecdotes from Alexander McKelway in Princeton's Barth archives.

imagine they actually wanted my little old desk for a museum piece." He marveled at this strange fancy for artifacts.[2] But then he grew serious and sighed ruefully, "If only they would *really read* my books instead." That sigh seemed to breathe something of his experience at the hands of many Americans, who had read only fleetingly, largely in his earliest works, but were ready to caricature and label him.[3]

It struck me as astounding that the entire *Church Dogmatics* could have emerged from this small room, written on an antique desk that was miniscule by our standards. It measured only about two-and-a-half-feet deep by four-and-a-half-feet wide and was topped with a cubbyhole shelf that left him only about three square feet of writing surface (39 x 17 inches to be precise). This severely limited work space stood in mute testimony to the inner organizational powers of the man. Small wonder that someone from Pittsburgh wanted to have it on display.

The belated tour Barth finally made in America during the spring of 1962 was obviously something special for him: "an intense pleasure," he said. (It was not so wonderful for me,

---

[2] This was only one of a number of American enthusiasms that evoked smiling puzzlement from Barth.

[3] Pittsburgh did later include his son, Marcus, on its New Testament faculty for some time, and Princeton Seminary now has a center for Barthian studies. His work is much more widely read today.

personally, since it left me hanging for a time, expensively studying in Europe, without my doctoral advisor.) He was especially delighted by his meetings there with some American originals, such as the activist Harlem lawyer, William Stringfellow, and by his tour of Gettysburg Civil War sites in connection with a visit to the Lutheran Seminary there.[4]

He also made a point of asking to see for himself how Americans handle their prisoners. "You Americans. . . ," he later told us, sadly shaking his head. "You Americans treat your prisoners like caged animals."

Barth had put his finger on our most crying and often ignored social problem: our desperate need for a more grace-informed restorative justice system. (See Chapter 13.) He found it remarkable that despite such blind spots, "Americans, it seems, all want to do ethics." Yet at the same time—in a concession to their multicultural heritage, perhaps—many had been inclined to cut their study of social ethics off from the belief roots necessary for any enduring value commitments. The scowling portrait of Barth that appeared on the cover of *Time* magazine reporting on his trip[5] only reinforced the distorted

---

[4] For Barth's own rather charming description of these events, see his Foreword to the American edition of his *Evangelical Theology: An Introduction* (New York: Holt Rinehart and Winston, 1963).

[5] The Easter issue of *Time*, April 20, 1962.

stereotype of Barth as a stern, authoritarian figure, unrecognizable to those of us who knew him.

Since this is a retrospective, before going on with a description of Barth's later significance for me as an American teacher and churchman, I need to pause and explain that, as an international graduate student, I had been trying to extend my antennae as far as I could in diverse directions; so though I found some grounding in his approach, I did not feel tethered to his thought. I had even made a point of attending the lectures of a Prof. Faber whom the Tübingen students tended to shun, because he had been a Nazi-sympathizer. I wanted to examine firsthand his philosophy-of-religion approach which seemed to have been implicated.[6] Again, when I was later at Geneva, I took pains to follow the lectures of Auguste LeMaître, an honest-to-goodness liberal, who harkened back to Johann Fichte and Rudolf Otto, and was still trying to use our natural aesthetic feeling for a theological basis. As an American fraternal worker at this cultural crossroads, my commitments were widespread during these post-graduate years.[7]

---

[6] I was touched and rather embarrassed when, learning of my special interest, this professor went out of his way to work up a bibliography on the virtue concept for me in the hope of attracting an American doctoral candidate.

[7] I was fortunate to find companions who were patient enough to help me in German and French: Elizabeth Haug, daughter of a Stuttgart

Foyer John Knox, our Presbyterian Church-supported Geneva experiment in international living, housed a community of students from more than twenty different lands. With Dr. Paul Frelick's leadership we organized conferences around a number of concerns, such as one that brought together atomic energy researchers from The European Organization for Nuclear Research (CERN), to explore religious-ethical dimensions of their field. The liberation struggle was going on in Algeria and South Africa; so we often focused on areas of rapid social development. We also gathered together African students who had been studying in many European universities to consider re-entry problems before their return home to Africa. We were called upon further to shelter and re-locate a number of Angolan refugees in European universities. Meanwhile I was organizing student discussions engaging leaders, such as South African novelist, Alan Paton, or an Israeli diplomat who had business at the United Nations center in Geneva. We worked with the Student Christian Movement at the University and tried to keep worship opportunities as joyful a part of students' life as our

---

pastor, and young theologians: Wilhelm Dantine and Helmut Mach from Vienna and Henri Mottu of Geneva. Vacations included Council of Churches study tours across Germany and into East Berlin and trips into Austria and Italy, as well as longer visits in Denmark, where my cousin, Nancy Hughes-Brøndum, had made her home and then to Helsinki, where Gunlög and I were married in 1960.

holiday parties and to make our visits to Church renewal sites, such as the Ecumenical Center at nearby Bossey and the Taizé community at Cluny, as engaging as the Alpine ski slopes.

This recital is simply to underline the fact that though I was doing my dissertation with Barth, I was never exclusively centered in his work. In fact, like Barth, despite initial reservations, I found Calvin to be my primary teacher during these years. So I was not glued to Barth but was learning from a number of others as well.[8]

During the later period of the 1970s and 1980s, there was little incentive for an American professor to be labeled as Barthian; and I never sat down and systematically worked right through his enormous *Church Dogmatics*. Yet I could count on being richly rewarded whenever I pulled down a volume, as I often did, to consult as a resource along the way.

Despite a lifestyle I had acquired from my parents' strict frontier pietism, I had found my own way to become even more deeply committed than Barth to anti-legalistic spontaneity

---

[8] In particular I have found useful what Oscar Cullmann taught us on Paul and salvation history, Bo Reike on the Gospels and the emerging Church's historical surroundings, Max Geiger on Early Church history, the mysteries and gnosticism, and Hendrik van Oyen on social ethics and the gospel; Jacques de Senarclens on Reformed theology and its roots; and Jeanne Hersch on Simone Weil and the Catholics. Other notable teachers included Hermann Deim, Aldolph Köberli, Hanns Rückert, Matthias Rissi, Martin Auchard and Franz Leenhart. To all of these I am an unworthy but grateful debtor.

(though this, for me as a student had been tinged with political quietism).[9] As already mentioned, I felt Barth had failed to carry through on a christomorphic re-definition of justice relative to the core Christian doctrine of atonement.[10] Yet as I look back now, I must acknowledge that his voice has reverberated with persistent resonance through all my later thought and work in higher education and the ministry.

His approach to theology has turned out to wear well over time and has had much more profound and lasting effects than I might have anticipated. Dialogue with Barth evokes an ever-fresh christocentric corrective—especially now, as we in America find ourselves confronted by ever-vaguer notions of *spirituality*. This will-o'-the-wisp human attribute is being touted as an ostensibly universal, neutral and politically correct

---

[9] Once, when we were discussing the Sermon on the Mount, Barth was perturbed by my suggestion that Jesus actually might have meant literally his injunction in Matthew 5:3 not to oppose evil [or the evil One]. I never shared my friend, Henri Mottu's extreme position, however, when in opposition to Barth, this son of a highly placed Swiss army officer notoriously went to prison for refusing military service. Yet at this time Barth was speaking out against nuclear armament, while many of his peers, including Emil Brunner, had bought into the notion that since atom bombs trump other forms of weaponry, they should be stockpiled as the only realistic deterrent to aggressors. But ultimate security does not depend on us; and Barth, indeed, could finally say, "We are not in the situation of men who need to fight against evil. This fight is accomplished." (*The Faith of the Church*, p. 96). It is a sobering thought that there may well be a vestigial residue of natural theology in his readiness (and our own) to resort finally to armed conflict.

[10] See Chapter 9.

212

natural substitute for any life-defining faith.[11] Barth's defense against natural theology also works as an antidote to the myth of *American exceptionalism* with its attendant specter of nationalistic militarism, which sometimes swells to an almost fascistic pride among us. Apparently his works have the staying power of classics and are sparking more new thought and discussion than ever. Now, nearly a half century after his death, it appears that many are making that discovery—some by simply chancing to nibble at the edges of his theology.

Through the rest of this book, then, I intend to underline certain points at which I have found memories of Barth retaining key importance for my own teaching and "theological existence today." I will unfold this selection of themes from my own retrospective viewpoint; for I am not in a position here either to summarize the enormous literature or respond more directly to the many pointed discussions that Barth's work evokes. But in a personal way I will describe some of the important insights and approaches that rubbed off on me during my nearly six years of

---

[11] In the last thirty years hundreds of titles have accumulated that move in this direction. An especially telling example was the sociologically-based dismissal of the Church represented by a group at Lancaster University in the U.K. See Paul Heelas and Linda Woodhead, *The Spiritual Revolution: Why Religion is Giving Way to Spirituality,* 2005, in Blackwell's series, "Religion and Spirituality in the Modern World." See also Jeremy Carrette and Richard King, *Selling Spirituality: The Silent Takeover of Religion* (London & New York: Routledge, 2004 & 2005).

contact as his candidate. Here are some of the insistent emphases in his teaching that have prodded me along the way. In some of this I will be reinforcing widely recognized motifs. Yet others of his most useful insights remain virtually unnoticed.

In doing this, I intend to single out only a selection of those themes from Barth that have resonated with great significance and shown a tenacious holding power through my subsequent years as college teacher and teaching elder in the Presbyterian Church, U.S.A. These are themes, by the way, that have proved to be liberating, radiant and joyful for me in personal terms. Whether you have given much attention to Barth or not, you may find him prompting you here, as well.

"ORDER IS EVERYTHING"
FOR OUR CONFUSED WORLD

One of Barth's key emphases that have reverberated most significantly for me in the New World has been his frequent caution that "*in theology, order is everything.*" Given grace, we should always follow the inner order of God's own self-disclosure and be attentive to the *sequence* of how its discovery engages his creatures' lives. Despite the chatter that surrounds us, Barth would have us reflect the crucial order or "living *pro-*

cession"[12] intrinsic to God's own free action in Christ.

In reviewing with him his section on "the perfections of God," we had been impressed by how each successive set of terms was presupposed by and grew, organically, as it were, out of the previous ones, both to delimit and amplify their unfolding meaning. God's "perfections" could only be grasped as unfolding from the freedom of his prior wholeness in love.[13] Barth carefully made a point of using the word "perfections" in place of traditional talk about "the attributes of God," which could all too easily presume to confine or delimit God in our categories rather than acknowledging him as self-determining. So Barth begins to speak of God's *Selbstbestimmung* as his "being as the one who loves in freedom."[14] And since God subsists outside the sphere of our prior experience, our speech must honor and describe the ultimate priority of this love in an all-important *irreversible* order.[15]

---

[12] Compare p. 9f. in Barth's final *Evangelical Theology: An Introduction*. As would-be knowers, relative to God's self-revelation, we are in "the position of a fundamentally and irrevocably determined **subsequence** which can in no way be changed or reinterpreted into a precedence of man. It is the position of grace" (CD II/1, S. 21f. / p. 21).

[13] This order is unfolded in full across the second half of *Church Dogmatics* II/1, §§ 28-31. For a most recent review of this theme, see Robert B. Price, *Letter of the Divine Word: The Perfections of God in Karl Barth's Church Dogmatics* (Edinburgh: T & T Clark, 2011).

[14] CD II/1, p. 288ff.

[15] As Grover Foley has translated a characteristic summary near the beginning of Barth's *Introduction*, "in its perception, meditation, and discus-

UNPACKING THE PRIORITY OF GRACE

Should we mistakenly reverse this order in our minds, we are liable to misconstrue God's *freedom* as if it were a capricious free-for-all and tragically suppose his grace to be a fickle sometime-thing or power that we can pre-condition, qualify or control.

Following further, we discover the *holiness* of God. But again, this is first and always to be grasped as the holiness of the one he is. That is, it is not an abstraction, but the otherness of his *prior personal grace*.[16] Then, further, we can, indeed, come to know his righteousness. But again, this, the only true righteousness, is *pre*-defined and shaped by his unique mercy and not by our cultural presuppositions. Likewise, his wisdom is *pre*-defined and shaped as the wisdom of his prior merciful patience. So it never storms our minds with rational proofs or swamps them with ineffable, mystical force. For God in power takes infinite care not to tyrannize either the minds or bodies of those he loves.

---

sion, theology must have the character of a living *procession*. Evangelical theology would forfeit its object, it would belie and negate itself, if it wished to view, to understand, and to describe any one moment of the divine procession in 'splendid isolation' from others." It is like "a bird in flight" (*Evangelical Theology: An Introduction*, p. 9f.).

[16] Barth was avoiding the notion of an impersonal otherness, such as one finds in Rudolf Otto or Paul Tillich (as if that could be a higher level of numinous divinity behind the gracious and personal One we meet in Jesus Christ).

Similarly, his perfect unity is preconditioned and defined by his power to be everywhere present, as he is, wholly *gracious;* while his exercise of all-power is itself predefined and circumscribed by this person-tendered loyal constancy. Finally, any appropriate *glorification* of God on our part must mean regard for his prior action, which has unfolded for us as *love, grace, mercy and patience.* So there should be nothing pompous or bulldozing about how we represent it, and no abject kowtowing before him. All of this is given in an unfolding sequence.

With his slogan that "in theology, order is everything," Barth meant that if we are responding to God's Word, our discourse should always reflect the priority of events that already have taken place on our behalf in both creation and redemption. For considered in the light of God's *simultaneous grasp and lordship* over all our times,[17] his essential, life-giving events come to us in an irreversible *subsequence,* as a drama, that has behind it a full past-perfect actuality and permanence with God.

We cannot even know that it is a savior we need, before we discover we already have one. Although from our side we can experience this reality only in part now, and as forward-tending promise, it is no hyperbole to say that we are invited to hope for and anticipate as our future in grace what is already

---

[17] See Chapter 10 on simultaneity.

accomplished fact with him.

Although Barth's almost Baroque writing had its skeins of thought looping through a paisley of variation across fugue-like recurring themes, he tried to be highly disciplined where the prior divine order that is to be followed is concerned. Theology must always be attentive to the unfolding of God's own drama as it enters our history. There is an intrinsic sequence of events and unfolding consequence of meaning to be respected and communicated, regardless of the many angles from which we view it.[18]

We've noted how some have spoken dismissively of Karl Barth as "never having had an unpublished thought." But anyone who has read closely into his work knows that despite its cumulative nature and massive architecture, there is little unstudied or random in his organization. For in his view, Christian theology must seek to reflect the inner sequence that unfolds as a historical drama where its Subject enters time. This he discerned in the original Pauline language which described an

---

[18] "*Jede Umkehrung dieser Ordnung der Nötigung ist durch den anselmischen Bergriff des Glaubens ausgeschlossen* [i.e., every reversal of this constraining order is excluded through the Anselmic concept of belief]. (*Fides quaerens intellectum*, S. 15).

Reformed theology follows Paul in clarifying that God's election and saving action (i.e., his adoption and justification) always precede, occasion and motivate any appropriate renewal in our lives (i.e., sanctification) in an order which is always to be gratefully acknowledged and reflected as his initiative (and never to be spoken of as if it should or could be reversed).

irreversible sequence: God's prior election, rooted in his freedom to be wholly himself, loving, and so to take sovereign initiative to justify us.[19] His election and revelatory actions always retain for us a temporal and covenantal priority. They always anticipate further Spirit-mediated gifts that we gradually come to experience as our vivification: our communal faith-response and re-oriented life, (i.e., our "sanctification").[20] We find new behavior motivated as, touched by his accompanying Spirit, we reflect thankfully on what subsists for us—already complete and permanent with him.

It is particularly important to us, over and against American revivalist tradition, to be clear that God's righteousness and justice flow out of his prior mercy and are never to be pre-defined or abstracted from it. No divine omnipotence subsists prior to or separate from his constancy. There is no divine law that is not first principled by his prior freedom in grace (so law is not to be split off from gospel). There is never a fire-and-brimstone threat prior to or cut off from God's promised re-creation. There is no inhuman justice prior to or abstracted from the one who embraces us in love. Since his eternal truth and wisdom are functions of his grace, the Lord is never dismissive

---

[19] E.g., see in Romans 8.

[20] Here Barth holds true to Calvin's oft-repeated Pauline claim: "Those God justifies, he also sanctifies."

of those who are foolish or have been in error. Likewise, there is no divine glory prior to or separate from his passionate service to the least of his creations. Yes, order is everything.

So Barth always stuck by the priority of grace:

> As God has made self known in revelation, his is the fullest freedom. But this is the freedom of his love. He has [freely] bound himself. He has made a covenant. We don't bind him. His is a covenant of grace. He is the man-loving God, the God of *philoanthropia.* We have now (*after* revelation)—because it is true love, the faithfulness of God—not to worry about the possibilities of his not being faithful. We're on the firm ground of God's grace, which always has loved freely. We can only give thanks for the free gift.[21]

Yet for Barth such insistence on theology's Subject-defined order did not imply that there is a hierarchy of importance between the events of adoption, justification and sanctification or covenanted community, as if priority made the one

---

[21] English Colloquium, May 5, 1959.

220

more important, finally, than the others;[22] nor does it imply that every theologian should begin speaking at the same point or employ the same form.[23] One may approach or describe this intrinsic order of Christ-revealed event freely from many angles and seek out new expression forms with the fullest creative latitude. Such freshness is the theologian's manna or daily bread. But to reverse the unfolding order of God's own saving drama, as if his initiative here could in any way be jump-started or juiced-up from the human side, would short-circuit its significance and turn theology into gnostic speculation.

So the "beautiful science" remains deliciously free to focus in on any point in this drama. For God's self-bestowing grace grants freedom to our response and evokes unlimited creative innovation. Nevertheless, the prior giftedness and inner dynamic of its living Subject will reassert themselves wherever we attentively hear and follow. Each of us is called to reflect and follow loyally (from her or his own perspective) God's underlying drama of creation, redemption and salvation. Each of us can and should reflect the flight path or trajectory of our

---

[22] In early works Barth had described this as dialectic between God's eternity and our times. See in his study of the Reformed faith: "The reforming of life must flow naturally, as it were, from faith if that faith is authentic." (*The Theology of John Calvin,* pp. 75f.; 80). He came to emphasize, however, that God's eternity is not devoid of human time and event, but commands them in rich plenitude.

[23] See *the Faith of the Church*, p. 54f.

living Subject from our own angle. Our responding imaginations have free play for whatever variations we may hit upon to communicate and celebrate the ordered divine event and radiate its joy. But we are never in a position to reverse its order.

In other words, no matter where we dig in or begin to trace our own faith journey, a given order, intrinsic to the inner-connectedness of revelatory events, discloses itself.[24] This means a christological ground and reference for every imaginative flight in our "beautiful science." An order of event is "all-important" for theology precisely because our key to knowledge is incarnational—based in God's believed self-revelation and advent as event in time. We celebrate in gratitude, but may not speculate or collaborate in attempts to re-shape or sidestep that prior happening.

I would stress again: when Barth said that in theology order is everything, he did not mean that you should not re-examine everything from your own point of view (as indeed, the biblical authors themselves had done). He meant, rather, that if we are attentive, we'll find God's self-presentation in human terms, retains priority as our subject. (That, as we saw above,

---

[24] Barth, of course, was with Calvin following Paul here. As we saw previously, in Barth's seminal *Fides quarens intellectum* he exhibits the basis for ordering faith's intellect as a prior ontological necessity that is God's own, from which our minds may discover an unanticipated liberating noetic necessity that rationally they can but follow and enjoy in gratitude.

was for Barth precisely what Christians' *"Ge-hör-samkeit"* or obedience must mean.)

As we move into an age atwitter with electronic texting, Barth's insistence on being cognizant of, and obedient to, the ontology of God's prior action on our behalf as a meaningful and irreversible sequence of events could steady our communication of the gospel. It is all too prevalent among us in the chatter of popular religion to speak as if that order can be reversed. One hears many marketing claims for various prescriptions that are supposed to enhance an independent something or other called "spiritual growth."

As Barth would point out, it is the common error of pietism to speak as if the order of election and conversion could be reversed; that is, as if our own decision, or what we have been or undertaken to become, were the source of our renewal. He insisted that we can speak legitimately only in terms of faith's discovery that we have been already long-since chosen, elect and justified in God's grace. Any meaningfully restored life must flow out of this as a drama of discovery; i.e., as a free, Spirit-accompanied response—always gifted and always engendering unalloyed gratitude.

This is never to be vaunted, as if something within us or some method that we have capitalized upon, some spiritual exercise, guidance or growth program, were its agent or cause "lest anyone should boast" (as Ephesians 2:8 warns). Ministers of the gospel are not called to patent, bottle or sell spiritual steroids. Faith's attitude and subsequent action are always to be grasped in terms of their intrinsic order as essentially God's own prior action and gift, and never as a result of what any of us, enmeshed in our common human egoism, have managed to decide, accept, or undertake on our own. Here Karl Barth would upend our familiar Anglo-American notions about free will:[25]

> *Metanoio* [i.e., *re-orientation*, which is only loosely translated, "repentance,"] means looking to him who was, is and will be present—going forward and not looking back like Lot's wife. We are on the way: *iustus simul et peccator.*[26] There may be one special moment, like by Wesley. But even he must go on. As in Luther's 95 Theses, the Christian life is a continuing *Busse,* a continuing *metanoio.*[27] We are on the way, *iustus simul et peccator*—not half and half, [but fully both justified and sinner. It's our whole] story. It's all behind us, tapping us on the shoulder.

---

[25] See Chapter 9.
[26] I. e., simultaneously both justified and sinner.
[27] I. e., a reorientation (repentance).

224

That's true of all men; but Christians are *aware* of being on this way—and so, *con-verted*. This changed state is realized in Christ. But *liberum arbitrium* [so-called free will], without Christ, is our state of bondage. Freedom in Christ is **the positive order**.

If the message is ordered in the wrong way, then the instruction loses its freedom and becomes sad, distorted, and [there is ground for] persecution.[28]

Recognition of God's prior choice and action on behalf of all, finally, is the great equalizer in the world. Here, Barth's insights have special importance for us who, as Americans, have been bred to individualistic activism, spanned between traditions of frontier revivalism and the urban social gospel. God's initiative or "election" in, by and for grace is already there *for* such as us and already in force to heal all that has been broken in us. "You are to be completed, perfect, as he is already perfect."[29] Jesus' word here stands as a sovereign promise that is in no way dependent upon our subsequent actions, even as it

---

[28] English Colloquium, Dec. 18, 1963.
[29] Matt. 5:48 The Greek here significantly carries both indicative and imperative force.

confronts us also as divine command. "One must not make of election and reprobation equal partners. One must always speak of acceptance and rejection in such a way that acceptance is always the real [and all-embracing] context of God's decision."[30] Yes, order here is everything.

The priority many American evangelicals give each individual's determinative will in conversion, of course, comes into question here. Billy Graham, for example, typically read into *metanoio,* his own iffy concept of conversion. Thus in a broadcast sermon Graham announced: "Jesus said, you *must be converted.* It's all yours *if you are willing.* The word *conversion* means turn around and become a new creature." Thus the revivalist was in the habit of subjecting Luke's sovereign inclusiveness to an unwarranted precondition: "If you are willing!" Such an iffy business seems to imply that we are the ones who finally are in control, as if God, despite his sovereign grace, may be left wringing his hands, a helpless bystander, completely subject to our "hour of decision." But as he orders all things, is the gracious Lord of the Universe to be so easily defeated?

---

[30] Compare; Robert Jenson, *Alpha and Omega,* pp. 141-5; CD II/2, pp. 12-16.

Chapter 8

Natural Theology's Push
to Monopoly

A related motif in Barth's teaching that has proved to be crucial for us in the most practical terms is his oft-repeated caution about natural theology: that even the smallest concessions to it are deadly and will tend to shoulder their way toward *monopoly* every time.[1] One should note how this warning comes as a corollary to his observation that we've already stressed that in theology *order is everything*.

A tendency to begin with some aspect of natural experience, rather than with the holy God's self-revelation, is the most prevalent and calamitous reversal of theological order. Here was not just a warning, but Barth's call for a kind of sensitivity, so we may recognize the offshoots of a hydra-headed monster even in apparently innocuous, self-evident-seeming popular notions.

---

[1] Compare KD II/I, 152f. = p. 137f.

Theology is doing its job if it gives advance warning of how even apparently innocent minor speculations threaten to grow into idolatry.

FAITH SIDE-STEPS EVERY NATURAL THEOLOGY

Guarding against this slippery slope, as we have already seen, should be our Anselm-like reverence for the otherness of the holy God, who, in his grace, is free to be himself, quite apart from all experience-based speculations. Given grace, we may explore faith from the inside and resist every natural theology— every attempt to define, domesticate or prove belief, even in prior religious, spiritual or ethical categories.

Natural theologies are forms of gnosticism; and Quispel was quite right in describing gnosticism as the most prominent world religion; for its speculative mentality reasserts itself with seductive, new permutations in every generation.[2] Barth's life-long effort here is reminiscent of how the first great Church theologian, Ireneus of Lyon[3] found himself in mortal struggle against *"the Falsely So-Called Gnosis"* (AD 180/89). Whenever this busy bishop of the young churches in Gaul managed to get

---

[2] See Gilles Quispel's *Gnosis als Weltreligion: die Bedeutung der Gnosis in der Antike* (Zürich: Origo Verlag, 1972 = 1951 [Jung Institute]).

[3] Ca.142-ca.190. See also in the pseudonymous late Pauline epistle of I Timothy (6:20).

a spare moment, he would sit down and write still more of what would become five entire volumes against the Gnostics, even though he had early dismissed them with the phrase: "You need not swallow the whole ocean to know it's salty." This had become, and still is, the perennial survival struggle of the Christian Church—just as actual and pressing for us as it was for Ireneus.

Typically, an American student objected that since the same God that we meet in revelation is the source of all Creation, shouldn't we be able to rely on our general experience as one source for ethical truth and norms;[4] and why shouldn't the original creation be considered the ground of divine command, just as much as is the gracious deliverance promised us in the new creation in Christ?

Barth responded:

> It's the same God certainly. But what
> have we as "grace of creation"? It's hidden—
> covered by sin. We can't know him there. Our
> real starting point is the grace of revelation.
> From there we detect points in nature—but not

---

[4] I.e., "why must 'the metaphysics of being' (which is the starting point for a natural theology) be considered outside [and alien to] the grace of revelation?"

lights which are immanent."[5]

Further acquaintance with Barth only made one increasingly aware of how there is no more salient generalization to be made about the thrust of his work. It is not just that he was opposed to natural theology; his entire life was devoted to struggle against the Gnosticism that had so fatefully carried away the German Church. And America is not immune.

THE SPECTER OF THE
NATURAL AS BASIS OR NORM

But why would Barth regard people's natural and most obvious experience as a hydra-headed monster in theology? Why was something so perennial and near at hand, so seemingly self-evident and foundational for most religions, to be avoided like the plague? Why has Barth's basic challenge here found such resonance with us?

Charles Darwin summarized his observations of organisms' natural defense systems by declaring, "Nature will tell you a lie if she can." This certainly is also true where our intelligence regarding ultimate meanings is concerned. Nature, as God has purposefully left it, though awesome and wonderful, is

---

[5] English Colloquium, Dec. 18,1961.

often deceptive and at best, ambiguous.[6] Of all natural phenomena, our experiences of death and entropy, on one hand, and of our subjection to evil, brute forces, on the other, are always in evidence and can appear to have the last word; so both human and natural history are equivocal at best. Again and again we heard Barth's warnings here.[7]

The Unknown casts its veil over the fabric of our human existence, obscuring far more than we commonly allow ourselves to consider. For it precludes any clarity about the ultimate fate of time, space and substance. It blots out any factuality regarding our possible life after death and even any enduring coherence of our human personhood, love relationships, or named identity. And finally, it leaves ambiguous whether there is any meaning to life, any transcending substance to our value claims and sense of justice, good and evil, any model for the

---

[6] As Barth explained relative to his Barmen Declaration, "God has unambiguously spoken in *one* place. . . . Confessions will not help us if we put alongside them a second source of revelation." (E. Busch, *The Great Passion.* See notably p. 68.)

[7] As said, under title of natural theology Barth was speaking of the often tacit notion that we can find clues to the great unknowns (which elude us on every hand) on the false assumption that they necessarily must be analogous to our ordinary experience. Or we may be making the equally speculative false assumption that what- or whoever escapes us there *must be* wholly unlike what we ordinarily experience. So we presume to deal with the Unknown as if it must be a kind of spiritual opposite—like a jello-mold in negative contrast to the material world (e.g., the *via negativa* or the "pure spirit" speculations so common in mystical and gnostic thought).

wholeness of our human life. (The devotee of Theravada, for example, can quite rationally deny much of this.) All could stand or fall with the question of whether there is any transcending, meaning-giving, personal power behind nature—quite simply, whether God is for real.

So I would stress once again something that has not been enough appreciated regarding Barth. Much, perhaps even most, of his almost unbelievable output of writings continued to be motivated by his conviction regarding what had gone wrong in Germany—a crisis on the level of the beliefs that people live by. The specter of disaster spawned by German nature-based folk religion and its power-mongering master-race belief was always festering in the background for Barth. So he saw an enormous practical danger implicit in any natural-experience-based, speculative claims on the Unknown. I became convinced that virtually everything Barth wrote was keyed into his underlying impassioned drive to counter such deadly admixtures of natural-appearing speculations with the gracious revelation of the Scriptures.[8]

One often hears of his dismay, as a young Swiss theology student, when his famous liberal theology professors in

---

[8] See e.g., KD II/1, S. 165f.; 198. Also Robert McAfee Brown's Introduction to his translation of Georges Casalis's *Portrait of Karl Barth* (Garden City, New York: 1963), p. 12f.

Germany all lined up behind the militaristic nationalism of Kaiser Wilhelm in the First World War. Hadn't they uncritically corrupted their commitment as Christians with their own natural patriotism? Barth's awareness of distortions in the Church that fairly cried out for self-criticism was reinforced by the miserable later events of the 1930s, which saw a larger part of the German Church carried away by the power-appeal and racial supremacy doctrine—"blood, land, folk and steel"—of Hitler's National Socialism.[9] This movement, which Barth understood to be rooted in a form of natural theology,[10] was a major cause of the Second World War and would lead to the murder of six million Jews, and to that warfare's annihilation of five times that many people and the displacement of twice again that number. Barth perceived an insidious natural theology lurking, not only in Fascism, but also in the other great "-isms" of the age—

---

[9] Karl Barth explicitly placed his notorious "Nein!" to Emil Brunner in the sphere of his defense against the tragic flaw of the German Church in its bowing to Hitler. Brunner simply had not had Barth's harrowing German experience, so had a less vivid sense of the dangers involved. See W. Sykes Introduction to *The Way of Theology* . . . , p. 14 and p. 45 re Barth's letter to Max Schoch (in *Letters 1961-1958*, p. 270).

[10] Hitler explicitly mocked all revealed morality, religion and humanitarianism as a "*betrayal of nature*" and as such, "the original sin" and "a revolt against heaven." Claiming brute biological struggle for survival and a quasi-scientific social Darwinism as his basis in nature, he would declare that "what applies to apes applies to men too at a higher level." See Joachim Fest on Hitler's table talk and monologues of the 1940s. See *Inside Hitler's Bunker: The Last Days of the Third Reich* (New York: Farrar, Straus and Giroux, 2004), p. 167.

in godless Marxism, with its naturalistic interpretation of history, as well as in the glutted consumerism of the West.

I mentioned earlier how Barth once exclaimed, "We've not been fighting against windmills, but a real threat to Church and humanity. Look what happens when people are following such [nature-based] goals: It begins with great hopes, ideals, and illusions of all kinds, and ends with shooting."[11]

There is a real sense in which wars—perhaps all wars— have their roots in various natural theologies. For the ambiguities of Nature leave the speculative minds of different people committed to clashing values and ways of life. If these are seen simply to cancel each other out, they leave a mood of moral apathy or disdain; but if they are stubbornly maintained, they lead inevitably to mortal conflict.[12]

Nothing could be more crucial, then, for us in our present great-power situation than Barth's staunch "no!" to every form of natural theology. Unfortunately, Barth's insistent "no" to natural theologies and religions has often been styled as

---

[11] English Colloquium, Jan. 27, 1959.

[12] It is here that Robert D. Shofner's tightly argued choice of the philosophy of Charles Hartshorne's more broadly sourced epistemology over Barth's theological exclusion of general experience as basis for belief, while cogent and understandable as philosophy, strikes one as overly sanguine in not attending to the actual mortal dangers that exercised Barth throughout. See especially pp. 223-230 in *Anselm Revisited: A Study of the Role of the Ontological Argument in the Writings of Karl Barth and Charles Hartshorne* (Leiden: E.J., Brill, 1974).

symptomatic of a narrow exclusivity or sour negativism, although nothing could be further from the case. We cannot stress strongly enough that Barth's "no" to natural theology was but the obverse side of his much greater "yes" to all humanity. In this spirit he said "no" to the Germans' gut feeling claims to *Volk*-supremacy. And whatever else his Barmen Declaration[13] for the Confessing Church (1934) may have been, it was a manifesto of the full worth and dignity of *all mankind.* This is to be defended out of respect for God's own freedom and infinite power to be himself (fully gracious to all). Barth could be quite explicit about this: you may *only* speak this kind of "no" with force as an expression of the "yes" of grace, which *must be spoken at the same time* and much louder.

To recognize God as God, means to recognize him as he freely is in himself—as he is, personally and loyally God-man, having chosen undying relation to our lowly human selves. Barth's "no" then, was the expression of an ineffably greater "yes" to our fullest corporate humanity[14]—a "no" in defense

---

[13] While this Declaration against the idolatrously nationalistic Deutsche Christen Kirche was issued in the name of the combined Confessing churches, it had been crafted almost entirely by Barth. See his comments in CD II/1, pp. 172-178.

[14] See Raymond K[emp] Anderson, "Corporate Personhood: Societal Definition of the Self in the Western Faith Tradition," in *Becoming Persons,* Robert N. Fisher, ed. (Oxford: Applied Theology Press, 1995), Vol. 2, especially p. 571.

against all that would split us and leave our own spirit warring against our body or one limited human ideal, social pattern, value, or ethnicity set against others.

Having said all this, however, does not eliminate the possibility or even the apparent probability (as Thomistic scholars have been eager to point out) that God might make himself known *also* in his handiwork in nature alongside his incarnational self-revelation as attested in scripture. Here one must also be clear how and why maintaining ambiguity in nature may be an expression of divine grace. For if God does not impose himself, but has chosen to retain indeterminateness in our natural surroundings, it is important to suggest why he holds to that plan.

He takes the trouble, if you will, suffers the complex burden, takes great pains and is passionate not to force himself upon us with compelling power. That God enabled earthquake, flood, wildfire and all else that seems to equivocate the goodness of creation may, in fact, cohere with divine grace. For at the core of the Christian revelation is the paradox, that in representing himself, God resists a uniquely divine temptation[15] and would "rather die" in human terms, than lord it over his crea-

---

[15] See Matt. 4 and Luke 4. Also Mark's narrative on the disciples' fateful temptation to power (9:35 & 10:35-45).

tures with rapacious force or take their minds by proof. [16]That his all-healing Messiah does choose to submit himself and die in human terms has perhaps its greatest significance just here.

For Barth, God's unexpected self-revelation as transcendent grace always surprises. Like one of those transparent pages in an atlas, it overlays all of our highest and best projections regarding life-meaning with a translucent vision of something infinitely more astounding, relaxed and, finally, good-humored, than we ever could have imagined from the pages of our everyday experience.[17] Here is something more joyful, far, than our most highfalutin notions of spirituality; more open, far, than our most soulful claims to religious ascendency; more healing than our most deeply felt notions of tit-for-tat justice or morality.

THE OLD LIBERALISIM—BARTH'S FOIL

What was at stake for us in the academic discipline of theology should be kept in mind. Some sketchy historical reminders could be useful toward understanding Barth's thought here.[18] In the wake of confessional wars in Europe, during the period

---

[16] Compare Mark 10:42 ff.

[17] "There is no faith without experience; but experience apart from faith is equivocal" (K. Barth in English Colloquium, Feb. 24, 1959).

[18] See further in, e.g., H. M. Rumscheidt, ed., *The Way of Theology in Karl Barth*, p. 72 f.

before America's founding, many young thinkers were fed up with the zealotry that claimed religious justification for endless warfare. Those who had arrogated authority to themselves (those claiming Papal authority, on one hand, and on the other, Protestant Scholastics, who were making a paper pope of their Bible) came to be derided by intellectuals, who were fed up with religious sloganeering and bloodshed and had been educated with an Enlightenment awareness that the Bible of "Christian Europe" is itself a quite human book, with its own errors and obsolescence.

To counter this attitude, which permeated the sophisticated salons of Berlin, the young Friedrich Schleiermacher in 1799 wrote his *Reden über die Religion an die Gebildeten unter ihren Verächtern* (talks on religion for its cultured despisers). In this popular little book, he tried to win back young skeptics' flagging respect for religion by pointing to a universal *feeling*. Presumably, we all experience a natural feeling of complete dependency upon something beyond ourselves (an *Abhängigkeitsgefühl*). Thus, God-thought was to be recognized as founded in this most natural of feelings. Schleiermacher would then rehabilitate the role of Jesus Christ, mainly as a great pioneer witnessing to this natural sentiment that all might discover in themselves.

238

In similar vein, Deists such as Thomas Jefferson or Tom Paine, who expressed themselves in America's founding documents, looked to what "Nature and nature's God" teach: presumably, including the notion that all *men* are created equal. (Never mind millennia of ambiguity surrounding quite naturally occurring slavery and women's subjugation!)

Immanuel Kant (1724-1884) picked up another strand of general human nature: the felt need to have moral reinforcement. God becomes a natural necessity, a postulate or projection of our Practical Reason (as backing for those universal principles, the "categorical imperatives" we must settle upon, in order to act according to our rational nature). Following Kant, the theologian Albrecht Ritschl (1822-1889) tried to bolster traditional Christian faith, on the notion that Jesus was the one who most clearly intuited such natural ethical rules and values. Meanwhile, the philosopher Jacob Friedrich Fries (1773-1814) took an analogous and parallel tack, as he focused on universal aesthetic values: a natural sense of beauty.

Following his lead more than a century later, Rudolf Otto developed one aspect of Fries's ideas[19] to posit a special religious-aesthetic experience of "the holy," as a tremendous

---

[19] Viz. the subject of Otto's doctoral dissertation.

natural mystery that can set your hair on end.[20] (Again Jesus presumably had made himself a religious pioneer, in that he had *felt* the holy so immediately.) Otto would go so far as to ascribe a special virtue to the incomprehensibility of the Mass spoken in Latin, for example, inasmuch as its strangeness triggers a natural response to the mysterious and uncanny, the holy. More recently still, we saw Paul Tillich in similar vein, pointing to a feeling we all presumably share: that there *must be* something that we intuit as our "Ultimate Concern." Such a natural feeling or in-sight becomes his base line for theology.

From the skeptical, philosophical sideline, a whistle was blown on all such speculations by Ludwig Feuerbach:[21] You say all this speech is about God (*"theou logoi"*)? Yet the whole time, you're really talking about people—about what makes people feel good, perhaps—their biggest and best ideals, perhaps; their wish-fulfillment, most certainly. But what you've been calling theology is still only man-talk—fancy-brand anthropology. The mature Barth would tend to agree with Feuerbach's assessment of such speculation.

On a more faith-positive side, Kierkegaard, as we have seen, had taken seriously that God has been Unknown—the Unknown that Reason at its height must acknowledge, but can-

---

[20] *The Idea of the Holy* (London: Oxford University Press, 1928).
[21] Ludwig Feuerbach, *Das Wesen der Religion* (1845).

not fathom or grasp. Your ordinary natural experience says nothing about the subsistence or non-existence of the Unknown. It can not even say with any surety that the Unknown must be unknowable and cannot make itself known in human terms. How might that be?

Couldn't the Unknown . . . An absolute paradox, this. . . Couldn't the Unknown, as far as we know, make itself known in our terms and give us a new condition or happy "passion" of mind (whereby we might accept this extraordinary self-presentation as representing the otherwise Unknown) and thus giving an alternative basis for our rationality?

Indeed if truly beyond us, the Unknown may (for all we know) be free and capable of presenting *itself* to us and maintaining *in itself* a humanity of its own to be known by us. In short, the Unknown could become man and so give a new frame of reference for our Reason, a new Occasion for a new Condition which would contextualize everything we know in a new perspective.

What should we call this weird, but real, possibility? Asks Kierkegaard tongue in cheek, "Let us "assign a word to it," a brand new word, no one has ever heard: "we shall call this passion '*Faith*.'"[22]

---

[22] Søren Kierkegaard, *Philosophical Fragments* (Princeton: Prince-

Karl Barth was deeply influenced by Kierkegaard while, as the young minister of a Swiss village, he struggled to have a life-saving message garnered from the gospel he was interpreting and especially from Paul's Letter to the Romans. The living God of grace he met there was far greater, better and more engaging than the insipid, watered-down notions of God of the so-called liberalism in which he'd been schooled (with its admixture of human-nature-filtered religious talk).

The counter-slogans Barth fired off in his early writings became one-sided, as he later would readily agree, and tended to slight the humanity, gentleness, kindness and humor of Christ's actual incarnation. But to clear the ground of all speculation, he stridently called for a purge of all attempts to fund our ideas about God with notions based in our equivocal natural human experience: "Let God be God." The Lord's Word comes, *"senkrecht von oben nach unten"*; that is, like a bolt of lightning, "perpendicularly from above downwards." You will find his faith claims lifting you from the minefield of your mind's natural assumptions about spirituality, morality, justice, absolute power, and other notions that have seemed most "natural" to you in speculating about who or what a great god, ought to be or require. Only then can you be truly attentive to God's

ton University Press, 1936), p. 47.

astounding loving humanity.

MISREADING BARTH ON HUMAN NATURE

One of the common caricatures of the early Barth in America
was that he was saying "no" to human rationality and depreciat-
ing the human being—as if he were of the opinion that God is
everything and man is nothing. Whereas, as Barth often observed, it is when self-experience funds natural religion and
pushes toward monopoly that regard for human wholeness and
diversity invariably falls victim and dwindles. In Christ-based
faith, by contrast, while recognizing that "by taking thought,"
we could not "add a cubit" to our own stature,[23] we find ourselves within the human community imbued with undreamed-of
worth and permanent promise—no longer experienced only as
tiny specks of protoplasm out in the boondocks of the universe.

Barth's "no," as we said, is always intended as a liberation from anything that is getting in the way of a greater "yes"
to mankind. The revealed Word's "yes!" is *for* the people of
varied intelligence of all religions—and for those of all athe-
isms—in a grace that embraces them all.[24] So it intends to ad-

---

[23] Matt. 6:27.

[24] In his second Gifford Lecture Barth risked remarking that the
modern Church might "be in a better position if she had remained suspect of
atheism" in the same sense that the Early Church was in the Roman world;
i.e., if it were clear that Christ's Church is not founded on any of the popu-

dress a louder yes-claim to each person, in the same word and
movement in which it says "no" to any less hopeful undertow—
"no" to repressive moralizing and to exclusivist individualizing.

THEOLOGY OF NATURE (NOT NATURAL THEO-LOGY OR DENATURED SPIRITUALITY)

When he inquired about my Calvin findings, Barth wanted to
know, was it my observation that, although Calvin appreciated
nature and respected philosophies based upon it, did the Reformer not, nevertheless, regard nature as so ambiguous for us,
that it could never be an ancillary basis or support for faith (as
Aquinas so fatefully tried to make it)? Indeed Calvin went to
great lengths to bring these subjects into the curriculum of his
Geneva Academy and could speak strongly of how nature
would mirror its Creator, **if only** human vision were not clouded
by sin. But it is. So unaided, we read only mixed messages
there.[25] Everywhere we look death casts its pall.

Barth's defense against nature-based theology is completely misunderstood, when it is assumed that he was somehow
downgrading the natural creation or the importance of natural

larly taken-for-granted speculations (p.19). In the same vein, one might
comment that the Church might be in a better position today, if she were
suspect of not being at root "spiritual."

[25] See e.g., *Institutes* II/ii/12-25.

244

science or ecology, however.[26] Quite the opposite is true. Whereas the bulk of nature-based speculative religion tends to dualize the world (setting a higher, spiritual side of life in tension or conflict, over and against a lower physical side), incarnation-based revelation takes positively the bodily wholeness of man. This faith can delight in the intrinsic goodness of God's entire creation, while it evokes our caretaking stewardship within it. It is a matter of record that, nature-based speculation, which has recurred throughout history, virtually as a dominant world religion, has time and again scorned our physical nature as a trap or mortal burden which man's ostensibly higher spirituality would do well to escape, or at least repress, either with detached cool or through a sated exhaustion.[27]

The mature Barth, who began always with the incarnate Word, maintained a pithy body-spirit holism against all such gnostic tendencies. Astoundingly, divine grace can regard each person and each point in time/space *simultaneously*, as equally a

---

[26] See for example R. H. Roberts, who assumes that Barth's "denial of natural theology comes dangerously close to a repudiation of natural reality itself"; while quite the opposite can be true. Time and again, it has been nature-based gnosticisms that typically have tended to seek escape from the death-bound natural world through some form of body-spirit dualism. Incarnation-based theology, by contrast, calls us to share God's love for his good Creation. (In view: "Barth's Doctrine of Time," Sykes, *op.cit.* p. 110.)

[27] The latter, the "ethical" tactic of the early Carpocration gnostic sect, has its modern parallels where some try to neutralize their disturbing sexuality through "cool" overindulgence.

center for the whole;[28] but no individual man is to assume an attitude of tyrannical possession. Indeed as Calvin had said again and again, "We are not our own." Even our selves are not totally at our disposal. How could we degrade the wonder of God's universe by regarding the rest of nature as our unqualified possession and chattel? Barth's grace-based appreciation of the wonders of nature, then, reached far beyond any anthropocentricity. Considering that he wrote long before the anti-technological backlash and ecological movement had come into vogue,[29] his grace-based theology of nature became remarkably clairvoyant here. Yet again, God's grace remains constant and is also *for* the gnostics, who despise nature, in spite of their dualistic apperceptions, just as it is *for* the rest of fallible humanity. But it remains a simple fact: gnostic attitudes were and are rife, both in the world of Jesus' day, and in our own; and they are not to be shrugged away or ignored.[30]

---

[28] See Chapter 10.

[29] In Godsey's transcription of *Karl Barth's Table Talk* (p. 51f.), we find Barth already volunteering a sweeping self-critique over his early myopia on this score, recognizing that he had neglected creaturely life spanning through the gift of time in favor of its eschatological *terminus ad quem*: "At the time I wrote this I did not know that God was Creator of heaven **and** **earth**! Man is too important here! . . . Barth intended CD III to be as better balanced in recognizing how "the greatness of God's dealing with man is *in nature*" (p. 51f.).

[30] See Geddes MacGregor, *Gnosis: A Renaissance in Christian Thought*: (Wheaton, Illinois: Theosophical Publishing House, 1979), pp. 17-27; 74ff. *et al.* This author seems to be unfazed by Barth's critique, but does

THEOLOGY AND PHILOSOPHY

Significantly, for Barth the natural creation that we are to respect includes the empirical embeddedness of our own minds and the entire range of possible rational responses to the world. Contrary to rumor, he was highly interested in, and respectful of, natural philosophy and philosophical rationality in general.[31] Our liberated minds are to deal with natural knowns, chart their limits and enjoy full play with alternative theories. His brother, Heinrich, was a professor of philosophy (not always in agreement, to be sure), and he himself had spent much time and energy in that discipline. However theology—gifted with faith's revelation-base regarding the great Unknown—should never be confused as if it were either in conflict with, or could be supplanted or supported by, natural philosophy or natural science.[32]

---

well to caution us against simply ignoring Gnosis, as we, much more critically than MacGregor, perhaps, strive to avoid syncretistic admixtures with the Apostolic Word.

[31] A number of theologians have described Barth as using reason in an "attack on reason." He saw himself, rather, as respecting its limits and its hidden source—i.e., its foundation and funding. He was cognizant of Kant's distinction between *a priori* and *a posteriori* knowledge, but regarded faith claims as historical givens to which reason may, and finally in all honesty, must objectively relate. One is not being irrational when one recognizes the fact that a divine reason may have priority over our own and considers the orientation that such a possibility would entail.

[32] See further Barth's essay entitled "Philosophy and Theology" from the 1960 *Festschrift* celebrating his brother, Heinrich's 60th birthday, translated in *The Way of Theology in Karl Barth,* H. Martin Rumscheidt, ed. (Allison Park, PA: Pickwick, 1985), pp. 79-95. In the introduction to his final *Evangelical Theology,* Barth, with tongue in cheek, speaks of his own

The separation between theology and philosophy should be visible in the order they adopt. (Remember, "order is everything"!)[33] They both have truth as their subject and object and are called to be reflective of and governed by it. But the theologian begins with God's self-revelation which then puts all human experience in new perspective; whereas the philosopher begins with ordinary human experience and, when honest, seeks to clarify not only its scope, but its limits and inconclusiveness where truth itself remains unknown. Asked the source of his method, the theologian "must answer directly and without qualification, without being ashamed of such naïveté, that Jesus Christ is the one and entire truth through which he is shown how to think and speak, just as strictly as the philosopher is given his task."

Finally, Barth's opposition to seeking to know God through natural analogies does not mean that one will not begin to extol in nature the traces of the Creator whom faith has already known. Barth acknowledged that "fingerprints" of the gracious God become visible among the enigmas of nature, as

---

modern parallel to Abraham Calov's seventeenth century criticism of what Calov called "*mixophilosophicotheologia*"! (p. xiii). Barth never nourished the illusion that he or anyone else could become chemically pure of the philosophical notions and terminology that permeate our thought world—a fact that van Til thought counted against him and Brunner. (See his *The New Modernism . . .*)

[33] See Chapter 7.

faith gives us eyes to recognize them. So it is a wonder of grace to be delivered from the threatening aspect that veils God's presence behind dark and often catastrophic ambiguity. One can mine nature, as Jesus did, for parabolic suggestiveness. And though the death-bound mortal world is equivocal, shot through with earthquake, flood and famine, we are enabled to apprehend it with joy. For given a faith full of promise, we are heartened to dance even when our way is lined with tombstones.

As Barth's faith is not against people, in their rational struggle for scientific and philosophical truth, neither is it against them in their spiritual struggle, but for them through it all. So he pointed us to the gracious One who remains veiled in our philosophies and philosophies of religion, even while revealing himself to be greater than, and better than, our most daring conjectures.

Chapter 9

Grace for the Religious
And Godless World

"RELIGIONLESS" CHRISTIANITY

Did reverberations from Barth study make us dismissive of the study of religions, then, as some have supposed? I would hope not. Heightened civility, respect and a desire truly to understand should express the stance of grace, especially here, where humanity is so deeply entrenched. For everything pervasively or even perversely human is to be regarded as the object of sovereign grace. But since religion is, in our general experience, one of the most persistent dimensions of human nature, Barth's caution against natural theology's toxic drive for monopoly does apply with special force where particular religions are concerned.

Yet, just as Barth's "no" to man-based theology has been turned inside out, where it has been taken to denigrate human nature—and just as his rejection of natural theology has been misconstrued, where it is supposed that he downgraded material nature or was indifferent to natural science, or was anti-rational in respect to philosophy in general—now, something similar must be stressed, where it is a question of the theologian's relation to religion per se and our release from religious forms of bondage.[1]

Admittedly, Barth would sometimes express aversion to the very word "religion" when it intruded into faith-based discussion; and his "religionless Christianity" was the aspect of his thought that evoked the most vehement opposition from some of my American colleagues (since it could so easily be construed as a chauvinistic disdain for cultural diversity). But it needs to be stressed that in his efforts to keep the ambiguity, confusion and despair of general human experience at bay, Karl Barth was no more *against* religion or religions per se, than he was against humanity or human beings per se. Barth's "religionless Christianity" does not signal disdain for human cultures and the multifarious religions which infuse them. Rather, when we regard the devotees of various religions as embraced by Christ's grace, we are liberated to explore their beliefs as a fascinating dimension of scientific sociology and even to treasure them as a multicultural heritage, without becoming

---

[1] Compare E.Busch, *The Great Passion*, pp. 141-151.

enmeshed or captive to them or embroiled in confessional warfare. "There's nothing outside a man that can defile."[2] And yet the hour is coming when true worshippers will not worship only in the high places of one or another religion, but in spirit and in truth.[3]

To recap here, let us remind ourselves that the humanity-in-general of our era has been gored by brutal totalitarianisms. We have experienced as our everyday banality what Zbigniew Brezinski called a century of *mega-death*. If you look to broad human experience for your truths and values, the quiet message of the cross will seem to be drowned out by the noise of gunfire and terrorist bombings. Yet for apostolic faith, it is our post-traumatic humanity that God infinitely loves and will restore. That Barth would not have us fund either theology or Christian anthropology from the ambiguity of this general human experience does not mean he was against humanity, but quite the opposite that he was radically, supra-rationally, for it.

Let us put this another way. We found that faith is not opposed to empirical science when it sticks to a non-empirical hope that undergirds it with a belief that can redeem science from its involvement in the mass weaponry of mega-death. Likewise, faith is not against human sexuality, when its belief

---

[2] Mk. 7:15; Matt. 15:11-20; KD IV/2, S.195f., 191.
[3] Jn. 4:21: KD. IV/2, S.197.

would heal even faithless promiscuity with the promise of restored covenantal relationships. Now, by the same token, Karl Barth's faith is not against peoples in their various religious heritages and spiritual quests, but *for* them all, in pointing tenaciously to the gracious one who, while remaining effectively hidden, reveals himself to be greater than, and better than, has ever been intimated as the highest and the best, even there—in our religions.

The story of how Paul was misunderstood on Mars Hill[4] may have its parallel here: For in the name of Christ Barth represented One whose grace embraces *equally* all the animists and the witches and Taoists and Hindus and Muslims and atheists and Catholics and Presbyterians alike. Such non-religious commitment is apt to be misunderstood from both right and left, just as the first Christians were taken to be either heretics or misanthropic atheists by Jewish and Hellenistic neighbors.

But if one begins to surrender to the kaleidoscopic gnosis of natural experience as source and listen to the cacophony of human religions for one's grasp of the ultimate Unknown, then Zeus, Daemon, mana, Satan, Wicka, Gautama, all seem to have equal natural footing and crowd in with equal force until, finally, they begin to cancel each other out and fail us. Any

---

[4] Acts 17:22ff.

Unity that actually subsists behind such diversity will be clouded beyond recognition by the contradictory claims championed in warring religious speculations. So sophisticated people today, as those Schleiermacher addressed in his time, will tend to shrug it all off—as if this source of conflict, the truth question, being beyond reach, is not worth pursuing.

For Barth, the one who comes into history and grasps us through our faith puts our prior religious endeavors in perspective and shows how humanly flawed and ungracious to each other they all may have been.[5] This goes quite as much for clubby exclusivity of some post-war Protestant churches or for the vindictive tribal warfare of early Hebrew scripture as it does for the *karma*-bound fate of the Upanishads, or the person-negating detachment of Theravada. William Stringfellow commented that Barth was "a remarkably unreligious man" who could say he had had no desire "to build a Christian home" lest it become too conscious of itself as *religion*.

But nevertheless, those of Hebrew religion, of Christian religion, and of every other genre of religion, all become *equal-*

---

[5] This is the point where (as von Harnack pointed out) the congenial second century heretic, Marcion, with his one-sided grasp of grace understood St. Paul better than anyone else of his day, and yet misunderstood him. For Marcion, still awash in a nature-derived dualism, tried to wrench the gospel free from any attachment to the creator of a seemingly misbegotten material world.

ly the objects of grace. As all things human are subject to God's saving intention and election in Christ, all are believed to be equally in need of his re-creative restoration. In each of our religious traditions we stand ever again with the distraught Jewish father in Mark, "Lord, I believe; help my unbelief."[6] Not bound to this or that mountain, we may "worship in spirit and in truth."[7]

Let us repeat: a religionless theology of grace is not against religious people, but everlastingly and rather scandalously *equally for those of every genre*. And that can be, only if its promise has broken in from beyond to transcend them all. The gospel of God's grace discovered in the Christ events relativizes whatever Christians have made of it as a chauvinistic institutional religion, just as resoundingly as it transcends all the perennial natural profusion of gnostic speculations.

In sum, to re-vision our humanity in the light of grace does not set us against humanity, but most forcefully motivates the opposite commitment. The same goes for our natural religiosity, as for all other dimensions of our common humanity. Though religion is a human work "scarred with dualism,"[8] it is a natural expression of the creature God loves. As we find our-

---

[6] Mk. 9:24.
[7] Jn. 4:21-23.
[8] *The Epistle to the Romans*, p. 231.

selves reoriented through Christ, the light of divine grace scours and re-visions it all—bleaches out, dries up, sloughs off, all that was hopeless, ungracious, anti-human, life-threatening, fatalistic, compulsive, onerous or divisive in our diverse religious experiences.

PATIENCE FOR IMPATIENCE

Barth's treatment of mystical experience and mysticism becomes another case in point in his general warning against natural theology. That mystical experiences can and do come upon people, both inside and beyond scriptures, he would not deny.[9] But while these may be provocative as signs, they always retain the ambiguity that is present in every other form of natural experience. So, as Barth would often observe, whenever this particular form of natural experience is presumed to be a clue to the Unknown, such claims to mystical revelation wrongly imply that God *loses patience* with us in our identity as separate selves (and begins to take over our minds or absorb them into himself). Yet such impatience would countermand his grace. For the God

---

[9] Quite naturally, about one person in ten of any population will have had a mystical experience. Though these, like all else in nature, are subject to diverse religious interpretations, in Barth's terms it would be misleading to think of them, with all their "ineffability" and ambiguity, as especially *super*natural or "religious," as did William James in his *Varieties of Religious Experience* (1902), or to confuse them with explicit revelation of the Unknown.

who loves us will take care never to violate our minds. He would rather die, so to speak, than domineer his creatures or even compeo them intellectually. Hence his Word as the crucified Messiah.

As all nature is full of suggestive hints, but is too polyvalent to be our basis for understanding, the same must be said even more forcefully of that fraction of the common human experience which has an ineffable, mystical quality that defies concrete description. Where knowledge of God is concerned, any experience beyond Christ can be only a vessel, finally for experience in and of Christ himself.[10]

It probably needs to be acknowledged here that Barth recognized mystical elements in the Bible, just as he recognized that other elements of natural theology can play a limited preparatory role along the road toward theological discovery in faith. He would say, "I agree with those who think there is a preparatory natural theology. But it can only show the way to Christ. If man is not enabled to accept what God gives him, then man does not have a natural preparation. The world is full of natural theology."[11]

---

[10] Cf. E. Busch, *Karl Barth*, p. 447.
[11] English Colloqium, Jan. 27, 1959. Barth expressed similar insights in his Colloquia of Jan. 13 and Feb.10, 1959.

"FREE WILL"—A NATURAL THEOLOGY

Barth's treatment of so-called free will is another case in point in his general warning against natural theology. One of the most taken for granted bits of natural theology for those of us within the Anglo-American tradition must be our inherited habit of ascribing a foundational role to people's native pride in exercising a life-determining free will. Billy Graham's loudly heralded "hour of decision" had broad resonance among us. Grace may be essential, but doesn't everything still depend on whether we decide to accept the gift proffered to us or not? Here Barth was careful to note that the freedom we are given in and for faith's spontaneous response, though a real and intentional gift of God, is something radically different from our natural notion of possessing a sovereign *liber arbitrium,* as an unlimited power for the final disposition of our lives. Does he abandon us to our own resources here?

Barth's response to a student's question here is telling. The student asked whether our freedom in and for grace does not imply that God's ability to be gracious to us depends on our act of free will in the traditional sense, as a prerequisite necessity. Or did Barth mean something else by our freedom—something more consistent with the sovereignty of God?

The professor replied:

I would prefer to differentiate between a true and a false freedom. True freedom is not a choice between alternatives. Our one freedom is obedience to the will of God.[12] What we call freedom as "free will" is not real freedom. We are free, if we are in agreement with God; [i.e., with the giver and free spirit of life itself.]

This came at the end of Godsey's *Table Talk* transcription, where students repeatedly asked whether we don't have a natural ability *not* to "choose" freedom—as an assertion of free will. Barth's jarring response: "The liberty of 'free will' is sin. It is the shame of humanity that we live as if we could choose."[13]

Such choice against freedom could only be an enslaving compulsion. In our English Colloquium[14] a student voiced confusion at this point: "Aren't we faced with two apparently incompatible things that you claim must be affirmed alongside one another (i.e., the sovereignty of God and the freedom of

---

[12] See Chapter 4 on Barth's use of the term, "obedience." It is not meant to be coercive in tone, but describes a spontaneous attentiveness inspired by the Spirit still present in grace.

[13] John D. Godsey, ed., *Karl Barth's Table Talk* (Richmond, VA: John Knox Press), p. 99.

[14] Feb. 26, 1962.

man), in spite of the fact that even after our best thought, their relationship remains a mystery for faith?"

Barth answered that God gives a real freedom, an *allowance*. "His command is an allowance."

If we are sinning, we are not sinning within the realm of our freedom, we are contradicting the very nature of [our humanity and] our freedom. Sin is terrible because we are choosing that which cannot be chosen—going against the rule of our own nature.

The fact that man disobeys is "only a fact," but does not defeat his relationship with God. God in sovereign grace will give *full* freedom.

The "potentiality for bad decision"? Sin, *peccare, hamartia*—it means "out of the way," abyss, *nihil*. That's not a potentiality."

Our freedom, the freedom we're given, is potentiality (to be what we *are*, his people), given by him, who by his freedom makes us his people. The sinner is still *his* person, still within his sovereignty. It is a sovereignty which is grace, his love—a burning fire. Here's real freedom, real choosing: the positive [action] of

God's will, as he has chosen us.

The student protested: "You say, 'an imperative to which I owe absolute obedience must necessarily come in the most radical sense from within,' but three lines later, you state that such an imperative 'must come to me as something alien, as the command of another.' [15] Which is it?"

Barth again pointed to the popular notion of free choice:

Hercules in Greek saga with the two ways, or Paris with the three women?—that's not freedom. Real freedom, a truly good [and liberating] thing, is not within their choice. (This woman or that?) "Free will" [so-called] is a *servum arbitrium*, [an enslaved will] as Luther speaks of such choices. Choice—but not free!

You are truly free, then, only when, gifted with a confident and untrammeled sense of direction, you can be completely yourself.

Barth's radical side-stepping of such a broadly accepted concept as "free will" is probably the sort of thing Stanley Hauerwas had in mind when he commented that Barth's ethic

---

[15] CD II/2, p. 651.

"exemplifies a position whose substantive insights are constantly in tension with the conceptual categories used to express these insights."[16] The problem for Barth lay in the alien baggage common nature-based categories, such as "free will," always bring with them. It also awkwardly encumbers such other general-experience-rooted categories as that of human *character* and of habitual *virtue*, which Hauerwas sought to rehabilitate as more appropriate "correlatives" to Barth's view of life as a journey, than his theme of obedience to commands.[17]

"SPIRITUAL GROWTH"—A NATURAL THEOLOGY

Both within and beyond our churches today you hear frequent marketing claims for various prescriptions that are supposed to enhance an amorphous something or other called "spiritual growth." But to Karl Barth's critical eye the spiritual development *of persons* is either a misnomer or myth. Instead, we are given to live modestly with the dynamics of day-by-day direct

---

[16] Hauerwas, celebrated ethicist of Notre Dame and Duke Universities, though he had come to theology with more Methodist than Reformed predilections, perhaps, "was attracted to Barth" and has worked valiantly for a critical synthesis with some of his key insights. (See especially his Gifford Lectures and his autobiography, *Hannah's Child: A Theologian's Memoir*, pp. 59, 63 and 87f.).

[17] Stanley Hauerwas, *Reader,* pp. 85-7, especially n.16. We have explained previously how the natural concept of "obedience" takes on a completely different meaning when oriented to the revelation of God's grace, rather than to general, natural-appearing "conceptual categories" (see Chapter 4).

263

response to, gratitude for and attestation of the one who is always equally *there for all*. The Christian message makes us increasingly aware of our corporate solidarity with all the others.[18] This is not a matter of *our* having grown to some new level of achievement. For in a real sense, as Barth says:

> One never is a Christian, one can only become one again and again, in the evening of each day somewhat ashamed about one's Christianity of the day just over and in the morning of each new day glad that one may dare to be one all over again, doing so with solace, with one's fellow man, with hope, with everything. The Christian congregation is of one mind in that it consists of real beginners.

When we deceive ourselves instead with a natural-theology-based notion of *spiritual growth* (as if the essential here could be analogous to muscle building or intellectual development), we have crippled our Church's mission with self-centered, will-o'-the-wisp aspirations foreign to its gospel.

A church youth worker slides into some inappropriate behavior and *The Washington Post* captions a three-page lurid

---

[18] Cf. e.g., *Fides quaerens intellectum*, p. 68: "...there is a solidarity between the theologian and the worldling."

report with some reporter's lament: "He shattered people's idea of what being part of a church is."[19]

Actually that particular notion of "what a church is" is more alien to the New Testament memory of Christ than the young man's culpable actions had been. (For in St. Paul's or Augustine's or Luther's or Calvin's or Barth's view of the Church nothing is less surprising—although it's sad, to be sure—than human transgression.) If the gospel's appeal really could be stymied by that old saw, "They can't hear what you're saying, since actions speak louder than words," the Church never could have spread. But the Spirit outflanks us all the time. Ours is always to be a here-and-now fresh immediate response to the accompanying One, and not a gradually achieved level of progress or growth in ourselves.

VESTIGIAL REMNANTS OF NATURAL ROOTS?

It is a patent fact that even the great Reformers could never completely purge themselves of habitual residues of some of the medieval accretions they intended to search out and discard. The same, of course, must be said of Barth's attempt to root out something so widespread and generally taken for granted as natural theology. Inevitably, there are elements, even in re-

---

[19] *Washington Post* article with front-page spread, April 3, 2011.

ceived orthodoxy, which have their actual origins in speculation from nature, rather than in Christ-mediated revelation. Certain notions of this sort are so habitual that they remain atavistically entrenched even for Karl Barth, despite his urge to purge all such assumptions.

"What? Natural theology still active in Karl Barth?"

The man never claimed a finished system.

A serious example of one such notion, I believe, lurks at the heart of his treatment of the atonement doctrine, which he could sometimes call the "real center of dogmatics and church."[20] *Cur Deus Homo*, why God assumes humanity, is much clearer in Barth's thought than *why* God's Christ must suffer. For an essentially culture- and nature-based penal-satisfaction "explanation" for the inner significance of the cross still hovers around some of his references to its efficacy. I find this sort of appendicitis sometimes obscures the priority of grace that *should* be seen to pre-define God's justice according to Barth's best insights.

A Roman-law-tinged conjecture regarding justice, based on mechanical tit-for-tat equity, had become current in the Church long before Aquinas gave it the prominence that has

---

[20] CD I/2 (§24). See p. 24

persisted to this day.[21] So a "satisfaction theory" of the atonement, often is still bannered above the gracious nature of God, as if further suffering and sacrifice is necessary to restore harmony, according to some overarching mechanical equity—an idolatrous abstract, shopkeeper justice under which even the Holy One is assumed to be subservient.[22]

This is not the only purpose and meaning Barth finds in the cross of the Suffering-Servant Messiah. Not by a long shot! Yet he sometimes explains Christ's significance in language that can be taken to imply a supra-divine necessity in these terms, and remnants of such natural-seeming mercantile conceptions of justice do persist in Barth's language, along with related notions of mere equity, recompense and punitive retribution.[23]

Yet such presuppositions may be alien to the gospel, where in the Lord's own hands, justice is grace-defined as sup-

---

[21] This view was rightly countered already by John Duns Scotus O.F.M. (1270-1308) for whom Christ's work showed God's direct forgiveness and acceptance, without reference to an abstract "justice" of mere equity or pay-off recompense. See Karl Heussi's *Kompendium der Kirchengeschichte*, §62, n.

[22] The doctrine of atonement formulated at Session Six of the Roman Catholic reforming Council of Trent was grounded in this idea.

[23] Thus to Questions 71-2 of Calvin's Catechism, Barth typically began his explanation of Christ's crucifixion with received language: the cross "is a sacrifice by which he expiates our sins in the sight of God, and so appeases the wrath of God and restores us to grace with him" (p. 95). See also in *Credo* (Engl. tr. pp. 92-96).

portive, re-creative and restorative. "You have heard that it was said, "an eye for an eye and a tooth for a tooth, but I say to you, do not resist." (Turn your cheek; and let them add injury to insult.)[24] For as Barth himself would say, our true "judge has not judged."[25] God's justice from first to last remains contributory, self-giving. At this point, however, the commonly received atonement doctrine was early infected with an atavistic, natural law notion of retributive justice.

SLIPPAGE ON WHY CHRIST MUST SUFFER

We probably should dwell on this a moment. The problem here is that where the atonement doctrine is concerned, Barth tends to include and pass along certain culture-bound notions of the requirements of an abstract justice that tacitly root into speculative human presumptions. For we are prone to suppose that there must be an overarching, impassive equity—a line that must be toed even by God—above and quite apart from his freedom to be himself and from his gracious justice that is essentially contributory, supportive and restorative.

---

[24] Matt. 5:38f.
[25] KD IV/2, viz. S. 190 & 199. "He was the judge and had judged nothing."

When Barth, following much in the prophets, says "the flesh is abandoned to punishment, suffering and death,"[26] does he really mean God is abandoning us, or is it that we have committed ourselves to despair? Again, when he says that man is demonstrably guilty before God, does he really mean a punitive necessity is superimposed upon God's grace, as if God were required to impose further suffering to "pay a price" in the abstract. Or should he not believe such meanings are to be viewed only through the optic of resurrection promise?[27]

He does intend the resurrection to be axiomatic for evangelical theology. Yet Barth will say that man, having become incapable of knowing and loving God must incur the wrath of God and be "exposed to death because he has sinned against God."[28] If "the wrath of God *must* fall on man," it is "not as a fate, but as a *righteous, necessary wrath.*"[29] The Law of God does not just expose sin, but *punishes* it (at least as a means to healing). But nothing could be further from Barth's often-stated main intent in all of this than to portray a vindictive Father. For God's most serious and imperious "no" to our evil, does not displace his love with hatred (as not only the Qur'an,

---

[26] CD I/2, p. 428.
[27] See e.g., CD I/2, p. 92.
[28] CD I/2, p. 151ff. See further *in loc.*
[29] CD I/2, p. 157. [Italics mine.]

but isolated passages of the Bible might imply).[30] Rather, it is the voice of God's suffering with and for ones he loves, whom he has acted with finality to restore.[31]

> According to belief in the New Testament witness, God's son is coldly beaten and crucified to death, whereas in the Isaac story it is held off.[32] What may not happen there *must happen in the New Testament.* On Golgotha God has borne himself the thing that is gruesome and frightful in the Old Testament.[33]

Thus Barth would refer to Kierkegaard's treatment of the shocking readiness of Abraham to sacrifice Isaac. Confronting the Unknown, the first patriarch could have no prior assurance that God would be trustworthy and keep earlier promises regarding Abraham's progeny.[34] God finally reverses the field for him by redeeming Isaac; but the as yet unshaped content of what justice and righteousness might require in terms of retribu-

---

[30] See some of the Psalms (e.g., Ps. 5:5; 138:8f. 139:21f.) or the bald Deuteronomic interpretation of history (see e.g., Deut. 32:35) and a number of prophetic utterances, such as Na. 1:2.

[31] CD I/2, p. 882.

[32] Genesis 22.

[33] Barth in discussion with his *Sozietät*, May 8, 1964.

[34] See *Fear and Trembling* on Abraham's *Anfechtung* and "a teleological suspension of the ethical."

tion and punishment still hangs, threatening and unsure, for the emerging Hebrew people.[35] "They said to you of old, an eye for an eye and a tooth for a tooth;" but Jesus had something different to say.[36]

The danger of misunderstanding is strong: for in saying that Christ bears our punishment, one may well appear to be saying that God is subject to hateful retributive passion.[37] Whereas in Christ we find God acting to "satisfy" man's passion (i.e., to neutralize, tranquilize and *dispose* of man's nearly universal bloodlust and cruelly vindictive natural law sentiments). Barth does tellingly cite Augustine and Luther here. They knew that it is the wayward *people's* own ugly, retributive demand which has been projected onto God that would have to be satisfied *if God were like us.*

"But he is not like us."[38] (Not in this.) His Christ on the cross reverses that field; and the harsh human demand for retribution is stamped "Paid in Full," once and for all. That is, for our sake God passionately acts "to satisfy" even this, *our* most pernicious "need"—puts it to rest for good and defuses our

---

[35] This issues into the Deuteronomic interpretation of Israel's drama which was impatiently challenged by Job and finally delimited by Jesus.

[36] Matt. 5:38ff.

[37] See e.g., KD I/2 p. 391; 428.

[38] CD I/2, p. 380.

natural resentments and forebodings.

I remain unsure whether Barth did not continue to attribute the vestigial demand for blood vengeance to God himself in this connection, where an abstract, natural-law demand for equity has all too often moved to monopoly in people's minds. This speculation has virtually idolized a mercantile Roman notion of "justice" as proportionate payment and slighted God's gracious sovereignty, as if he were a kind of Demiurge subordinate to it.

The unregenerate hate-filled notion that "somebody's gotta pay" is all too natural. Even today, the satisfaction of someone's cruel lust for vengeance is prominent among us as the most common theme for cheap films. There is Rambo's deep-seated conviction that blood must flow, before a broken past can be wiped away. Our natural feelings are engaged. But as the apostles saw it, was it not this very human need to assuage this godless abstraction—this putative punitive "justice"—that was being *satisfied* by the Lord's suffering? Was it not this ugly, all too human sentiment that was being gratuitously requited and expunged by Christ—this virtually universal and very American gut feeling that "somebody's gotta pay"?

That God in Christ freely acted to satisfy and bring closure even to our most primitive retaliatory feelings may be a measure of the depth of his kenosis, in bending to our lowly

272

human nature through his self-bestowal in Christ. But who is it who is "satisfied" by this gracious action but natural man?[39] The cross can and does satisfy and assuage our most alienating natural-seeming needs.

A crime victim's vindictive heart is as alien to God's love as was the crime itself. A vengeance-obsessed victim has become just as tragically entangled in the alienating coils of evil as was the offender. But wonder of wonders, God loves his *enemies*, on both sides of such a tragic equation, and by his own initiative, people's resentful "price" has been stamped "paid." Every victimized person's agonized cry—"Give gravity to my loss: make someone else suffer!"—has been damped down in the most vivid terms by sovereign kindness: "Cool it: for if you feel such a necessity, God in Christ has covered it."

It is, finally, our own stingy and perverse resentment against simple, unqualified forgiveness and restorative kindness that cries out for satisfaction. And it is our *natural* block against grace here that is crucially set aside through Christ's sacrifice. Thank God, our lingering resentment, too, has been forgiven.

---

[39] In a letter, responding to my CSE paper expounding this subject, Donald Shriver, retired president of Union Seminary, calls it "a strong case for delivering Jesus (and Christians) from any version of justice not intimately infused with health-giving restoration" and "a great contribution to our thinking about restorative justice," one of the most burning issues he finds confronting American society today. (See further in Chapter 13.)

In this perspective, the so-called satisfaction doctrine of the atonement does cohere with the rest of Christian revelation. Barth does not lack this insight, and punitive retribution is certainly not the only purpose and meaning he finds in the crucified Messiah's suffering-servanthood. But apparently, many of Barth's references to Christ's work do retain natural-law-based baggage and would not be particularly helpful towards reining-in our often graceless criminal justice system. Here, Barth's attitude in preaching in and for the Basel prison gives a much clearer light. For Barth's conception of the legitimate use of punishment certainly had evaded any knee-jerk penal-satisfaction theory. Eberhard Busch tells us that when a group of prison chaplains began to press Barth on the issue of punishment for crime, he answered, "It must be understood, administered and accepted as a pastoral measure, and *not as expiation*" (italics mine).[40] This insight certainly informed his attitude toward criminals in his own prison ministry and could well have been brought into sharper focus in his all-important doctrine of atonement. Justice itself has been entirely redefined by grace. His insight here has resonated so insistently in my own later work that I will pursue it further in connection with Barth's much disputed doctrine of election in the next chapter.

---

[40] This discussion took place May 10, 1960. See E. Busch, *Karl Barth*, p. 442.

Chapter 10

Holistic Election Discovered in Christ:
God Is For His Enemies

THE CHALLENGE OF GRACE-DEFINED JUSTICE

We have been saying that if Christ's actions express who God is, freely himself, in grace, they do not "cause" or change God's judgment, which is gracious to the core, much less satisfy some abstract "justice" that hovers above and prior to him. This latter view, prevalent in second century Gnosticism was initially condemned by the main church.

Most in the earliest church followed Paul's redefined sense of *justice*. God's kindly justice means much more and is often quite different from mere fairness. His kind of justice is and is to be supra-reciprocal—with uncorked, foolish-seeming love—and need never be limited to the popular minimal notion of stingy sameness for all.

The Christian exercise of civil authority is a matter of self-bestowing service,[1] and may be creatively unique in every instance. It need not, and in fact must not be constrained by a popular wooden equity. The overarching rightness of gracious generosity need not be tight-fistedly even-handed. Jesus was remembered to have made this clear. That the later Johannine Church saw justice in this redefined sense is reflected in familiar texts, such as I John 1:9,[2] which says God is faithfully "just" [δικιος] in that he intends to forgive our acknowledged sins and cleanse us from all injustices [α-δικιας].[3]

For God, then, it is not an either-or question of justice *or* mercy. For his justice is predisposed as loyal and loving kindness. It is supra-reciprocal and more individually supportive than could ever be mechanically "fair." Covenanted life is not merely or simply fair because God's grace knows no outer limits or shortages. It is right and good that the organist should have at her disposal a costly instrument as she plays for all of us; it is just that the airline pilot should serve uniquely by controlling a multi-million dollar craft. To be merely fair is not just. Grace-bound, justice requires us to treat each unique person

---

[1] See Mark 10:42-45.

[2] See e.g., Jn. 21:22.

[3] The divine initiative is represented here in the Greek by what I call a royal purpose clause [*hina* + the infinitive].

with a supra-liberality. Life itself is not fair, because God graciously keeps a low profile (to let us be free); and when he does suggest himself for faith, his revelation is not merely "fair," because it claims unlimited grace for all. But notions of abstract equity and retributive justice gradually pushed their way into early medieval Church teaching since they jibed with popular, natural-law-based perceptions.

Sad to say, some of the most recent articles by evangelicals, "engaging with Barth," still take him to task for having been for their taste far too evangelical here (in the root sense of that often abused word).[4] Troubled spirits seem to cling to the

---

[4]See for example, *Engaging with Barth: Contemporary Evangelical Critiques,* David Gibson & Daniel Strange, eds. (New York, London: T & T Clark, 2008), and especially Garry J. Williams' article, "Karl Barth and the Doctrine of the Atonement," pp. 232-72. Severe criticism of Barth here seems to issue from William's rather scholastic notion that the death of Christ somehow causes or "effects" salvation (instead of being expressive of God's own being, as he is freely himself, gracious). Note especially p. 267f. [See also David Gilson's take on Barth's doctrine of election, notably p. 158ff.] One of Barth's earlier critics from this same fiercely denominational tradition, Cornelius Van Til, not recognizing Barth's line already in Paul, dismissed it as a "non-Christian metaphysics" and declared "Barthianism" to be "even more hostile to the theology of Luther and Calvin than Romanism." This is not the place to engage with Williams' hardening within a massively and scholastically conceived "historical Reformed" tradition, though one wonders whether those of us who stand in other branches of this Reformed tradition are to be consigned, along with Barth, to outer darkness.

It is notable that this tradition seems blind to the divine simultaneousness we describe below, where Barth was faithfully following Paul's view of created time-space.

Williams does give us one of the best summaries of Barth's atonement doctrine and he, too, documents how Barth speaks ambivalently re-

notion of God's retaliatory back hand—almost as if a demiurge who nurses a rancorous natural law "justice" still looms in the background—a deity whom they imply can only in a limited way be represented by the free grace we have met in Christ. The criticism Barth still evokes at this point from present-day guardians of the scholastic hardening that took place in "historical Calvinism" underlines how challenging his interpretation of Reformed Church roots can be.

Although, given his apostolic grounding, Barth might well have been even more explicit regarding how God's justice is redefined by Christ's grace, we must stress here again Barth's

---

garding commonly received understandings of penal substitution. But the "historical Reformed" tradition (which he defends here as a putative, logically coherent mass) may have become all too ready to lock God inside the strictures and either-or necessities of human logic (e.g., God must *either* elect some to damnation *or* fail to prove to *our* rational satisfaction that he is truly free). So Williams comes to the conviction that Barth's conception of Christ "excludes eternity and history." (This I believe could seem true only if time and eternity are naturalistically conceived.)

Equally strange to Paul, I find the language, which seems to be axiomatic in this branch of post-Reformation thought, that *Christ's work is "effective" to cause salvation.* (It is as if the concept of effectual calling that changes people according to Reformed statements of faith has been displaced to describe a change effected upon a vindictive God.) Barth would be truly saddened by how mean-spirited this notion can appear with its reluctance to accept that natural justice has been re-defined by Christ as revealer and mediator of the Father's own intentionality and initiative. Isn't God's nurturing and healing purpose (as he expresses himself—loving even his enemies in Christ) to be understood as sloughing off our natural notions about untouchable purity and our mercenary preconceptions of justice (as abstract equity, *lex talionis* retribution, fair punishment, etc.)? What here becomes clear in Christ was only foreshadowed in the Hebrew Scriptures. God was not changed by Christ but expressed himself in and through him.

underlying insight regarding theological order: God's *law* is rooted in and requires gospel love; his *justice* embodies kindly grace. These are not the either-ors of logic.

Barth's basic position here is far more than mere "rhetoric,"[5] but represents his wholehearted attempt to be respectful of God's freedom to be himself. However, as said, Barth's theology does waver sometimes, seeming occasionally to buy into a culture-bound doctrine of retributive "justice." His personal actions on behalf of Basel's prisoners spoke with far greater clarity.[6] We recall that he pointed out how American prisons, with their tradition of de-humanizing retribution for felony, present some of the most pressing social-ethical problems of our day. Our criminal justice system needs to be leavened by our belief in a more contributory and restorative definition of justice. (See further, Chapter 13.)

---

[5] Thus W. Kreck.

[6] Barth's understanding of the descent-into-hell motif of 1 Peter 3:19 and the *Apostles' Creed* is a bit slippery. For a natural law or cultural definition of justice seems to creep into the meaning he finds here (as if God's justice describes a demand for retaliation and retribution that must be assuaged before he is capable of restoration and forgiveness). Barth takes the creedal image of Jesus' descent as a sign of his submitting to God's hateful retaliation and not just as an expression of his radical "no" to all that is destructive of our lives (which is how Barth elsewhere describes the atonement). One wonders whether Barth failed to appreciate the descent motif as an image of Christ's gracious healing being even for the most evil people imaginable—in a kind of worst case scenario.

In the light of what has just been said, one of Barth's most significant, yet often misunderstood, insights for us today is that "in Christ" God's saving election may be hoped for as a free and decisive act on behalf of *all alien people*. For the Lord is not locked into some kind of preferential selection between his abject creatures. Such inclusiveness always sticks in the craw of some; and American students would try to pin Barth down and shake his position on this issue. But he saw the priority of God's freedom in grace as opening out into a Creation-wide perspective. By contrast, the spiritual scalp-hunt limited to individual souls that has been so familiar in America reeks of a churchly exclusivism and fragmentation of faith's corporate humanity.

"FORENSIC SANCTIFICATION"—A COROLLARY?

In my draft on Calvin's Doctrine of Christians' life, I coined the expression "forensic sanctification" to use alongside the familiar term "forensic justification" to describe how Calvin works out his cardinal claim that "those God justifies, he also sanctifies." In God's gracious, simultaneousness he already embraces and preserves our particular fallible actions only in terms of the restored perfection for which we, for the time being, can only hope. After he read my chapter, Barth grinned, "'Forensic sanctification?' *Das ist toll!* [That's really wild."]

280

I don't know whether he meant he got a kick out of an unusual, apt expression, or thought "forensic sanctification," was a bit over the top. (He was always kindly disposed, even when he disagreed.) But I was describing a little-appreciated aspect of Calvin's doctrine of Christians' life; and I think something similar was brewing in the way Barth himself followed Calvin here.

He too was recognizing that God in grace redeems and remembers even our most limited and broken actions, *as if* they had been fully angled into the permanent covenant community in which we are already bonded by virtue of God's re-creation. Perhaps a sovereignly gracious fiction actually has been brought to life as God's ultimate, recycled truth for us, inhabiting permanently his time after time. Thus already early in the *Church Dogmatics* Barth could say that in God's perspective "the believer is *already sanctified*," as well as justified—is "already God's child" for good,[7] although we experience our renewal only as a bumpy process.

By contrast, the movement that was gaining popularity in America, under title of Process Theology, must have appeared sadly entangled in natural theology, where it speculated that God in effect *must be* embedded in and subject to time in

---

[7] KD I/2, §14/3, S.131 = CD I/2, p. 119.

the same way we are. For John Cobb and a number of others had begun to project a God that is emergent within time and evolving, as we are, rather than recognizing the Creator as lord over time itself.[8]

THE SPECTER OF UNIVERSALISM

Over the years, I have encountered a strong suspicion among many of our church members against the kind of openness-to-all that the gospel, in Barth's view, must produce. "That's universalism," some would say in a dismissive tone that consigned the very notion to hell, along with a large number of people (perhaps even the vast majority of mankind), who because of God's "secret council" (a kind of lottery hidden in the divine basement) are not to be identified as fellow recipients of his grace.

This is not the place to review in depth Barth's much discussed doctrine of election; but I have found it crucially important as a corrective to the received Reformed tradition. Nothing is more carefully worked out; for Barth had a lover's quarrel with his great mentor, John Calvin, over this point. He would cheerfully agree with Calvin that aside from our special experience of God in Christ, we have no inner knowledge of

---

[8] See e.g., John B. Cobb Jr., *A Christian Natural Theology* (Philadelphia: Westminster Press, 1965); Check also James Luther Adams, *Taking Time Seriously* (Glencoe, IL: The Free Press, 1957).

282

God's ultimate judgment of anyone. Yet this is the very spot where Calvin, in Barth's view, had been most fatefully inconsistent. Though the Reformer insisted that we can never know of any person in particular that she is not elect, sometimes when he was especially angry at some group's behavior, he would seem to forget himself and dismiss them once and for all, as "reprobate."

We know that our judgments will always fall unspeakably short of the grandeur of Christ's kindness and God's restorative power. If we risk any judgment at all (forgetful of what Jesus said about not judging and his own refusal to categorize people),[9] we know that we are apt to err. For harsh experience has left us defensive and stingy at heart.

Here Barth would say that since we know we are apt to err, we had better at least make sure we err in the safer direction; that is, by laying claim, on anyone's behalf, to God's sovereign freedom to forgive and graciously re-create. We, who apart from Christ would stand condemned, had better steer clear of condemning any others. For only in Christ do we know who God is toward them—Christ who, it is claimed, shared a meal

---

[9] See e.g., Jn. 5, especially v. 45. (The verb translated "accuse" in Jesus' declaration here ("Don't think I am going to accuse you...") is *katagorizein* in the original Greek, which significantly already included the wider connotations of our word, "categorize.")

and thereby sealed a permanent covenant of salt even with his betrayer,[10] Christ, who, though agonizing on the cross, prayed for the howling mob, "Lord forgive them, they know not what they do," and claimed paradise even for the condemned terrorist hanging alongside.[11]

For Barth, the Father's "love for *all* people is like a burning fire." He wanted to be utterly clear here: "It is the rejected who are elected." That means "we cannot believe against unbelievers, but only for them," on their behalf.[12]

At one point, John Hesselink asked him, "[Since] you see the responsibility for reprobation assumed in Christ, aren't you in danger of universalism?" Barth replied:

> I know the danger may be what is called universalism. I do my best to avoid it; but I know it is a danger lurking behind me. Yet if I had to choose between this danger and the outlook of a definite separation between the elect and the damned, I'd choose universalism. But I don't, and I don't. Still, I *prefer* the one to the other. I'm not there where Staehelin[13] is—a decided

---

[10] Jn. 13:25ff.
[11] Lk. 23:34, 40ff.
[12] See further KD IV/3, S. 410f.
[13] Ernst Staehelin, *Die Verkündigung des Reiches Gottes* (Zürich:

Universalist. He told his hearers that there may be a hell, but he's not very sure any people will be in it.

We are free now—happy? "We *know* *we'll* not be in it"? This kind of happiness is a danger. If you look at Christ, then you cannot be happy [with yourself—with what you have been]. You're sure of the condemnation of Man; and it's not some [abstract] theory. In both Calvin and Staehelin, it's more *Weltanshauung*—not *evangelium* [i.e., philosophical world-views and not gospel].[14]

Some who, under title of "historical Reformed doctrine," remain defenders of a narrower scholasticism, react here against the way Barth sidestepped the most problematic Calvinistic assumptions; and they continue to speak as if Jesus' action (and

---

EVZ, *1968*). See p. 321ff. Compare K. Barth, *Die Botshaft von der freien Gnade Gotes* (Zürich: EVZ, 1947), p. 8. Hesselink, to this day, attributes to Barth the view that God's "rejection of some is impossible." See e.g., *Calvin's First Catechism: A Commentary* (1997), p. 98. Although Barth certainly sometimes gave the impression of holding this view, he intended to avoid hanging any such humanly-logical necessity on God, who being himself, gracious, acts in complete freedom to be himself at every juncture, person to person.

[14] English Colloquium, Dec. 5, 1960. Barth always declared himself against a bald universalism that would turn God's gracious person-to-person judgment into a mechanical principle. Compare, e.g., KD. IV/1, S. 61.

not the Father's own nature and purpose) were the *original cause* of saving grace (thereby presumably limiting its reach to a Christian lucky few). But if "God is in Christ reconciling the *kosmos* to himself,"[15] then, as Barth saw it, the saving intent is a cosmos-sweeping expression of God's own freedom, as he is in himself and so will be toward all.[16] If you are tangled up in a

---

[15] II Cor. 5:19. Recall John 16:27: "The Father himself loves you."

[16] See e.g., CD IV/1, p. 750 and IV/3, p. 487.

Many are confused by an isolated N.T. text, II Timothy 3:5, which describes a number of godless, vice-ridden peers and then says "avoid such people." Does this mean the Christian congregation is to be a closed clique, out of contact with the surrounding society? Barth has no place for this text in his *Dogmatics*. He does refer to a cognate passage in Timothy's first letter, however, which clearly is not of a mind to break off intercourse with other people, but simply to avoid mixing your teachings with their silly gnostic speculations or their related anomie (I Tim. 4:7). This stands in close relation to the sweeping apostolic affirmation that God is indeed, "the savior of all people—[which has become manifest (?)] especially to those who believe." This is the Timothy text Barth cites, as he insists on the congregation's solidarity with all the godless or, as he says, *"einer besonders qualifizierten und hervorgehobenen solidarität mit allen übrigen Menschen."* (See e.g., KD IV/1, S. 838, CD IV/1, p. 750 and IV/3, p. 487).

Second Timothy's exclusivist-sounding language in verse 3:5 is a small piece of the overwhelming body of evidence that the letters to Timothy did not come from Paul himself, but were pseudonymously written in his name for a later church, which was being forced to adopt a hard-shelled, institutional stance to ward off gnostic Christian incursions, and keep the gospel intact.

Indeed, Paul himself had been misunderstood in this direction when he had advised to withhold the Eucharist from those who would confuse gospel freedom with moral indifference. ["not even to eat with such"] So he later must clarify that he meant church membership should not give the impression that the gospel-centered community teaches such license. Paul, who is himself "the "chief of sinners," certainly did not mean to avoid association with and deny God's salvation to other sinners. That would be sheer arrogance; and to do it, you'd have to be a different person and leave God's

punitive or retributive presupposition regarding the function of Christ's atoning sacrifice, then, as said, you will be prone to read a vindictive twist into the assurances of substitutionary sacrifice and atoning satisfaction instead of a cosmos-wide expression of God's own triune freedom, as he is in himself. (Undeniably parts of the New Testament retain traits of the narrower view.)

But for Barth, the actions of Christ express to the depths who God, the Father, elects to be in his own prior freedom. It may be quite true, that, as von Balthasar puts it "a grace that, in the end, would automatically have to include and reach each-and-all would certainly not be a free or divine grace."[17] Yet, by the same token, a sovereign God does not *have to* give anyone an abstract, logical proof of that freedom by becoming inconstant and graceless to some, as the later Calvinists' rationalizing preoccupation with double-predestination would have it.[18] His

---

world entirely behind (I Cor. 5:9-13).

[17] Hans Ur von Balthasar, "Dare we Hope that all Men be Saved?" in K. Barth, *Die Botshaft von der freien Gnade Gottes* (Zürich: Zollikon, 1947) p. 8. Here too, Barth distances himself from Ernst Staehelin's truly universalistic stance. See Staehelin's *Die Verkündigung des Reiches Gottes* (Zürich: EVZ, 1968), p. 321ff.

[18] John Hesselink tells me he remembers a Barth Colloquium "when Fred Klooster, a professor of theology at Calvin Seminary and an anti-Barthian, led a session that dealt with double predestination." Hesselink says, "Klooster, was defending his position by quoting the Canons of Dort," a standard for Dutch Calvinism, until "at one point Barth in exasperation interrupted him and said, 'But Herr Klooster, our final authority is the Bible,

judgment remains the free and personal act of one who loves even his enemies.

Barth saw all people as in the same boat, God-less in themselves and in need of grace;[19] so the gulf of separation between victim and offender should be bridged. But despite his restored openness to all, many of his formulations regarding election, redemption and atoning sacrifice still lack the clarity and levity we might expect from him.

DIVINE SIMULTANEITY: HOW GOD HAS THE TIME OF OUR LIVES

Meeting with Barth's *Kleiner Kreis* in 1964 when much of our discussion focused on eschatology, I received the distinct impression, perhaps mistaken, that he was not overly concerned with completing the projected eschatological capstone for his *Church Dogmatics*. Wary of authoritarian tendencies to ensconce his work as a *summa*, he was wondering whether his overall purposes might not be better served by leaving his *Dogmatics* pointedly unfinished, as a fluid, open-ended work in

---

not the Reformed Confessions.'"

[19] Here Barth seems to follow Calvin's view that God commands of us what he knows we, being who we are, "cannot do, in order that he might show his mercy to all," which was in turn the Reformer's take on Paul's insight that God has "consigned all to disobedience in order that he might show mercy to all" (Rom. 11:32 *et al.*).

progress.[20]

Old age and semi-retirement had reduced his energy level; and as we met around the eschatological theme, it seemed to me he also was thinking of how his mature thought here would evoke a storm of protest that he now simply lacked the energy to counter. So he was reconciled to leaving the *Dogmatics* unfinished, as a large sampling of church thought "under way." Besides, he had already said so much. . . . Those who followed his work could intuit what his position here would be, for he had staked out the ground.

Clearly, his complete eschatology would have caused a stir, for an unresolved tension existed between his maturing thought on the subject of afterlife and the beliefs that are broadly held in our Church today. I remember being taken aback once when he asked me, "You don't really think that we'll go on and on having new experiences in heaven, as in our present existence, do you?" (or words to that effect).

---

[20] See further Barth's comments at the time in *Barth's Dogmatics for Preachers* by Arnold Come, p. 60. The unfinished *Church Dogmatics* section was to have included eschatology; and, as I explain later, Barth was well aware that his grasp of God's Time in contrast to ours (i.e., our ultimate future in relation to divine simultaneousness) would result in an afterlife teaching so unusual as to be almost unrecognizable in traditional terms.

In my naïveté I had not seriously considered alternatives and was quite startled. But his question shed new light on a tension we had already noticed between his views and those of his Basel colleague, Oscar Cullmann, over the nature of God's Time, beyond time. Barth was taking more seriously the trans-temporal eternity one finds suggested by St. Paul[21] as something quite other than the rather simple linear continuity of time (as we know it) that Cullmann had projected in his book, *Christ and Time*.[22]

If time, as we know it, is entirely God's creation and subject to him, his total sovereignty over it may include a *divine simultaneousness* that lies beyond our grasp and ability even to imagine.[23] His actual relation to our entire corporate lives, past, present and future, may "skein them together," as Barth would

---

[21] Paul frequently refers to his key concepts for new life and renewal (such as adoption, forgiveness, justification and even sanctification) in the past perfect, or present tense, as already permanently in force, so far as God is concerned; while at other times he speaks of them as in the future and not yet fulfilled from our perspective "in the flesh." Oscar Cullmann strongly emphasized this ("*schon-aber-noch-nicht*") character of Paul's key expectations too, but he did not go so far as Barth to take the "*already*, but not yet" as signaling an actual simultaneity in God's concurrent grasp of all the times of our lives. Compare Jenson, *Alpha and Omega*, p. 88f.

[22] See e.g., Oscar Cullmann, *Christ and Time, The Primitive Christian Conception of Time and History* (Philadelphia: Westminster, 1960). In his Basel lectures and seminars, Cullmann repeatedly reinforced this view.

[23] The prophetic insight that God's "ways are not our ways" carries crucial significance where the divine grasp of time itself, and so of our times in particular, is concerned. "A thousand years in thy sight are but as yesterday or a watch in the night" (Ps. 90:4).

say, grasping them as a living whole, such as the random access memory of the greatest computer can barely suggest. For we are invited to believe that the *totality* of our eventful lives is restored and preserved mysteriously in God's all-embracing grasp, with no worthwhile moment ever to be lost. So we can anticipate a future recapitulation and consciousness of this totality that we are promised to be enabled somehow to share. Given this hope, we may celebrate future life with enormous gratitude, rejoicing that it is already there for us ("like money in the bank," as I once heard William Stringfellow put it).

From his side, God may enjoy a never-ending simultaneous access to all our times, without being himself trapped in the irreversible time-sequence of our experience. He may somehow preserve in its entirety the restored substance of everything we have been or done together. Sovereign over time, he does not have to be left with only the dregs of our life at death, as if the final emergent state of what we've achieved or become were all that subsists or matters for him.

What lay behind Barth's view here? As mentioned above, he early distinguished himself with a nuanced Pauline grasp of God's own time after time.[24] I have often observed that

---

[24] E.g., Barth's *The Resurrection of the Dead,* (London: Hodder and Stoughton), 1933, p. 218. See further: Raymond Kemp Anderson, "Corporate Selfhood and *Meditatio Vitae Futurae*: How Necessary is Eschatology

many of the perceived problems or contradictions that are ascribed to Barth's work are a function of our uneasiness or inability to follow him in following Paul just here.

Many in the Early Church evidently recognized that our time itself, along with the whole spacious cosmos is God's creature. So God is not embedded or entrapped within or bound by historical sequence as we are. Paul's apostolic witness and the emerging kerygma shift attention back and forth between, on the one hand, our experience of the sequential history of our lifetimes and, on the other, our wonder at God's own all-enwombing embrace of the entire drama of our lives within his *simultaneous grasp*. Hence, as you may recall, Paul's language shifts continually between the future tense, in describing our

---

for Christian Ethics?" *Journal of the Society of Christian Ethics,* Vol. 23/ 1, Spring/Summer, 2003, 36f. and notes. Compare Robert W. Jenson, *Alpha and Omega: A Study in the Theology of Karl Barth* (New York, Thomas Nelson & Sons, 1963), p. 76f. in context and *God after God: The God of the Past and the God of the Future, Seen in the Work of Karl Barth* (Indianapolis, 1969). Jenson, who studied with Barth for a time, gives the most trenchant treatment of this theme: God "as the Creator . . . is one of His creatures. For He is the One who is His own decision."

Yet I feel Jenson could well have done even more to clarify how God's "having" or possessing time, as its Creator, does not mean he is himself embedded in our irreversible time sequence or that we will ever come to share his mastery over time and begin to experience his simultaneous "now" through some sort of *theosis*. Robert Jenson's recent endorsement of the Helsinki theologian, Tuomo Mannersmaa's rapprochement with the Russian Orthodox doctrine of *theosis* is subject to question at just this point. (See Carl E. Braaten and Robert W. Jenson, *Union with Christ: The New Finnish Interpretation of Luther* (Michigan/ Cambridge: Eerdmans, 1998).

expectation of the fulfillment of our lives in Christ, and the past perfect, for God's eternal grasp of these same realities. Unless we open to the possibility of this divine simultaneousness, Paul's language here seems riddled with contradiction.[25]

---

[25] Although nested in a number of philosophical presuppositions, R. H. Roberts' study of "Barth's doctrine of time" recognizes the central role of divine "simultaneity" or "contingent contemporaniety" (*kontingente gleichzeitigkeit*) in Barth's understanding of God, who, as the creator of time, is fully sovereign over it, yet free to act within it (see p.114). In view CD I/1 150ff. and especially p. 162.

Roberts, who finds himself unable to share Barth's belief here, as we noted above, jumps to the quite common, but unwarranted assumption that Barth's limitation of faith's *bases* to special revelation, must entail a disregard for the world of common experience and that his theology is "prized apart from the structures of contemporary human life." Anyone who knew the man and his lifelong political and social commitments will find this judgment rings hollow. To be sure, Barth was acutely aware of how the "structures" of our ordinary world are fraught with ambiguity and clouded by mortality until they are illumined by grace; but would Roberts have us suppose that Barth's obvious passionate engagement in and for this "real world" was not a coherent expression of his theology?

Was Barth, as Roberts supposes, cleverly reworking unrelated "aspects of biblical tradition" into an *idealistic* framework of his own, in order to resurrect a medieval metaphysic? (See p. 98f.) Was he not, rather, taking seriously the prophetic insight that God's thoughts are not our thoughts and his ways are not our ways? In my reading, Barth's doctrine of divine simultaneity was closely following Paul and other apostolic sources with taproots in Hebrew Scripture (see, e.g., Ps. 139).

Roberts' readiness to dismiss Barth's work finally, as "the most profound and systematically consistent theological alienation of the natural order ever achieved" (p. 124f.) may be closely related to my own initial misunderstanding of Barth's stress on obedience and God's sovereignty (see Chapter 4). Indeed, a sense of offense at what he supposes to be "a profound theological totalitarianism" seems to underlie Robert's judgment here (p. 144). However, we have sadly missed Barth's core insights if we jump to our nature's "logical" assumption that obedience to the gracious God entails a demeaning "subordination of the cosmic and human reality." Rather, Barth

The full force that the Reformers' *simul iustus et peccator* concept held for Barth is to be appreciated in Paul's dual time perspective. While we suffer our way through our persistent brokenness, God grasps us simultaneously as we have been, are to be and, yes, *are now for him*, with our entire drama wholly restored. Henri Bouillard in his attempt to come to terms with Barth's enormous work went so far as to conclude that this is "the most persistent theme in his theology and that everything else is built around it."[26]

FROM TIMELESSNESS TO DIVINE TIME-FULLNESS

Early in his career, Barth had been in the habit of speaking of the eternity of redeemed life and the time of our present life as virtual opposites. But he came to realize that to project such a

---

found the apostolic witness to the sovereign priority of grace signifies the very opposite: their fullest valuation and liberation is to be defended at every juncture.

[26] Arnold B. Come, *An Introduction to Barth's Dogmatics for Preachers* (Philadelphia: Westminster, 1963), p. 158. Paul's belief in the simultaneousness of God's grasp of time is incomprehensible in human perspective. So all our tentative expressions here are bound to be counter-intuitive. We find ourselves speaking of God's eternity, not as timeless, but as a time-full plenitude. We find ourselves believing that he grasps our entire singular lives both in their wholeness and in their detailed dramatic unfolding. For each event that God embraces and restores remains actual with equal force in his divine subsistence. Our moments may be place-marked, with everything worth keeping "working together for good"—preserved in the simultaneousness and wholeness of his grasp of our times after time. We anticipate personal participation in all of this, though the what and how of that remain completely mysterious.

mutually exclusive contrast between our time and God's eternity may actually be a vestige of natural theology. For according to Paul and the New Testament, God's own transcending grasp of time (which is itself wholly his creation) is not only incomprehensibly synchronistic, but is capable of embracing and preserving a vast wealth of times.[27] Here if anywhere, "his ways are not our ways and his thoughts not our thoughts." So those who continue to see in Barth a complete *antithesis* between time and eternity are caricaturing him beyond recognition.[28]

---

[27] Barth found this view of time already in the Reformers' grasp of the Creed itself. (See e.g., *The Faith of the Church,* p. 114). Compare CD I/2 p. 52 and context.

[28] Note how any insistence on an "infinite qualitative difference" between time and eternity has been modified here. Some of those with a British grounding in philosophy dismiss Barth's revelation-based thought (with its openness to the transcendent and apocalyptic) as a surviving vestige of a passé European idealism, a Hegelian "metaphysical" speculation, and suppose this to be "highly significant [for] his understanding of time." This fails to appreciate how such a time-eternity antithesis or "axis" would imply the sort of natural philosophical speculation Barth wanted, above all, to avoid and that Barth had no use for such metaphysics. Compare, e.g., R. H. Roberts on "Barth's Doctrine of Time," notably p. 93 and context in *Karl Barth: Studies of his Theological Method*, S.W. Sykes, ed., (Oxford: Clarendon Press, 1979). Roberts wrongly assumes that for Barth the temporal is "confronted by a consuming eternity" (p. 96), rather than by a grace that embraces, upholds, integrates and sustains its temporal drama and creaturely subsistence.

Recent work, such as that of Todd Pokrifka (*Redescribing God: The Role of Scripture, Tradition, and Reason in Karl Barth's Doctrines of Divine Unity, Constancy and Eternity*, 2010) shows scholarship finally coming to terms with Barth's grasp of God's own "unique temporality," and power of simultaneity (p. 281). This is something that few, such as George Hunsinger, have dealt with seriously. (See *Redescribing God. . .* , notably p. 260.)

On the basis of such *via negativa* contrast to our experience of time, gnostic speculation often projects divine *eternity*, as an abstract time-*less*-ness (which may parade itself as the *greatest we can imagine*). But God's sovereignty over time, as its Creator and Lord, is not a privation but is unspeakably greater and fuller than that—and better, too, in its positive human effects. As the young Barth began to discern with Paul, God treasures and comprehends our times in his own immediacy, as a living and detailed whole: "The ribbon of time, which to our eyes is unwound endlessly, is in God's view rolled up into a ball, a thousand years as a day."[29] God's untrammeled lordship over Time precedes and contains his loyal relationship to us in time; for he can create and command a rich panoply of times.

Barth gradually pulled away from any assumption that resurrection cannot include the grace of a new timeliness or time-fullness re-created and preserved on our behalf—time after time. So the promise of eternal life does not have to mean a negation or privation of time for us. The humanity of God may include, as his loyal gift, a plenitude of new time immemorial for a recognizable resurrected life.[30]

---

[29] K. Barth. *The Resurrection of the Dead* (London, Hodder and Stoughton, 1933), p. 218. Barth here read "the same 'synchronism'" in Paul's earliest letter (I Thess. 4:13-17).

[30] In Barth's early ethics, he tended to assume a greater discontinui-

Asked whether the same Holy Spirit who we believe acts among us in harmony with Christ was already active among his immediate disciples, Barth replied, "In the New Testament *before and after are not so important*. He is the same yesterday, today and for eternity." Given this perspective Barth felt it becomes rather silly if (with the historical Jesus school) we begin to distinguish between "a pre-and post-Easter Jesus" or make a wooden separation between his baptism, his righteous life and its pinnacle on the cross. "Eternity in God's time forms [*bildet*] beginning, middle and end of our time. There is no abstract eternity. There is no eternity which is not also *for* our time; that is, *for* us."[31]

Again, if time itself is to be understood as entirely God's creature, totally subject to him, and not as somehow containing and delimiting him, he remains free to relate positively to our lives' times in their multiplicity—not simply to their point of arrival or fulfillment in growth, but as a restored whole, with all the earthly times of our corporate lives preserved intact some-

---

ty between the present and any resurrected future life: "we exist this side of the consummation, in time and not yet in eternity [so we have to question about the Christian life" *The Christian Life* (London: S.C.M. Press, 1930 (tr. of *Vom Christlichen Leben*, 1926), p. 20f. Later, he stressed how a plenitude of times are embraced by God's sovereign grace; but we found him still very critical of any tendency to lock God's eschatological lordship into our linear time frame (such as he found in Oscar Cullmann's *Christ and Time*). Here he would find another symptom of natural theology.

[31] *Sozietät* discussion, May 28, 1964.

how, as an entire drama before him. This could mean all of our past interpersonal relationships are restored, finally, and preserved in an unbroken whole, for us to know finally "as we are known."[32] Yet although such a hope is to be proclaimed and welcomed, its full meaning remains beyond our comprehension now. At the very least it suggests that all the pressure we have been in the habit of placing on the end-product of "spiritual growth and development" is rather misplaced and may be beside the point.

To sum this up in other words, God is not excluded from time, nor is he under its thrall. Yet he does not simply exist in our terms, but, as we might say, *suprasists*, in being before, beyond, and transcendent to our times and yet still richly in possession of them all. So God's "eternity" is not to be thought of as time-*less* or being deprived of either time or bodily substance. For it is his freedom to create and uphold a plenitude of times and places however he will—time after time for us—with sovereign freedom to redeem and maintain alongside himself all our times as a persistent subsistent glory of his re-creative grace. Thus the mature Barth would tell us:

Eternity is not time*less*ness, but God's Time. His

---

[32] I Cor. 13:12f.

eternal decree is not a fixed [static] decision, but an eternal actuality to be unfolded in history in many, many new decisions—always a free choosing of God for the fulfillment of his will.

Underline: *"Predestination has nothing to do with determination."* There are new decisions. But God works it all out to his plan; [although how, and] how far it doesn't contradict, may be hidden to us. As a question of faith, we accept that God doesn't contradict himself.[33]

So in no way does this simultaneous matrixing of our mortal struggles and moral conflicts within their divinely grasped permanent reconciliation render their event-character inconsequential or denature our timely decision-making as moral agents. But it does shine a new, revitalizing light on our entire drama, while letting the pressure off our present moment. For if we believe God's promised embrace of our *lives-as-a-whole*, we may venture confidently from grace to grace.[34]

None of this set Barth against the classical Christian affirmation of bodily resurrection in all its deep mystery. Such a

---

[33] English Colloquium, June 14, 1960.
[34] Already in his Gifford Lectures of 1939, Barth had said the Lord "in fullest reality surrounds us on all sides" (p. 29).

hope is there, in the Bible, but our knowledge of the form future life may take and be experienced by us remains quite anomalous. Does this hope necessarily postulate an endlessly protracted interpersonal drama? Apparently, Barth was comfortable with the thought that our storied lives, even as restored and preserved eternally by God, might be graced with both beginning *and end.* For he was in the habit of thinking of the Creator's *limitation* of our human life-drama as itself a blessing, in which the final page may be as much a grace as the first.

He did, however, see the completed wholeness of our life-drama as being gifted with an everlasting permanence that we somehow will experience and share—as part of God's own glory. For "we are destined for a future which . . . consists in perfect life with Him."[35] Yet, as said, Barth was quite hesitant where it became a question of an everlastingly protracted coming and going, as if God's gracious re-creation will become an endless treadmill sequence of events (or as if we, finite creatures, are to become infinite agents alongside our Creator).[36] Such a presumptuous *theosis* would be no kindness in Barth's

---

[35] See e.g., the 3rd Gifford Lecture, *loc. cit.*

[36] See above. The Finnish Lutheran theologian Mannersmaa's Russian Orthodox-mediated notion regarding believers' final "theosis" would surely have seemed suspect at this point to Barth, though his former student, Robert Jenson, and Carl Braaten have done well to bring Mannersmaa's work before an American audience.

view.

Perhaps the most telling indication of how Barth's thought was firming up regarding afterlife belief is in a letter cited by his son-in-law, Max:

> Eternal life is not another and second life, beyond the present one. It is this life, but the reverse side which God sees although it is as yet hidden from us—this life in relation to what he has done for the whole world, and therefore for us too, in Jesus Christ. We thus wait and hope, even in view of our death, for our manifestation with Him, with Jesus Christ who was raised again from the dead in the glory of not only the judgment but also the grace of God. The new thing will be that the veil of tears, death, suffering, crying and pain that lies over our present life will be lifted, that the decree of God fulfilled in Jesus Christ will stand before our eyes, and that it will be the subject not only of our deepest shame but also of our joyful thanks and praise.[37]

---

[37] Zellweger-Barth, *My Father-in-Law* (Allison Park, PA: Pickwick, 1986), p. 49. Also in *Letters 1961-1968*, p. 9).

So to acknowledge God's simultaneous grasp of our times does not mean a fixity or inactive stasis on his part, but rather his active constancy and covenanted loyalty. We have to respect both God's sovereignty over time and his freedom to uphold or renew it or act at will within it, and for our sakes to create anew, somehow, its *wholeness* and interplay as drama. This lies beyond our capacities to imagine; but it does not have to entail either an ultimate uncertainty (such as is endemic to various notions of an emergent or evolving process-deity *in time)*, or a fatalistic stasis *over and against time*; although both of these notions have surfaced repeatedly as the highest and best that theologians could conjure.

Where it was a question of our ultimate hope, Barth was fond of citing the image from an Ibsen play, where a ship-wrecked sailor, waves crashing about him, clings for dear life to the very rock that could crush him.

FROM TIMELESSNESS TO DIVINE TIME-FULLNESS

It is striking how Barth could give value and importance to the creation sagas without being perturbed by their complex nature and by inconsistencies in the text. Creation is to be thought of as a *sagenhaft* event evoking unending gratitude. It melds into a dramatic unity with a future fulfillment and fruition while remaining completely open as to the ineffable process involved—

i.e., without saying a thing about either the exact time, duration or mysteriously evolving means behind the gratitude-engendering gift of creation. Even here, Barth found his revelatory key to be christocentric. Creation and redemption and salvation are to be understood as melded together in a single, dramatic whole. So there is no place for a downgrading or escape from the material world that God already declared good in the creation saga.[38]

It is important to Barth's view of our eschatological future that he had, as we've observed, a wholly positive assessment of nature, a theology *of*, or better still, a christology *of* nature. God's election to represent himself in human form charters human nature. The ambiguity of our temporary experience of a fallen state is superseded, and any pessimistic disregard for the physical side of life is excluded. Barth's affirmation of a unity of the covenant (with both creation and redemption coming to focus in Christ as the Word) should in no way undermine our critical attention to the unfolding drama of the scripture as a history of changing perceptions and gradually emerging, often revolutionary insights across the epochs of human history reflected there. The Bible is not to be treated as a massive paper

---

[38] E.g., Gen. 1:31. Some of the earliest doctrinal disputes came when popular dualistic notions rejecting the material world pushed their way into the Hellenistic Church in a number of gnostic permutations.

pope, as if its time-bound perspectives all should claim identical force for thoughtful people of different eras.

The cliché that Christianity is a historical religion or that God is the God *of history* should not obscure the belief that he, as Creator and Lord of time itself, freely relates to the times of our histories without thereby becoming subject to them or de-limited within them. Where we have said God is not destitute of time and freely embraces our histories, as such; that does not mean he is stretched or squashed into a linearity, whereby his alpha is separated from our omegas or vice versa.[39]

A THEOLOGY FOR OUTER SPACE?

While we may apprehend with Barth and Paul that God's simul-taneousness transcends our own time- and space-embeddedness, we can never comprehend it. It remains mysterious, wholly other. God's holy lordship over time and space, whereby every person, every point in time, every position in space are equally and simultaneously in God's "mind" and subsist at his finger-tips, so to speak, has no analogy in our experience. It was intuit-ed and apprehended, however, by post-exilic Hebrew prophets and psalmists as they reflected on how their own liberator could be always like himself and still accompany them across the

---

[39] See Jenson, *Alpha and Omega*, p. 74f. Re abstract "timelessness."

deserts into a foreign land.[40] Paul began with this desert-born faith and in Romans 8:38f. He glories in the belief that Christ's revealed grace has the same sweeping scope and simultaneity. For the Psalmist long since had cried that if he should go to the uttermost depth of sea or space, God would already be there and then stammered, "Such knowledge is too wonderful for me—high, I cannot attain it. In my mother's womb you did know me; your eyes beheld the days that were formed for me, every one of them, when as yet there was none of them."[41]

The same belief opens out onto a space-age grasp of God's omnipotence, omniscience, simultaneity and universal presence, while still respecting the irreversible order descriptive of his human initiative.

We may be in the habit of supposing anthropocentric and geocentric Ptolemaic cosmology to have been displaced, long ago, by the simple concentric orbiting circles of Coperni-

---

[40] See e.g., in Deutero-Isaiah (Is. 40) and Ps. 137 among many other texts.

[41] Ps. 139. The Psalmist, of course had not yet confronted God's attitude "face to face" in his Messiah, so he adds to this amazing insight a sub-Christian outburst, snarling, "Do I not hate them that hate you, O Lord? And do I not loathe them that rise up against you. I hate them with perfect hatred. I count them my enemies." He then asks to be led "in the way everlasting"! The Qur'an follows this O.T. view of God (which for some may justify terrorism). By contrast Christ reveals that the "way everlasting" leads in the entirely unexpected and quite opposite direction following God's love for his enemies.

cus that relegated man to the boondocks of a solar system; but today the enormous complexity of computer-assisted space navigation must revert again to centering in on individual persons—pinpointing astronauts soaring anywhere in space as if their spaceship were for the moment the practical center of the whole—a constant in the midst of a fantastic swirl of complex interstellar relationships.

A galactic-based natural theology promises no more holding power than the older earth-based systems, yet ancient faith-claims take on a new and crucial interstellar force today. Isn't the God we know in Christ already simultaneously there in whatever galaxy, in whatever worlds where other creatures may find themselves? Isn't he mysteriously able to center himself on each of them in love? His manifold presence is not limited by the speed of light. Don't the in-Christ faith-claims regarding God's presence and grace hold, out there, whether or not extraterrestrial persons have been graced already with their own independently revealed Word?[42] Wasn't the perennial truth-claim for interstellar creatures already present *in nuce* in ancient prophet and psalm, and enacted for the apostles; even though, as Barth was always intent to show, the scope and grandeur of

---

[42] In the Reformed tradition, Douglas F. Ottati, past president of the Society of Christian Ethics, has been making significant observations along these lines.

God's grace must be infinitely greater than anyone could have grasped?

Chapter 11

Resonance in Christians' Community
and Worship Today

Karl Barth once commented that if he had to come back in another lifetime, he might well opt to be a traffic cop. For he conceived his role in and for the Church as similar: signaling this way and that and helping traffic flow when and where it's safe to go. What follows are some of his green and red lights for the Church today—theological pointers that have most significantly impressed themselves on our own work in America. In the spirit of Barth, such counsel cannot be regarded as prescriptive, but I have found several of these considerations reverberating with insistent liberating force throughout my own teaching and preaching experience;[1] so I will round out this retrospective by

---

[1] That I am not alone here may be seen in others' observation of a contemporary "Barth Renaissance in America." See the "Opinion" with that title by Bruce McCormack, delivered in Basel on April 12, 2002: *The*

reflecting upon some of them now.

LOVE, THE LAW THAT DAUNTS US

As we have seen, Barth, in line with Calvin and the *Heidelberg Catechism*, would emphasize that it is for the godless that Christ came. And it is those already aware of this astounding grace and covenant purpose who should be most conscious of their own actual shortfall and so, of their complete solidarity with all the other godless for whom he came. The command to love as Christ loved, even our enemies in Sermon-on-the-Mount terms, finds us all wanting and has the effect of casting us back upon his grace, which is the same grace for all humanity.[2] If the law is summed up in one word as Christ said it is—"Love, as I have loved you"[3]—this love command is itself the law that Paul said defeats us all.[4] Whenever I find myself alienated from or despising those who are at enmity to God, I am showing myself to be still alien toward him and desperately in need of forgiveness. All of us find ourselves in the same impasse here—completely dependent upon God's forgiving and re-creative grace ("lest anyone should boast").[5]

Princeton Seminary Bulletin, Vol. 23, No. 3, 2002, p. 337.
[2] Matt. 5:43 *et al.*
[3] John 14:21; 15:12; Matt. 5:43f.; 22:34-40; Mk. 12:30f.
[4] Viz. e.g., Rom. 10:4; 7:10ff.; 9:31ff. *et al.*
[5] Col. 2:8f.

Barth, with his insistence that *all* are elect in Christ, framed his entire teaching to contravene the later Calvinists' encroaching presumption that some are, so to speak, more elect than others. For Christ displays the full deity and humanity of God—both as his judgment and his salvation—not just for a limited "in" group, but for all. God, in his innermost freedom to be himself, chooses to be toward all mankind the one who he shows himself to be in Christ, as both the diagnostic standard for the humanity we all lack and as healer.

The love command, clearly heard, daunts us. Already in an early talk, Barth referred to Luther as having been much too sanguine with his love imperative where our continuing life in the world is concerned.[6] Luther, he felt, describes our love response as something far too beautiful to jibe with who we actually are as *viatores*, wayfarers, who are only on the way. By the same token, Barth expressed puzzlement at the casual way so many Americans would center their theological interest in ethics, as if that held life's answers; whereas Christians' ethics actually flow out of their Christ-response. Our present life, at best, is but a sketchy caricature of what is promised and never even remotely becomes loving in his terms. To say God's whole

---

[6] Münster, 1926. See in *The Christian Life* (London: SCM Press, 1930), p. 20.

law is summed up in the kind of love for God, neighbor and self that Christ exemplified and taught, formulates the most severe ethical stricture known to man and *is not yet the saving gospel.*

In terms of this law, Jesus said flat out, "it is impossible for people," being who they are, to heal themselves.[7] Yet how many of our sermons make the deadly blunder of requiring love, as if that, in itself, were tantamount to preaching the healing Good News. In actuality the cheery-sounding exordium, "You must love!" reiterates the law in its most sweeping, excruciating form. This law, as defined by Jesus, evokes either a desperate prayer ("O Lord, have mercy on me, a sinner"),[8] or self-delusive hypocrisy and pride ("Thank God that I am not as other men are.")[9] So we have to remember and be clear: *in itself* the love injunction, the Law, though it is indeed God's word, is *not* by itself the gospel.

In fact, nothing is more out of joint with Karl Barth's vision of the Church than the notion that its witness in the world depends on its own godliness. God's chosen medium of proc-

---

[7] In regard to the man, who asked for a further rule ("What can I do" with my personal powers and wealth to inherit eternal life?) Jesus declares, "That's impossible for people." It is solely God's possibility—a gift. One may simply follow the healer (see Mk. 10:17ff. & 27).

[8] In classical terms this is the so-called third, *usus elenchticus* or preparatory, function of the law (as distinct from its guiding in the life of a Christian, *usus in renatis,* or in inspiring social organization, *usus politicus*).

[9] Lk. 18:10-14.

312

lamation is and has always been a completely human community of people who know they are godless *in themselves*, along with all others—"the many" for whom Christ came. Their calling is, in main, to point past themselves. The reproduction from the Isenheim altar that Barth kept above his desk expressed that calling for him. It depicts John the Baptist pointing away from himself to Christ.

Unless I discover Jesus' promised healing as well as being confronted by the Law of his love command with his Sermon-on-the-Mount redefinition of its shocking, holistic demands, I will either be cut to the quick by my failure to feel and do it (prone to slide into mortal depression), or I will try defensively to sidestep it (by watering down love's demands and deluding myself that I really am fairly close to being the kind of person it describes). You are to be perfect—as Christ was perfect. That is a regal promise, while it remains a legal command.[10]

As command, it exposes that we fall short. Should we wrongly make a program of love in isolation from the gospel promise of healing, its demands shatter us. So we need to make

---

[10] Matt. 5:48, for example, has this double meaning in Greek: "You are to be [and/or are going to be] perfect as your heavenly Father is perfect" in his love. Calvin made a virtual slogan of Paul's claim that God "shuts all men into disobedience, *in order that he might show mercy to all*" (Rom. 11:33; Gal. 3:22; Rom. 3:9-27, 7:7 *et al.*).

our people aware that Jesus' love imperative by itself is not his gospel. (In my experience, no single point is more smudged in American churches than this.) Rather, the gospel is Christ's astounding claim that God loves us despite our failure to love as he does. He loves us *nevertheless*. Yet as Barth reminds us, this is the gospel, which when internalized, and nudged into place by Christ's Spirit, does indeed begin to motivate greater love and change us, as nothing else can. The love Christ commands is not ours to command, but a gift to welcome with joy.

SOLIDARITY WITH THOSE AROUND,
AS NOTHINGNESS SLOUGHS AWAY

What does all this mean for our church life? Ministers in America sometimes confront in their congregations an unspoken attitude of moral superiority. Sadly, in the eyes of objective onlookers this becomes obviously so self-delusive or hypocritical that it is a prime cause of the alienation often felt by their non-churched neighbors.

A speculative viewpoint inherited from Pietism or late Calvinism may be implicated: that is the notion that since the Holy Spirit is active in the lives of God's special elect, their superior conduct will distinguish them from others. Sometimes this speculation is linked to a callous readiness simply to dismiss the stubbornly non-Christian as "reprobate" and consign

314

them to hell.[11] One of the root causes here is that preachers and teachers have failed to clarify, what we have recalled here from Barth: the *rule of love* they experience in Christ epitomizes God's daunting law but is **not in itself** the gospel of Christ that they are called to proclaim. As the James text says so flatly, if you fail to show love at a single point, you show yourself out of phase with God's nature and thus alien to the purpose of the entire law. For it has become manifest that you are not at heart the kind of person he commands and promises us to be.[12] This may sound extreme, but it is analogous to how the agent of a foreign government, need break cover but a single time to betray his true identity.

Eduard Thurneysen, Barth's close friend, who through their lifelong exchange became almost an alter ego, put the matter sharply in his book on the Sermon on the Mount:

> Confronted with the portrayal of the new conduct of the new man in the Sermon on the Mount, an attentive reader will be like a man who stands in the Alps before a mountain wall

---

[11] The *syllogismus practicus* or practical syllogism, a speculative derangement of Calvinist thought, is often implicated here. To wit: (1) God sanctifies and blesses his elect; (2) person X is unloving or unsuccessful in her behavior; (3) ergo X can not be elect, but is hopelessly beyond salvation. Woe to the inebriate whose crops are failing or whose ship has foundered!

[12] See Jas. 2:10.

without handholds. His way breaks off. And now it's said to him: Up there a thousand meters above you, the way goes further! Then let's stand by it: This life of the new man is certainly not our life now. There's been only one time—only once—only in Jesus Christ that it has ever been lived out. But it will be ours by way of Jesus Christ. With that we're saying once again, that The Sermon on the Mount is taught rightly only when it is taught in a Christological way.[13]

Promise is in command. The unmerited grace that promises our future restoration elevates us to permanent status, as children and covenanted friends of God. Yet, at the same time, it illuminates what a hopeless state would be ours if we were only to be judged by his "perfect law," the "law of liberty," the "royal law of love."[14] While the Christ-revealed grace illuminates who we are going to be, it also humiliates and humbles us. So, as both Paul and James tell us, God's law, summed up in the love command, slays all our pretentions to have possessed fully

---

[13] My translation from "*Die Bergpredigt*," *Theologische Existenz Heute,* Neue Folge: Nr. 105, 1936. Also published as *The Sermon on the Mount* (Richmond, VA: John Knox Press, 1964). See p. 39.
[14] Jas. 1:25; 2:8; 2:12.

human life in ourselves. Exposed in his light, we all cast deathly shadows.[15] Yet, amazingly enough, the law of love that would slay us describes simultaneously the one we find forever acting on behalf of such self-defensive creatures as we.[16] In that, Christians should be reminded of their promise-bearing solidarity with all mankind. If rightly framed in grace, the daunting law of love can indeed move any of us almost in desperation to cast ourselves back into the waiting arms of God in Christ. Yet in that renewed relationship our very life purpose is fulfilled, as in the dizzying swirl of grace we have been swept from our depths to the heights.

But what is to be said about solidarity with all mankind here means the Christian teacher or elder should neither seem to be demanding ideal love as a prerequisite for participation in the covenant of grace, nor speak of it as a touchstone for church membership. Fruitfulness in love is only indirectly a criterion for the Church and not the immediate goal of its proclamation. To reverse that order is not only psychologically damaging, but also anti-Christic. Here too, order is everything.

---

[15] See e.g., on Rom. 3:19 f.: "Every mouth will be stopped and the whole world rendered culpable [*straffwurdig*]. Out of the law's action—and also and in particular, out of the law of the gospel, as Jesus of Nazareth made it known—no flesh will be recognized as righteous before God." (KD, IV/1, S. 247).

[16] E.g., Rom. 7:8-11; Jas. 2:8-10.

317

People are incapable of becoming little Christs. If un-happily, "Love like Christ!" is our primary message, it is likely to be simply denatured or ignored. But should such a bald love-demand be attentively heard, it tends to make Pharisees of peo-ple—entangling them in a self-deceptive masquerade of works-righteousness. Or worse, if apprehended with deep seriousness, it can catapult them into self-rejection and despair.[17] Even such slogans as, "They'll know we are Christians by our love," can mislead. Rather, others will know our message when we point past ourselves to God's love in Christ even for such as we—or they—are. At those moments when we find Christ's kind of kindness welling up within us, it will have been motivated by his gospel, but was not its pre-condition or price. His love is a gift, not a mortgage.

So let Barth underline for us once again: we, just as all others in this world, are the godless ones for whom Christ came—*simul iustus et peccator.* We should have an attitude: we will continue to side with those of whom he said he came to seek and to save, the lost.[18] That the minister himself and his

---

[17] I have met this syndrome implicated in clinical depression. At one point it nearly took my elder sister's life. My need to come to terms with her trauma and her desperate retreat, finally, from the kind of beliefs she had been taught was, I think, the main impetus that shunted me from my earlier absorption with science towards theological ethics.

[18] Lk. 19:10.

318

entire congregation always remain in the same foundering boat, as it were, sharing the human need of all who surround them, is all-important for the Church's self-view, the quality of its actions and the manner of its message.[19]

REORIENTATION IN AND
FOR THE GODLESS WORLD

In view of what we've been saying, one of the most problematic attitudes current in American congregational life has to do with how the members regard their special identity and role relative to the surrounding secular world. Often we are given the impression that the Church should think of itself as a group of superior people who are, or should be, well on their way to actualizing a Kingdom of God, either in hard-shelled contrast to the rest of society, or as a kind of amoebic organism trying to ingest and digest as much of it as possible. The speculative notion of "spiritual growth" is perpetuated in this connection. Too often, ministers are thought of as purveyors of spiritual steroids for a congregation trying to fill the idealized role thrust upon them, as if the pastor were called as role model to head a religiously talented, hyper-loving people.

---

[19] It seems some will take an isolated N.T. text such as II Timothy 3:5 as a signal to wall in the Christian congregation as a closed clique, out of contact with the surrounding society. (See Chapter 10.)

Commonly our congregations have been subjected to the old cliché: "Your actions speak louder than your words." (But if the hearing of God's actions and Word were so dependent upon believers' having accomplished Christ's kind of love, it's difficult to see how the Church could ever have survived. For as human beings, believers have always remained more or less ornery, fallible creatures.) To be sure, actions can be responsive to Christ and suggest gospel faith; but our spoken word can and must point to a grace infinitely larger than our own—a light that vividly silhouettes our own shortfall. St. Paul meant no hyperbole when he named himself "the chief of sinners," nor did Jesus when he told the disciples it is *impossible for people* to save themselves (as the "rich man" of Mark 10 would have had it).[20]

A key passage in the *Church Dogmatics* has, I think, special urgency on the American scene, where televised politics regarding trade, immigration and military policy can become tinged with a claim to "American exceptionalism" that risks becoming almost fascistic in tone. Our congregations all too often style themselves as a kind of privileged association of those who have chosen to be a superior folk in social-gospel terms, busily transforming themselves into the divine Kingdom:

---

[20] See Mark 10:17-31, especially v. 27.

Here is my translation of Barth's crucial response:

> The congregation of Jesus Christ is there for the world, for all, for every person, for the people of every time and space. (It has in the *totality* of the earthly creation, its place, its object, its means—but also the boundaries of its life and work.)
>
> The congregation of Jesus Christ is also human and creature and therefore itself "world." Thus, since it is there for the people and for the world, it is also, to be sure, also there for itself. It is, however, the one human creature which is destined in its very essence to be *for the other human creature*, which is different from itself. It is in fulfilling this purpose that the congregation is what it is, and in so doing it is also *there for itself.* Only so and in no other way! It exists ecstatically and eccentrically, but also within the world to which it belongs—not oriented to itself, but totally toward its surroundings.
>
> It saves and preserves its own life inasmuch as it invests and gives itself for the "other" human creature. Even so—in that way—it is there for God, for the Creator and Lord of the

world and for the completion of his intention and his will with and for the whole human creature. And inasmuch as the congregation of Jesus Christ is first and before all *there-for-God*, nothing remains for it other than in its own time and place to be, also on its side, *for-the-world.*[21]

ACCEPTANCE—DECISION ON OUR BEHALF

So once again, fundamental to our Church's actual reality and function in and for the lost world is the recognition that *in ourselves* we are God-less, like everyone else. As human beings we exist from square one in complete solidarity with that world, sharing all the fragility and foibles of our common humanity. As such, we are one with everyone else in being confronted by the grace of God, whose distinguishing light, leaven and salty message is for the entire godless world (and only because of that, also for us). As such, we are called to point not at ourselves, but past ourselves to God's startling love in Christ, his self-giving, his promise and healing for the often wretched, confused, uncooperative and certainly godless humanity we all share. We too are those "lost" who he "came to seek and to

---

[21] KD IV/3, S. 872.

322

save."[22]

Too often forgotten, then, is the Reformers' basic claim that we are all *simul iustus et peccator,* simultaneously justified and **sinners** who are to call attention to God's decisive action on behalf of such as we. For we have hope for renewal and fulfilled love between us only inasmuch, and insofar as we, at the same time, relate that hope to every human being's life problems as well as to our own. That even in the face of death we may hope, is a gift, a message that we have heard and believed, as God's promise, a permanent positive hope for all.

It is as American as apple pie and frontier revivals, however, to add, "Ah yes, but it all depends on my individual acceptance" or, "It is the hour of *my* decision." (Thus is reiterated the speculative notion that we are in proud possession of a personal power to overcome whatever holds our will in thrall.) But wait a minute. "Lest anyone should boast. . . ."[23] Is it all dependent, finally, on my acceptance and decision?

Apparently my *inability or unwillingness "to accept" or rightly "decide"* identifies me as the "lost" that Christ came "to seek and save." Isn't this the beginning, rather than the end of my drama of salvation? Christ's gospel is most astoundingly

---

[22] Lk. 19:10.
[23] Rom. 3:27f.; Eph. 2:9.

also for those who are in this sense truly "lost" and have no will left to "accept" or do anything else "to inherit eternal life." In Christ, we meet a God who truly loves his enemies and is not defeated or helpless in their regard. "Blessed are the spiritually impoverished"—those languishing for lack of a righteousness they do not possess in themselves.[24]

PUBLIC WORSHIP:
THE PRIESTHOOD OF ALL TO ALL

Barth's insistence that in theology, order is everything, finds its corollary here in the congregation's worship. Spelled out, it means that in public worship, proclamation of the gift of grace and the assurance of full acceptance and promise of pardon are to come first every time, then to be followed, by a responding mutual confession of sin. At that juncture all believers present actually can and do act as God's priesthood, absolving each other in a declaration of mutual acceptance and celebrating together the promised renewal of all their tenuous relationships.

Following in the Reformed tradition of Calvin, then, Barth posits public worship on the believed reality of God's presence as a grace. Worship service is fundamentally God's service to us. One honors God by attentive reception of his

---

[24] Matt. 5:3 & 6.

service to us, rather than in abject kowtowing before him, or presuming that our service to him has become the vital thing. According to this faith, we don't need to invoke or persuade God to come to us. He, who knows and loves even his enemies, is already closer to us than our skin and bone.[25]

So with the *priesthood of all believers* comes this necessary recognition of auricular confession *of all to all* followed by a reciprocal priestly proclamation *by all* of *pardon* and acknowledgement both of sin's full absolution and a renewed recognition of each other as fully restored in God's sight. Mutual forgiveness and acceptance are to be publicly welcomed, pledged and celebrated between us in worship. Compassion to be there to share this support for others (who are perhaps confronted by moral failure, illness or death at the moment, or have some other desperate need) can be a much greater motive for attending public worship, than any thought of what I can get out of it as a spiritual consumer. Others urgently need to hear our hope for them and our assurance of acceptance, as we pass "the peace of Christ" between us.

The promise of renewed acceptance, which radiates between us at this point, may be expressed through something as

---

[25] Barth's sermon of Oct.7, 1960, "You Shall Be My People," has a lovely reflection on this theme. *Deliverance to the Captives*, p. 60ff.

simple as a hug, a handshake, or direct eye contact. This interpersonal drama, then, is to be a key dynamic in the Reformed worship service. Here in the liturgy, as in theology itself, appropriate "order is everything."

Since it is essentially God's self-bestowing service to us that is being celebrated, we will want it to be simply our honest selves in response. It has little consequence, therefore, what worship style is ours—whether our own language is more folksy or formal or whether our music is more pop-oriented or classical.[26] In any case, there is an infectious challenge in believing that our own individual presence is profoundly needed by others in witness to what God has already done, and then to act as priests and absolve and reassure each other in the face of our worst ethical shortfalls, current illnesses and death itself. Here is surely our greatest incentive—to be there next Sunday: *for each other*.

Since worship essentially celebrates God's service to us, it becomes badly skewed when we appear to puff up what we're doing into a kind of benefit performance on his behalf. It is through his action that we can be and are his Church at worship "in spirit and in truth."

----

[26] Here Calvin would speak of *adiaphora*—choices of little consequence.

Yet one hears a lot of loose chatter about *serving the Church* and giving offerings *to the Church*. While well-intentioned, such talk is misplaced and misleading. We are not in a position to give *to* the Church, since we *are* Christ's Church. Everything we have is gifted; and that means every moment and every dollar that we save or squander anywhere is a free self-expression of the Church. To be sure, those earmarked offerings we collect to buy choir robes, support preachers' work, enable relief efforts and all the rest are a part of our common-cause expressions of who we are, *the Church*. But if we slide into the attitude of making donations of time or money *to the church* out there, as one institution among others, the meaning and purpose of our worship is undercut. Use such language for stewardship campaigns, and we shoot ourselves in the foot every time.

Chapter 12

Barth's Challenge to Church Leaders:
A Liberating Liturgy

Busy pastors are not going to sit down often to read systematically through the thousands of pages of Barth's works, and much has been written on how they might mine his resources topically to use in their preaching ministry. But there are certain suggestions and cautions, deeply rooted in the theology he shared with us directly as students that have reverberated continually in our later pulpit and classroom efforts. Other church leaders may find them helpful.

First, it follows from what has been said, that to identify with the godless world for which the Church is there, makes all the difference for pastors as well, since it clarifies what is expected of their proclamation.[1] To engender piousness, inspire

---

[1] Compare KD IV/3, S. 410.

godliness, or coach in "spirituality" is not at all their purpose or function.[2] Such things are welcome gifts and spin-offs, but there is no place for discouragement when you confront the symptoms of godlessness and pernicious sin persisting within your congregation or deep-rooted in yourself. These should be no surprise. As Barth once responded, "Can a minister be saved? I would say that with men it is impossible. But with God all things are possible. 'Be of good cheer: I have overcome the world.'" Again, nothing is more important for the minister's grasp of her or his own role as well as the congregation's sense of self than Barth's continual reminder that the Church *is for the godless world and only therein also for itself.*

We might recall that Barth, as academic scholar, had never forgotten: how his own struggle to find his footing as a pastor in a small, rural, but partly industrial, parish had set him on the theological quest that catapulted him into prominence without an advanced degree to his name. It is no exaggeration to observe that he intended his whole theological endeavor to underwrite and support proclamation in the churches. His was

---

[2] Robin W. Lovin rightly observes that "Christian life and Christian ethics understood [in Barth's terms] are quite different from spirituality and ethics as these are understood by many Christians today. . . . For it is not the human spirit's search for God that interests Barth but the Holy Spirit . . . . The center of attention . . . is not about our deliberations, but about God's determinative action." (Foreword to Barth's *The Holy Spirit and the Christian Life,* p. ix.)

truly a *Church dogmatic*—crafted in and for the revelation-founded, scripturally-funded, covenant-bonded congregation.[3]

In the last paragraph of his first volume of *Church Dogmatics* he made the sweeping statement that all exegesis, and all the dogma that dares to base itself on the text in exposition and explication, finds that its sole purpose is to ground a further courageous step outwards: to address the people and proclaim the message.

But what of our liturgy? Eberhard Busch mentions Barth's remarks regarding some high church Anglican dignitaries who led worship in connection with an Ecumenical Meeting. These remarks, I think, are indicative of his fresh, bread-and-butter matter-of-factness toward liturgical practice:

> If only the Anglo-Saxons would not make their phylacteries so broad and so long! I went to an Evening Prayer at which the Lord's Prayer was said twice and the Gloria five or six times. I said to them afterwards, "If I were the good God, I would reply to you in a voice of thunder, 'All right, that will do, I've heard

---

[3] Compare Arnold Bruce Come's *An Introduction to Barth's "Dogmatics" for Preachers* (Philadelphia: Westminster 1963), p. 14f.

you!'"[4]

Enough already!

Barth could laugh that his allergy to complex liturgical forms might well stem in part from his Swiss Reformed roots. But remember, his experience of the *Deutsche Christen* under the Nazis made him especially resistant not only to the introduction of flags or pictures on the altar, but to other extraneous symbols. We heard earlier how he would point out that the Bible itself has little concept of symbols per se. In scriptural perspective worship "in Spirit and Truth"[5] needs no such props.

Given what he called his "perhaps all-too Reformed view of liturgy," Barth confessed that already in his youth he "had a disinclination to all cultic formality."[6] But as theologian, he took seriously that in worship it is God who is taking the initiative to reach out and be present to us. If the Power of the Universe is behind this intentionality, then liturgical pleading for divine presence or obsequious begging for mercy may obscure the joyfully frank simplicity of Christ-responsive worship as primarily God's gracious service to us. It is the leader's role to proclaim grace in hopeful confidence, not to have the people chanting a woeful plea, *"Kyrie eleison"* [Lord have mercy].

---

[4] *Karl Barth, His life* (Philadelphia: Fortress Press), p. 399.
[5] Jn. 4:23.
[6] Foreword to *Selected Prayers*, pp. 8 & 5.

By the same token, as we have indicated, proclamation of pardon should always come first in a Reformed order of worship. For as God's gift, it precedes and frames our subsequent public confession of sins, followed by mutual reassurance of his absolution and of the peace of Christ that we are all to share.

THE BIBLE IN WORSHIP:
THE SCRIPTED AND THE LIVING WORD

That all our proclamation should be biblical is patent for Barth; but his means of accomplishing that show great change between the young preacher of Safenwil and the mature Barth of our acquaintance.[7] In his early sermons one finds Barth pulling together four or five to as many as sixteen ancillary texts to display a web of theological convergence. In Barth's late sermons, by contrast, almost all of this theological attention to horizontal coherence, between doctrines and diverse texts, is left in the preacher's study. "Of the many thoughts" the text

---

[7] Yet in his published early sermons one observes already hints of what was to become Barth's theological pathway. I.e., one tasks oneself to analyze and expose the inherent correlations between the diverse articles of faith along with the texts supporting them, remaining always within the parameters of faith, without pretending to prove or disprove any of this from general experience or philosophical standpoints external to faith.

calls to mind, Barth is apt to "choose just one."[8]

That the search for theological coherence is left in the minister's study does not mean that such study can become unimportant to his preaching. Rather, it is his legitimization. For Barth the whole of his vast theological enterprise has proclamation as its flower and primary goal. So the sermon is based upon and must take as its ground the cross-scriptural and creedal coherence of Christ's revelation and the intrinsic irreversible order that the theologian has worked so hard to discern. But we need not dangle the process before the Sunday congregation.

Neither should the sermon be an improvised affair in hopes that the Spirit will fill our mouth with something other than straw. Every concept, every term, should be thought through in advance as an accurate vehicle, accessible to the audience at hand. This is why Barth insisted that no matter how script-free we might aspire to be in our final delivery, sermons should be written out in full and subjected to careful reflection and self-critique. Although communication gifts do vary, extemporaneous speech easily issues in self-referential and shoddy thinking.

It also must be emphasized that the careful drafting of a closely related pulpit prayer was for Barth an indispensable part

---

[8] *Ibid.*, p. 25.

of sermon preparation.[9] In point of fact, the restored relation-ship, first manifest in prayer, is to be the real goal of one's preaching. As Calvin had discovered, prayer (which can be a conversant attitude, as well as actual speech) is the "chief part of gratitude" and as such the "principal practice of faith." For the active relationship it expresses is the rightful goal of our entire life.[10]

Look at Barth's late sermons, and you find they tend to focus stringently on a single text, chosen carefully in each case for its cogent encapsulation of some aspect of revealed grace. As said, he uses these texts to proclaim elements of the Creed, without much dialectic argument or reference to the complex of ancillary texts that crowded his own mind. His titles reflect a tight focus on the gracious claim of the text at hand without much wordplay or adornment. His sermons are not only exposi-tory in a general sense, but each tends to be limited to rehears-ing, paraphrasing and illuminating the single text chosen—often chorusing it with a word for word, phrase by phrase, exposition of its particular implications for us today in connection with the

---

[9] *Ibid.* p. 11.

[10] Raymond K. Anderson, "The Principal Practice of Faith: How Prayer was Calvin's Key to Living Well," in *Christian History Magazine: John Calvin* (1986). See also Allen Verhey, *Remembering Jesus* (Grand Rapids: Eerdmans, 2002), p. 62ff.); John Hesselink, *John Calvin on Pray-er—Conversation with God.* (Louisville: Westminster/John Knox, 2006. p. 32, n.7).

larger Creed.

Bolstered by the preacher's conviction that these gracious phrases are indeed all-important and are bound to evoke grateful response in prayer and life, he seemed to feel that such exposition is enough. Christian pastors should shake off the popular misconception that would have them speak primarily as moralists.

One of our liturgical practices that is liable to mislead those who may not be schooled in the complexity of the Bible is our common habit of baldly heralding the scripture reading, as "The Word of God!" The casual visitor can scarcely be expected to know that this is a shorthand way of expressing that Reformed faith grasps Jesus Christ himself as the living self-expression or "Word" of God; whereas the scriptural text is believed to be but the "cradle" in which his story comes (Luther) or the "eyeglasses" through which, with the Spirit's help, we may come to see him (Calvin). One of the most pernicious heresies on the American scene has been the historically recent notion that the scriptures themselves were handed down from on high, virtually word for word.

Barth looks in faith to the prior, living Word; but he would have us be clear that the various scriptures, as they point toward Christ with more or less clarity and at greater or less proximity, do not always say the same thing. As the Reformers well knew, there are profound historical developments within them regarding basic expectations and significant differences of perspective and interpretation—not to mention ordinary human blind spots and errors. Calvin would go so far as to suggest that the Spirit had inspired the inclusion of an occasional sniveling by the Psalmist to exemplify the very opposite of faith!

Sharpened awareness of such discrepancies, is one of the things that caused some Enlightenment thinkers to despair of biblical religion altogether. Sad to say, they were prodded towards such a turn-off by a misrepresentation they had met at the hands of some Protestant Scholastics regarding what was meant by the key Reformation claim: *sola scriptura,* [that the scriptures uniquely confront us with God's Word].[11] Even sadder to say, that same turn-off is apt to recur in the minds of untutored visitors today who, after some bloody Old Testament saga or vindictive Psalm has been read,[12] hear our liturgical cry: "the Word of the Lord!"

For Barth the scriptures point toward the living Word (as the obedient Church will do), which is Christ himself. Our liturgy should reflect this relationship and not slide carelessly

---

[11] It was only in the seventeenth century that certain Reformed Scholastics—notably John Koch (Coccejus) of Bremen—began to assume that Luther's *sola scriptura* principle implied a wooden, verbal inspiration. (See e.g., in H. Heppe, p. 17f.)

[12] See e.g., Ps. 137:7-9 with its glee over bashing in babies' heads.

into language that smacks of the last century's apostasy, where some would-be fundamentalists were in danger of idolizing the seamless block into which their own Procrustean imaginations had crammed the Bible text (similar to the way orthodox Muslims claim the Qur'an to have been dictated by God).[13] The Bible is in fact a canon of diverse witnesses to God's self-revelation in Christ written at various levels by truly inspired, but humanly limited persons from their different points of view. Barth was quite clear that to be truly *biblical*, necessitates frank openness to the diversity of witness that is manifest in the canon itself. For Christian faith, then, the self-revelation of God is discernible at the focus of all this responsive diversity.[14]

FROM GRACE TO GRACE: SPEAK OUT WITH COURAGE, GOOD HUMOR AND JOY

A beautiful study evokes a beautiful message. Barth's most sweeping advice to young preachers that has reverberated again and again in my own work has been that oft-repeated urging I mentioned previously: "When you preach, begin with grace, continue with grace and conclude with grace. They'll never tire

---

[13] Especially portentous was the work of J. Gersham Machen who turned toward this dead end, hoping to find here an antidote to theological liberalism, which he saw to be out of sync with the gospel. (See his *Chistianity and Liberalism,* 1923).

[14] Compare *La Proclamation de l'Évangile,* p. 19ff.

of that!" This in a nutshell was Barth's most mature and serious counsel for preachers. As he was quite aware, his own earliest sermons had not well embodied this positive poise; and he often shook his head over what the patient Safenwil villagers must have endured from his own pulpit there.[15]

This simple rule for sermon preparation ran counter to the homiletics many of us were taught in seminary, where much had been made of beginning with a negative in people's life-experience and then moving toward an upbeat positive climax. This often meant getting people to grovel in their human condition, their impoverishment and need—convicting them of their failure before the Law and of their sin—in order then to lever them toward the promise of the gospel, which one was to cast out to them finally, like a life preserver, as a psychologically welcome relief. Something similar was recommended in social gospel preaching: Soften the ground, portraying human problems and needs; so you can finally press hearers to some definite corrective action. In homiletics a final "practical application" or concrete challenge was deemed essential: Tell the hearers what they should get busy and do. Press home a drive to action.

---

[15] See *The Early Preaching of Karl Barth*, Karl Barth and William H. Willimon (Louisville: Westminster/John Knox Press, 2009).

Instead, for Barth sharing the Evangel with others means to project good news from first to last. "They'll never tire of that." As they begin to find themselves *re-oriented* to it (which was the original meaning of the New Testament's key word here, *"repentance"*), actual change will indeed begin to occur within your hearers' lives, like fruit, fed from the inner roots of what they discover themselves to be in response to the loving presence of Christ.[16] But that's not our primary problem. Such results are not ours to control or manipulate.

All of this is a far cry from the presumptive sort of "spiritual guidance" that is so often expected of pastors today: as if their role is to dupe people into supposing they can "by taking thought add a cubit" to their stature before God, ramp up goodness in themselves or grow in his love through churchy cheerleading or prescriptions of spiritual steroids.

Begin With Grace! One is reminded of the small boy who when asked what letter comes after the letter "A" exclaimed, "All of them!" Everything we are given to say comes after and out of grace.

Unhappily, the so-called "evangelistic techniques" of the American frontier's sawdust trail, that have lingered as an influ-

---

[16] See especially Galatians 5.

ence among us, were not unlike the priestcraft that was practiced by the mystagogues of ancient mystery cults to manipulate their devotees. This knock-them-down-in-order-to-lift-them-up formula for saving individual souls in the interest of a spiritual scalp-hunt came with no guarantee that the poor sinners subjected to it would recognize an antidote in the preacher's subsequent salvation rant or find in themselves a real ability to change. So the technique risked triggering either hard-shelled defensiveness, or hopeless guilt, clinical depression or even suicide.

Such indifference to the hearer's need for assurance not only clashes with the spirit of Christ's gospel message, but also violates the order intrinsic to the theology of grace, and thereby distorts the meaning of salvation and hampers the communication of Christian freedom. Again, as Barth was fond of pointing out, no person can know from her general life experience that a savior is the answer to her deepest problems and what she really needs—not until she hears the gospel claim that she *already* has one.

He would chuckle to us over his choice of the prison pulpit. "Because I am an old man, I am retiring to the jail. It is easier for an old man, because the prisoners know something is wrong." In early January 1959, he confided to us:

I had to preach on Christmas day again [in Basel Prison]. I can't ask from [my hearers there] their problems. My problem is just how I can tell them the story of Christmas. Like Peter on the sea: Looking at Christ, you go ahead; but look at the sea and you sink. Christian life is turned about: look at the full light and have behind us the full darkness. It's *not dialectic*, [or] a scales [to balance]. The question is whether you find yourself in this *Wendung* [re-orientation].[17]

I don't like that word—"dialectic." [Rather,] it is a story! (See Romans 7 and Chapter 6.) Having died to sin and living with Christ! In Romans 5, 6, 7 and 8 is all one trend—one history of Christians' life. Don't occupy yourself too much with weakness, shortcomings, wishing, delivering, etc. etc. That's not helping. That is everybody's abyss: busy with self! We mustn't look in this abyss. (Having trouble? A nose full!) Don't deny reality, but look forward; don't be like the wife of Lot, looking back at burning

---

[17] Note again, this corresponds to the Greek *metanoio*, often styled as "repentance," that signified a grace-oriented turning which enabled one to leave shame, sorrow and guilt behind.

Sodom and Gomorrah.[18]

[This is a matter of] daily bread each day and not a consideration of our whole life. That would be psychology and not theology. We should live theology and not psychology. (It is not good science *here*.) [19] Be joyful—a clue! That is the clue. Look on Christ and the *Good News* from Christmas.

An American student protested: "But what about the habitual past, say, of an unregenerate drunkard. Should we simply ignore it?"

Barth answered:

It's again speculation to ask if a Christian can remain an alcoholic. Perhaps the person has a tendency in this direction. (I don't think a Christian will [actually want to be] a drunkard; but there is no need to have an answer for this kind of question.) *Your* question is only what you can do for him. If you fail, you as a pastor

---

[18] Gen. 19:26.

[19] *"Wissenschaft"* usually is translated as "science" in English, but, as we have seen, Barth had in mind here the wider connotations of the German term: the intellectual craft, which includes different forms of knowing in the broadest sense.

have failed to show him his real freedom.[20]

Barth, then, did not conceive of the minister's primary role as being *to change people.* It is a matter of simple fact that *simul iustus et peccator*[21] describes everyone in one's congregation, as well as oneself as minister. In his sermon introductions Barth does not wallow in the plight of the human condition. That is already familiar enough and needs no massage for the sake of emotional traction. "If you begin a sermon with [love and gospel, as opposed to fear], you can end it with that too; because it is so interesting."

The last charming sermon in his *Deliverance to the Captives* collection from the Basel Prison does begin with a negative of sorts: a rather disarming admission of a tendency to grumble over the way things are, that Barth says he shares with his listeners.[22] But this negative is framed almost in the same breath as missing the gratitude that might well be ours from the first. He makes no attempt to gain emotional purchase by pulpit pounding on the Law or rubbing-in people's depraved state.

---

[20] English Colloquium, Jan. 13, 1959. Barth at this time preached frequently to convicts in the Basel prison. For the sermon in question, see the collection, *Deliverance to the Captives: Sermons and Prayers,* New (York: Harpers, 1961), p. 136 ff. (first published in German, 1959).

[21] I.e., Luther's insistence that Christians should know themselves as at best sinners, who are accepted, justified, by grace ("simultaneously").

[22] *Op. cit.*

Grace itself makes our shortfall sufficiently felt.

Yet to begin and continue "with grace" does not mean that the sermon should begin on a saccharine note and be blind to the evils that grace casts into the sharpest relief. To lead with our liberation is not to trivialize the contrasting ugly forms of compulsion to which we are subject. The sermon should not be lacking in dramatic development appropriate to its theme; but it should be framed in grace.[23] In other words, to begin with grace did not mean for Barth that one should side-step or ignore our actual situation with its ugly injustices and social problems. He did not envision a Pollyanna flight from reality, but the very opposite. To view even the worst injustice from the first through an overlay of grace, is to see it illuminated in shocking contrast to God's love. Only thus will the evil in us and our situation be etched out and clearly shown for what it is, casting its starkest shadow.

I know Barth was unhappy to discover that the precedence he maintained for grace could be heard as either unrealistic or soft on the life-destructive horror of evil. Criticism he received there took him by surprise, since in his early ministry he had been caricatured in just the opposite direction as "the red

---

[23] E.g., Barth could fault a sermon that failed to unfold a dynamic appropriate to its contents: promise → forgiveness → thankfulness → and joyful fulfillment. (See e.g., Max Zellweger, *op. cit.,* p. 68.)

pastor," and had been seen by many as far too directly engaged in his people's concrete social problems—especially in the industry-labor struggle of the day. (That in itself, of course, is no guarantee that his emerging theology was consistent.)

It would be easy to misconstrue Barth here, so I underline. To begin with grace does not mean he would have us avoid confronting people's pressing problems or the social structures that oppress them, but rather to keep even these sharply illuminated from the first as they are *nevertheless* surrounded and outflanked by promise of sovereign grace. This will make alarm bells really ring at need, but at the same time it will evoke hope for all without feeding discouragement or partisan resentment.

Thus the prior witness to grace he counseled, was in his view the only light that exposes evil or injustice for what it is, in its starkest, life-negating contrast, a hollow nothingness. So to begin a sermon with grace, as he would have it, you must speak to people's immediate needs in the real situation that cries out for concrete justice and social renewal. It is up to you, the preacher, with skill and imagination to show that *concrete situation already illuminated in the light of grace.* Hopefully, this will mean that you will also keep clear your own and your church's solidarity with all who find themselves on all sides of that situation—whatever their involvement or guilt—and not become self-righteous, partisan or vindictive.

For if our actual corporate brokenness is sharply exposed by grace, we are not apt to slide into a self-defensive "we-they" alienation, as if it were only the humanity of some offending individuals or group "out there" that has been broken by injustice. For the wholeness or goodness of our own corporate humanity is implicated. In the background here (more strongly even than for Luther) there should be clarity that *justice* itself has been redefined as demanding first supportive (and finally, restorative) grace for all. God's Law itself is to be understood as synonymous with Christ's all-inclusive love command. Barth would leave no wiggle room for natural sounding dichotomies that separate justice from love, law from gospel or brand some as innocent, while tarring others with guilt. We are all part of the same broken humanity that is tendered in God's embrace.

Continue With Grace! Proclamation that appropriately begins with grace and continues therein need not cloud the atmosphere with shrill polemics or fritter time away with apologetics. We may apply our full creative energies to portraying the beliefs we are given in grace in whatever expression coin may be available in our current cultural and social-ethical niche. It certainly never becomes the minister's task to defend religion per se or promote some kind of spirituality, abstracted from the specific kerygmatic claims to be made for Christ, as Word. The works and words of Jesus are simply to be made understandable in all of their non-natural and counter-cultural implausibility, as vivid occasion for a contagious new hope and an outrageous re-calibration of justice in our present situation.

I suspect that the older Barth we knew had long since come to terms with motivational realities, where there is not much future in pulpit-pounding or church-political posturing that seem to lay claim to superiority by labeling and bad-mouthing offenders. But he remained confident, as the Heidelberg Catechism has it,[24] that Spirit-inspired new life and concern for practical social ethics will take root and bear fruit out of sheer gratitude wherever the witness to Christ has been understood and his presence acknowledged. If grace is God's attitude, it motivates our gratitude, and this becomes the motivational spring for new life.

Continuing with Grace, means for the person in the pulpit to employ the full range of her creative imagination. It means seeking out colorful storied illustrations, as Jesus did. Entertainment values are real and certainly to be freely engaged

---

[24] See Part III from question 86, "On Man's Gratitude and New Obedience," where Christians' entire life is regarded in the light of Galatians 5 as "fruit of the Spirit" under a single rubric, "New Life Through the Holy Spirit." (*The Heidelberg Catechism* (New York: United Press, 1962), p. 87ff.

with relaxed good humor, but they are not to overbalance or displace the underlying message. The sermon is to proclaim the astounding, undeserved affection proffered in God's Word.

Word-appropriate word-smithing, the artful invention of colorful parabolic illustration, becomes one's craft. But in seeking vehicles for the message of grace the preacher's primary need is not to drape it with decoration or humor. For the message in itself is always dramatically counterintuitive, always surprising, always of ultimate importance and, let us hope, always underwritten by the Holy Spirit. Fear not, as a pastor your message is in itself intrinsically beautiful and interesting. A jewel is not enhanced by attaching bangles. We see far too many beautiful bodies today desecrated by cheap tattoos. Continue *simply,* with grace.

Faith may be given its credence in hearer's minds by the gentle impulse of God's own Spirit, but our proclamation is to remain graciously free of any pretense to compelling proof. It is calibrated to be liberating when it is simply suggestive of believed possibility. In other words, an appropriately suggestive proclamation should be reassuring and persuasive, but never seek to be coercive or aspire to transmute faith into indisputable knowledge—as if God would remove his people's breathing space.

It is natural to raise or lower your voice with the intensity of your feelings. Barth seemed to expect a normal, calm demeanor. But when one raises one's voice to be *compelling*, it can have an opposite effect, betraying what Kierkegaard used to call an acoustical illusion—as if shouting could cover faith's fragility.

Once, when a San Francisco reporter "testily pressed Barth on his reservations in a generally affectionate description of Billy Graham," Barth said, "Well, Dr. Graham and I are heartily agreed on the love of God, for instance, but I just don't happen to believe it should be pointed at someone else's head, like a gun."[25]

Referring to Graham on another occasion, Barth said, of the sermons he had heard,

> I have nothing against speaking loud and waking people up. But the question is, what one speaks. Graham makes a cheap contrast between moral good and damnation [and] breathes of the old magician. In a sermon on the Nicodemus account in John 3, the only thing Graham saw was "either be born again, or you won't see the

---

[25] Cited by Theodore A. Gill in an unpublished paper, "Barth as Artist," p. 11.

Kingdom of God!" He left out the whole picture of the Holy Spirit etc. in that context.

How to bring someone to believe in [the gospel-] history? I can't bring them to believe! I can invite them to go this way: to consider this account that lies there before the church in the New Testament. But there is the reality of the inner testimony of the Holy Spirit to be taken seriously. We can't give them belief. But present them with a history [*Geschichte,* storied-], events—not simply with an idea or a concept."[26]

Given confidence in the Holy Spirit's own inner testimony, the preacher may confidently anticipate the hearers' eventual joyful, free response to the suggestion that they are, before and above all else, loved just as they are.

Should the preacher draw illustration from her or his own fallible co-humanity and failures? Asking about this Ben Riest, Professor from San Francisco Seminary, said:

You make clear that this line *from* grace *to* sin may not be reversed. This [cuts to] the heart of preaching: Can the preacher, as *the real*

---

[26] Comments to the *Sozietät*, Ap. 30, 1964.

man—i.e., as *the sinner*, who participates in the grace of God—so bring to light the reality of his own true humanity that the fullness of the gospel is enhanced. May an argument for faith be adduced on this ground?"

Barth basically agreed that one indeed could. "But 'argument,'" he added, "is too much said? 'Persuasion?'— perhaps! Faith may not be grounded on argument; but as parable, it may be helpful."

Conclude with grace! By the same token, in the sermon mentioned above, Barth makes no effort in his conclusion to lever or tweak emotions, or "convict" the convicts in his audience. Instead he is content to declare how, if attentive to the revealed grace he has unfolded from the start, anyone (himself included) might find self freed from grumbling so much and discover inward freedom from larger captivities.

The grace that founds and funds the sermon is never allowed to appear as if it is posited upon or somehow subordinated to such a positive end result in himself or his hearers. Personal growth is not idolized. In other words, to "conclude with grace" means that the changes in attitude and behavior that proclamation may occasion are never allowed to reverse the theological field on grace-given promise. (Remember, "order is everything!") Whatever cubits have been or will be added to a hearer's stature, be they physical or spiritual, are not going to determine the full acceptance in which she has been addressed from the first by the one who also in this sense "is no *respecter* of persons."[27]

Although the sermon is expectant of free and joyful response, such results are not to be paraded, first or last, as if they were either pre-conditions to, or the ulterior purpose of the grace we proclaim. Like Calvin, Barth avoids as poisonous the kind of mentality that was canonized by the Council of Trent,[28] where a person's initial acceptance by grace was explained away as a temporary and conditional lever, merely a *preparatio,* not to become permanently hers, unless she achieve a fully implemented faith-in-action (*fides formata*).

TRINITARIAN PREACHING:
"LEAVE THE DRIVING TO US"

In concluding a message, then, we need not drive for moral response. It is enough that the present proclamation be offered as an occasion for faith. "The decision is not in our [own—or

---

[27] Gal. 2:6.
[28] See *Session* 6.

our hearers'—] hands."[29] It is enough to suggest that there are avenues for free response. The preacher may take to heart the claim that the Word must be and will be sealed in hearers' hearts, not by his or her urging or argument, but quite literally by the internal testimony of the Holy Spirit, who in his freedom, may take occasion, in our proclamation of grace. Miracles will happen: Spirit-inspired, ordinary thinking people will be led into their own creatively appropriate actions.[30] So we may, in hope and good cheer, leave the proclamation's effectiveness to the Holy Spirit. For that is to be expected and accepted quite simply, as miracle.

For Barth, then, a preacher does well to respect our intelligence by leaving political implications "entirely to our conscience and our inclinations."[31] He felt little need for apologetics and would not waste energy trying to establish God's existence or confronting detractors. Instead, he would try to share our common ground with the whole of godless humanity

---

[29] *Deliverance to the Captives*, p .25.

[30] Barth, then, did not see it as the church pastor's proper role to be doing the congregation's political thinking for them or feel compelled to spearhead their attack on specific social-ethical problems. The people are themselves called and capable of responsive political commitment in their own right. Grace-motivated they always will be taking thoughtful new initiatives. This is a point where Reinhold Niebuhr scorned what he considered to be Barth's "political naïveté." See e.g., his review of Barth's *Against the Stream* in *Christianity and Society,* 19/3 Autumn 1954, p. 29.

[31] *Deliverance...*, p. 156. See further in my next Chapter.

while pointing to the one who comes and is already present to all in grace.[32]

Those who feel (as some of us had been taught) that each sermon should end in the preacher's application or call to a particular concrete action would find themselves sidelined by Barth's typical sermon, as would those who try to bolster revelation with experiential proofs or argument. Proclamation remains just that; while appropriate response in the hearers' inner life and their behavioral expressions are entrusted to their own unpressured freedom, intelligence and creativity, which are to be respected throughout. The Sermon properly funnels into prayerful gratitude and relies on the motivating power of grace, rather than modeling proud achievements.

As the American Methodist Bishop, William Willimon, tells us then, "Karl Barth's preaching is counter to just about everything contemporary preachers have been told that we ought to be in our preaching. After all, God does not load us with a burden: *We* are the burden which he was willing to take upon himself, which he now bears. And his bearing us up certainly includes *his bearing with us.* We cannot pull ourselves up by our own bootstraps."[33] It is as though Barth thought the Holy

---

[32] Compare *La Proclamation de L'Evangile*, pp. 18-20.

[33] *Deliverance*, p. 157f.; *The Early Preaching*, Introduction, p. ix. Contrast Billy Graham's "Hour of Decision" slogan and the common homi-

Trinity long since was using the old Greyhound slogan: "leave the driving to us!" Shouldn't we, even here be fools for Christ in self-abandon.

They'll never tire of that! Compassionate grace inspires and evokes impassioned response. We saw that *obedience*, according to Barth, is a whole-person response that will include feelings, reflection, interest, bemusement and even amusement. A message that unfolds grace is and will be intrinsically interesting and evoke passionate feelings and compassionate response. If you communicate grace, it will be delightful. No question about that.

The neo-Kantian line in Protestant ethics that Joseph Fletcher, John A. T. Robinson and others popularized in the 1960s had become coldly one-sided with its rationalistic slogan that loving is not something uncontrollable, such as feeling or liking, but only acting on others' behalf.[34] Barth had left far behind his own youthful enthusiasm regarding Kant's mechanical imperative (where Christian action could be reduced to a rational, servo-mechanism response). For since Christ's passion

---

letic goal—to "convict of sin" in order to push people onto the sawdust trail of conversion, or to promote specific social-political action.

[34] See the thesis of Joseph Fletcher's *Situation Ethics,* or in Robinson's *Honest to God.*

is fundamental to the message, both impassioned feelings and compassionate service are going to be evoked whenever the gospel is well heard.

On the other hand, ostensibly good deeds which are not motivated in part by passionate affection would be hypocritical and even sub-human. How could they masquerade as Christian? That Christ's grace anticipates and engenders affections which we cannot control is not to be watered down. Rather, that fact exposes our profound need for resources beyond our own and evokes prayer. And as we discover ourselves, "poor in spirit," reaching out for a grace we lack, we find his Spirit, even in our yearning,[35] has already drawn us obliquely toward his underlying intent: a love-dependent relationship. "Blessed are the spiritually impoverished."[36]

Yes, if a sermon begins with grace, continues with grace and concludes with grace, it will be passionate and compassionate, bemusing, even amusing; and it will evoke a prayerful gratitude in others. It's not likely they will tire of that.

This brings us to a last important counsel to preachers, almost as insistent as those already mentioned. This one is perhaps surprising, coming from this man who wrote thousands of

---

[35] See Rom. 8:16, 26 and Gal. 4:6.
[36] Matthew 5:3-6.

pages for the pastor to study:

"Be brief!" Your labor may well be "a beautiful science," but to reflect it in kindness to a worshipping congregation be succinct. Don't exhaust them. "The spice in each part consists not in spiritual and theological verbosity, but in brevity!"[37] When Barth shared the text of some of his mature sermons with us, we found them surprisingly short, though designed from first to last to resonate and interpret the biblical witness to revelation.[38] Often he took a small, crucial passage from scripture and then explained and brought to value its every word in a running exposition. Along the way he used pithy illustrative examples from different areas of life—sometimes bringing several of them to bear in a clump, on a single point of the text.

His preaching, like his teaching, sparkled with humor and warmth. He seemed to feel that our full creativity should be engaged but that any storied narrative we use should have a clear parabolic purpose. Since the gist of grace is counterintuitive, its exposition will always be intrinsically fresh and

---

[37] *Op. cit.*, p. 7.

[38] For an early expression of this conviction see Karl Barth, *La Proclamation de L'Evangile* (Neuchâtel: Delachaux et Niestlé, 1961), p. 15ff.

challenging. As said, long jokes and other entertainment or attention-getters aren't really much needed and may dilute or fuzz the message. Barth's sermons are pared down. They speak with perennial surprise and compressed, good-humored earnestness to the import of the text at hand.[39]

Needless to say, it was easier for someone like Barth to say, "Be brief," than to follow his own counsel. We heard the story of how once, when invited to talk to some women's group, he had taken the occasion to launch into a long lecture that sailed over their heads and exhausted them. But his late sermons were concise and to the point.

THE SACRAMENTS AND GOD'S WORD

It is pretty clear that Barth was of a mind to rank the sacraments alongside the readings and proclamation as a further communication medium of the Word, who has promised to be in our midst "wherever two or three gather" in his name (and not just where they celebrate the sacraments).[40] There is no hocus-pocus about these ceremonies, no mechanical *ex opere-operatos*.[41]

---

[39] For good examples see Karl Barth's sermons at the Basel prison: *Deliverance to the Captives* (New York, Hagerstown, etc.: Harper and Row, 1961).

[40] Matt. 18:20.

[41] I.e., without a magical result caused by the sacramental action per se, as Medieval superstition would have it.

Clearly, the doctrine of the sacraments, as he was spelling it out, would disappoint many. For as Barth read apostolic sources, the Augustinian definition of sacrament (as an "outer, visible sign of the inner and invisible truth")[42] could only fit one unique case. The only sacrament *in that sense* has been the actual life of Jesus of Nazareth. The Church's forms of witness to that living Word, scripture, proclamation and sacraments (i.e., both its verbal and nonverbal witness) are of a piece—nothing magic about any of them, in themselves.

In the European situation he would get rid of the automatic infant baptism that had been denatured into a kind of secular folk festival or rite of passage, and restrict the sacrament to those who will be given to understand and remember the event. God in Christ will be there for the sacraments—all there—just as he will be there as the Word is preached and to hear every prayer. All of these bear the same sovereign promise and witness to the Spirit's *real presence.* As Calvin repeatedly reminded us, God may not be divided. If he is there at all to hear, he is all there to all.

---

[42] I.e., Augustine's familiar characterization of *sacrament* (as an outer and visible sign of an inward and invisible truth) was too loose for Barth. He held that only the historical life of Jesus Christ should be so described; for no human ceremony entitles us to strip bare the graciously veiled presence of God. However, when paired with Scripture-based proclamation, the sacraments (themselves dramatically portrayed *signs* of the Word) can and do *occasion* belief.

Similarly, one of Barth's most oft repeated lines is that from Christ's perspective *unity* in his Spirit is always supportive of *diversity* and our personal individuality is always upheld within God's own unity. So our communal celebration of unity in Christ in the first line affirms and supports our personal diversity. This is not a dialectic that has us somehow poised or tossed about in a balance, played off between contradictory principles. Rather, the unity and single-heartedness visible, as "the Father himself loves you,"[43] is ordered from first to last in God's freedom passionately to affirm and defend your personal uniqueness and preserve your named identity.

There is no such thing as a Christian unity which does not understand itself as *co-* or *com*-unity. Christ's body, his unity, is always corporate. Yet through his own self-humiliation the one Spirit everlastingly affirms and enhances our separate individual selfhood as well and requires no demeaning self-effacement.

I don't remember how Barth applied his frequent reflections on diversity-supported-in-unity to the communion ceremony itself; but the following reservation has suggested itself insistently to me.[44] It may become a misleading half-truth, when

---

[43] Jn. 16:26.

[44] This, of course, ties in with his equally frequent observation, mentioned above, that mysticism in all its forms wrongly supposes that God

361

we habitually speak of the Eucharist as simply "a celebration of unity." The one loaf [*Leib*=body] of bread is vividly broken into chunks and the wine splashed out into liquid clunks. The primary imagery here is of a corporate body so broken apart by distinct personhood, in time and place that our promised unity subsists as an invisible, spiritual bond.[45] To a large extent it is our *separate, discrete identity*, which God bears with and patiently upholds within his covenant community that is being affirmed in gratitude and celebrated here. It is not just the overarching mystic unity.

At one level then, the "my body" reference alludes to the actually dispersed corporate community, which exists as the unified "body of Christ," only by virtue of God's costly, creative and self-limiting action. But this communion, thank God, always will be supportive as well of our separate, named personalities and not violate them through some mystical absorption. So at another level, the crumbled loaf *"signifies"*[46] this believed truth: At the heart of our faith, God for the sake of

---

is impatient of our separate existence and ready to take over our minds by force or collapse our distinctive spirits into his own. Rather, it is through a passionate self-limitation that God adapts and mirrors self to communicate in terms of what for him must be the child's play of our lives. See, e.g. CD II/1, p. 52.

[45] Compare Paul's reflections on our awareness of the "one body with many members" in "spiritual worship" (Romans 12).

[46] This was Zwingli's favored term.

relationship will always support the complete individuality of those he has created.

At one essential level then, the broken bread and outpoured wine celebrate how God passionately suffers with and maintains our diverse personhood. His freedom in this is of the essence to the unity of his ineffably complex and nuanced plan. The Eucharist, then, affirms and receives in thanks his gifted constancy toward our discrete *individual subsistence.* So it does not just unify, but should also attune us to prize and uphold our own permanent uniqueness and that of all the others (which our creed affirms with the promise of bodily resurrection).

Barth would have questioned attempts to concoct extraneous communion symbols, as if further to convince ourselves of our promised unity. For instance, it has become customary in some congregations, to hold onto the morsel of bread until all have been served so all may partake at the same moment as a further symbol of Christian unity. (Or perhaps it is simply to follow Miss Manners's table etiquette!) The problem here is not that this practice may jar some ex-Catholics' superstitious horror at defiling the "very body of Christ" by holding it in their own sweaty hands, but rather that this focus on superficial momentary unity only blunts the sense of individual separateness that is here being both affirmed and transcended within the body of Christ. For God's mystical union is truly distributed,

363

"broken for you" and *"poured out* for the many."[47]

Again, I doubt that Barth would have liked some ministers' use of intinction to let them personally place the elements in each communicant's mouth, thereby implying a controlling role for the cleric, at the expense of the open priesthood of all in service to all.

TOWARDS CONCOMITANT RESPONSE:
PRAYER AND PRACTICE

For Barth, as for Calvin, the Christian community's entire on-going life is to be a continuing response within the relationship expressed in the first instance as prayer.[48] As Paul has it in Galatians, it is a spontaneous prayer response (*"Abba,* Father!") that first manifests a Christian's nascent faith.[49] And whatever else it becomes, real prayer can be childlike, frank and whole-hearted.[50] It is even more important to grasp that Christians' further behavior, in its entirety could and should become a vir-

---

[47] Mk 14:24; Mt. 26:28.

[48] See Raymond K. Anderson article on "Prayer as the Principal Practice of Faith" in the *Christian History: Calvin* issue, 1986; I. John Hesselink, "Karl Barth on Prayer" in 50th anniversary Engl. ed. of Karl Barth, *Prayer,* p. 74ff.

[49] Gal. 4:6.

[50] See e.g., KD III/4, §53, where prayer under title of "the freedom of God" is seen to be engendered as a "whole-hearted spontaneity" (S. 125f.). Barth's organization follows this with our concomitant "freedom of community response"—in his detailed sections on social ethics.

tual extension of prayer. For Christians' life unfolds in conscious free intercourse with God, as he is believed present; and that is prayer in action.

Barth's recorded seminars on prayer in the Reformation catechisms show he followed Calvin here in seeing that prayer, as direct conversation with God, subsumes the whole practical life insofar as it entails our further immediate response to his living presence—our *"action de grace."* This means there is no substantial separation between the verbal and nonverbal forms that express our total life-response.[51] Christian ethics have become the extension of prayer and vice versa, prayer phases into practical ethics. Christians' prayer and practical action become concomitant. Paul's "Pray without ceasing" evokes literally their entire way of life, the actual substance of their behavior.

The pastor's public prayer, which should follow out of the sermon, is to anticipate and funnel into that holistic life-response. Just as the joy of living communion is to be understood as the culminating purpose of life itself, public prayer is to be regarded as a culminating, integral part of the sermon and should be prepared with the same care. For this reason Barth

---

[51] K. Barth, *La Prière d'après les catéchismes de la Réformation* (Neuchatel: Delachaux & Niestlé, 1953). See p. 30 in particular. It is seldom appreciated how for Calvin, prayer (an ongoing communion with God) is "the principal exercise of faith," and that he wrote far more about prayer than any other subject.

"always avoided having sermons printed without the prayers which belong to them."[52]

For him, a sermon is simply incomplete apart from the prayer toward which it tends. So is life! But this does not mean prayers should ever be treated as magical incantations or spun out liturgically, as if they could be reinforced by repetition beyond their first simple expression. As said, he had no place, for pious cant or a groveling pleading for mercy before the Lord, who is from the first already sovereign *in his mercy*.[53]

Instead, Barth echoes the Reformers' assurance that since God cares infinitely more for us and our concerns than we ever could ourselves, prayer is never to be regarded as a lever to persuade or win over, the one, who is already at our side as the source of all concern and movement. By the same token, we may be assured that God, on his own initiative, hears all prayers and acts to fulfill them—"greater than" or "better than we can think," despite their shortsightedness and inadequacies.[54] The Lord's answers, of course, being far-sighted may be deferred— even remain eschatological in force.

---

[52] Foreword to *Selected Prayers by Karl Barth* (Richmond. VA: John Knox Press, 1965), p. 6.

[53] Voices raised here may betray the sort of "acoustical illusion" Kierkegaard described as symptomatic of repressed unbelief.

[54] *La Prière*, p. 15. "*Amen* means that the certainty of divine fulfillment [*l'exaucement divin*] is greater than the certainty that we feel in ourselves regarding our own needs and desires" (p. 59).

NO MANIPULATIVE MAGIC,

YET EACH WORD IS HEARD

That God hears and answers all prayer does not mean we have here arrogated a new power unto ourselves. Our short-hand references to the "power of prayer" actually misstate the case and risk serious miscommunication. Strictly speaking, prayer itself has no built-in magic to move mountains or anything else.[55] God has that power, in his grace; and our prayers, though at the very heart of Christians' life, are not to manipulate him. Theirs is not a virtue that is increased one whit by our psychic intensity, protracted pleading, or obsequious repetition. Here, one is reminded of how Paul seemed satisfied to have prayed a grand total of "three times" about one of the most tenacious problem of his entire life. Believing God heard him the first time, Paul leaves it in his hands.[56]

Since "the Father himself loves you,"[57] as Jesus said, "ask anything in character with me and he will act on it."[58] But his sovereign response may be, "There's something better in

---

[55] Bo Reicke would point out that "this mountain" to which Jesus here points was, in fact, Mount Zion on the Jerusalem skyline. I.e., faith's prayer "in spirit and in truth" has no need of the official prayer center, but could tell the Temple Mount "go jump in the lake," and do quite well without it. (See Mk. 11:23f; Mt. 21:21 & Jn. 4:21).

[56] See II Cor. 12:8ff.

[57] Jn. 16:27.

[58] Jn. 14:13; 16:23f.

store for you" or "Wait for the time being." Remember the eschatological dimensions of his grace.

In reading Barth's public prayers we find no repetitious litanies. They are intended simply to share a frank conversation godwards. Though theologically informed, these prayers do not pretend to instruct either God or the congregation. There is little theologizing and a minimum of stock phraseology or specialized language. We find no whiff of the magic prayer-wheel quality that some cultivate, no cozy, first name reminders or lists of persons (as if we needed to explain things, persuade or jog the memory of a reluctant or forgetful Lord).

Since they are public, these petitions remain general in scope, address God quite simply, and "bend under his judgment and praise his mercy."[59] In public prayer Barth almost always alludes to a vast community, beyond those present.[60] This is in the spirit of Calvin, who would almost invariably close his public prayers with a declaration that we pray these things "not just for ourselves, but for all people everywhere."

The Lord's Prayer was shocking in its daring, wholehearted intimacy, directness and yes, brevity[61] (originally com-

---

[59] E.g., *Deliverance to the Captives*, p. 92.

[60] *Ibid*, pp. 100, 92 & 116.

[61] The ascription now appearing at the end ("Thine is the Kingdom," etc.) was appended to Jesus' prayer in the Early Church, probably out

prising less than sixty words). And this trait is also a hallmark of Barth's public prayers, which were seldom a full page in length.

COUNTERPARTS IN MINISTRY

A word, finally, about co-workers in the ministry. . . The symbiosis between the two collaborative scholars, Karl Barth and Charlotte von Kirschbaum impressed us especially as Americans.[62] I certainly had never seen anything quite like the kind of scholarly existence it signaled, where the major portion of these people's lives were given over to a single great work. In retrospect, his students have been dogged by a more problematic aspect of the spirit in which Karl and Charlotte worked together where it suggested itself as a role model. I wonder whether others of Barth's ex-students have felt a drag of nostalgia for that kind of total support. For I must confess that as an American professor, working in a completely different social milieu, I felt a certain unrealistic yearning for some sort of theological partnering, not often found on the American scene. The temptation to lever our life-partners or faculty secretaries toward such a role could be insidious.

---

of misplaced desire to buffer its audacious directness.

[62] See Chapter 1.

This, of course, was before sharp criticism by some in the women's liberation movement began to question all possibility of a woman accepting a supporting role in any man's work. Offering it, wouldn't a woman be demeaning herself and fall short of her full potential? Our wives and colleagues, who had their own professions and fields of study, could not contemplate the sort of collaboration that no one has the right to require of another. (That, along with my years as a feminist advocate at a women's college, has called for some re-thinking.)

Yet the kind of professional partnering that one observed between Barth and von Kirschbaum may be an option that, thanks to the women's movement, has become more open for persons today without reference to gender. As we have noted, there would have been no *Church Dogmatics* without the providential support Barth was given by his gifted "counterpart." The achievement of these two, who persevered despite many raised eyebrows, might remind us that whenever the larger covenanted community can enable the full collaboration of any of its men or women in a yoked calling, far more may be accomplished than when each works alone.

Chapter 13

An Evergreen Social-Ethical Challenge

The Christian minister is not really in a position to second-guess what her or his hearers' practical response to the proclamation of grace should be. In fact, there is a danger that pastors may fall into the trap of attempting to bring their congregations' more or less Spirit-responsive action into line with their own programs as leaders. Barth's insistence that ethics is always an indispensable function of theology has a grassroots implication here. For all are called to think *and act* theologically for themselves.

Some Americans, missing their familiar activist harangue in Barth, suppose that in leaving us so confident of God's grace, he trivializes social concerns. Here one should remember it was the search for an adequate message in defense of the exploited factory workers of his parish that led him in his first study of Romans. The young "Red pastor" at first following the Christian socialism of Ragaz, Kutter and Blumhardt, however, was eventually led to become even more radical in his consequent social concerns by refusing to elevate and confuse any extant social order with God's ultimate will for man. People living in a democracy can be as shot through with godlessness as those trapped in Communism. True, God in Christ is always for even the most resentful underdog, but he is for the offending elite, as well. His Word is not captive to any ideology or party. Barth's thought enlivened the Latin American theologians of liberation, such as Gutierrez, but was not captive to their movement.

Real social change will come from the re-orientation of your hearers to grace and from the Spirit's initiative with each of them and not from churchly directives. They will soon discover that if there is any hope at all, it is there as a hope for all; and their corporate political action will be engaged. They will not long be reconciled to a situation where some go hungry, while executives gobble up hundreds of times more remuneration than some of their workers. Social initiatives will ripen among your hearers as fruit of the Spirit, and they will be agents for political change.

DYNAMICS OF SPIRIT-RESPONSIVENESS

Thus, it is a given that where the Holy Spirit is leading among the people, there will be political consequences. These, of course, will include increased sensitivity and attention to each others' concerns and greater civility when disagreements or cultural differences emerge. Christ always confronts the Church with new challenges or *Anfechtungen* [countering critiques], as Luther would say. The critical contrasts between Christ's promise and our present state arouse and orient the Church underway, but our political commitments are always to be freshly minted and situation-aware. So they may never be unqualified, unconditional or final.[1]

How would Barth have us act politically today? Where would his theological orientation have him coming down on the social issues that exercise our churches? We can only imagine what his counsel to pastors might be; but one thing is certain; he would not simply follow one or another party stereotype. He would have us pray to be responsive, first to Christ's all-embracing grace, and then to the actual situation, while trying to be considerate of the attitudes of those concerned on all sides of each issue. Barth's politics would be flexible and pre-set casu-

---

[1] See further: William Werpehowski, "Karl Barth and Politics," in *The Cambridge Companion to Karl Barth,* John Webster, ed., p. 228ff.

istry would have little bearing here.

He would not be happy with ostensibly "Christian" party labels or case-hardened positions. Where politics becomes the art of the possible, he would not want to stall negotiations by withdrawing into a shell of abstract ideals. So if he lived in today's world, Barth's political actions would continue to surprise many who are in the habit of taking sides, with knee-jerk predictability.

Spirit-accompanied, we should respond anew to the dynamics of each situation.[2] Where our political alignment becomes responsive to the Word of God, we will seek to be graciously uplifting to those embedded in the here and now. We are not called to override any of them, in the name of some favorite abstraction, but are free to respect the personal values and cultural differences that confront us and even to accommodate ourselves, as occasion may warrant, to a non-Christian dominant culture.[3] No party should claim its political positions to be non-negotiable or affect the mantle of being more Chris-

---

[2] Barth would be discerning and selective regarding which issues require us to take a confessional stand, *status confessionis,* for which we are willing to go to the wall. See Robert McAfee Brown, *Saying Yes and Saying No* (Philadelphia: Westminster/John Knox, 1986), especially pp.19-26.

[3] For all his zeal, Barth would not be a social irritant or firebrand but with Philippians 4:8 would expect Christians to be respectful of the existing ethos and considerate of whatever is generally considered honorable and proper, making politic concessions in the spirit of the freedom Paul championed. (See Barth's *Erklärungt des Philipperbriefes*, S. 122f.)

tian than others. "Christendom is not an Ethic and it has no special ethic. As a Christian one can only consider what all have to consider. . . . Do what is asked of you in the moment" in company with Christ.[4]

FREE POLITICAL ENGAGEMENT

Given his personal history, Barth was amazed when some assumed that, as one preoccupied with theological belief, he could or should be quiescent on social issues. For his theology would evoke strong practical involvement on each new issue.[5] Ministers of grace are not called to dominate others here, but to support them in their own freedom. Yet by the same token they will find themselves freely taking part personally in political life, seeking to influence social structures while puzzling out more grace-appropriate pathways for themselves and their institutions. We can be sure that Barth would have engaged himself in the pressing social issues of our time and would have had something new and surprising to say on each of them. For, as he would stress: "It is inevitable that Christian ethics will constantly surprise man and his moral standards again and again."[6]

---

[4] *Ibid.*
[5] See Gary Dorrien, *The Barthian Revolt. . .* , p. 142 ff.
[6] *God Here and Now,* p. 90.

JUSTICE IN ACTION TODAY

As a first example, let us imagine how Barth might have addressed that most pressing issue on the American scene, our vastly overblown reliance on harsh imprisonment in our criminal justice system. We have already observed his engagement with the prison issue a half century ago.

For a start, Karl Barth would be glad to see that concern for restorative justice has been recognized by a number of Christian thinkers as one of the most serious issues of our time,[7] and he would have listened attentively. Then his theology would, I think, have had him making surprising, even radical-sounding claims especially on two fronts:

1) First, following the revealed Word, there must be a critical focus on the Christ-molded meaning of justice or rightness itself. We have seen how the very concept of justice had been redefined as Barth understood our apostolic sources. *Dikaiosune* is always supportive and up-building, always a free function of loyal love.[8] So even in its response to the most egregious offense, God's kind of justice will maintain a forgiving attitude, without his wrath giving way to vindictive retalia-

---

[7] This is acknowledged by a study group of the international Society of Christian Ethics on restorative justice, spearheaded especially by Donald W. Shriver and Howard J. Vogel.

[8] I.e., Hebrew *Chesed* or Greek *agape*.

376

tion. In this perspective, a just civil discipline must be restorative and not become merely retributive.

Where Jesus' keynote address in Luke heralds liberation of captives,[9] his Church is to regard imprisonment as at best a necessary evil and focus its energy on redeeming people from jail, and not on keeping them there. A redefined justice is bound to uphold each person's integrity without giving way to our ever-popular, natural-law-based lust for payback that renders evil for evil and harm for harm. God's Word in Christ does not bow down to a shopworn abstraction of equity or fairness as getting even. We noted in Barth's reflections on prison ministry his insistence that our society's pragmatic use of incarceration as discipline or in defense of public safety not be misconstrued as expiation according to some perversion of God's justice.

2) Further, the solidarity Barth saw between all persons as justified sinners should preclude the stigmatization and isolation of some by others. If we appropriately embrace each other in humility and good humor as "we poor sinners, equally beloved of God despite ourselves," then there is no place left for any presumption of ethical superiority. The perpetrator of a crime and his or her victims (who are perhaps themselves seething with anger and resentment, eager for payback vindication

---

[9] Luke 4:18.

and cloture) share the same alienation from God, an equal need for shared restoration and renewal. Our human brokenness is corporate, finally, a fact weighing fully on all. It never becomes more your problem than mine. Our attempts to separate and insulate ourselves by drawing moralistic distinctions are sadly symptomatic of the problem. Here, finally, we see the most self-deceptive and insidious manifestation of our basic crime against the corporate humanity we are to share in the Reign of God.

With Barth we would eschew the American habit of turning our prisons into cages or oubliettes where some are, labeled "the bad guys" and left forgotten to languish, isolated from their families and the rest of us.[10] In both its military and its judicial systems our society's simplistic white-hat vs. black-hat, victim vs. offender categorizations must be challenged in the name of the Lord who says, "Do not think that I'll categorize you,"[11] and who tells you to love, in the way he does, even those who have categorized themselves as your enemies. Whenever we expect our prison wardens, tough on crime, simply to punish the bad guys, or our soldiers as mechanized killing machines to annihilate them, we show our whole society to be broken. Thank God his salvation is also corporate in nature and

---

[10] See Hebr. 13:03.
[11] John 5:45.

378

for all of us, "nevertheless!"

Needless to say, the biblical text would set the parameters for Barth, where Jesus, as the one who came "to seek and save that which was lost," proclaimed liberation for captives as a keynote. What Barth would have said is, I think, reflected in his son, Marcus Barth's thoughts on the topic:

> A Biblical summary . . . reads "deliverance of captives." It is still of the very nature of the church to be connected with those who imprison and who are imprisoned. . . . Mercy is greater than condemnation (James 2:13).

> The church . . . must seek to help and encourage every member of every congregation to take up a ministry of knowing and caring—not only for possibly innocent or over-punished prisoners, but precisely for those considered guilty by everyone. A congregation obedient to its crucified and risen Lord will not leave them alone. Since, according to the Bible, Jesus . . . is found by Christians as having preceded them into prison, Christians are encouraged to expect that any given prisoner may be a servant of Christ and a

379

most important member of the congregation.[12]

As said, Karl Barth would not have wanted to second-guess what our Christ-responsive action on any of the pressing social-ethical issues of our time and place would or should be, though he would want his teaching to embolden our corporate, living-faith response. Where he focuses on the "freedom of the community" in Book III of the *Church Dogmatics* there is a feast of practical food for thought for us both as individuals and as a church in society.[13] We could mention example after example:

Where we grapple with questions regarding international trade or immigration, he would have us remember that those at greater or less distance from us in space or culture are equally members of a single humanity embraced by God in grace. He would surely warn Americans not only against their individualism, but also against a precarious national exceptionalism, which can slide easily toward the kind of idolatry he had experienced in Nazi Germany. And no doubt he would call for greater openness towards immigrants where his own Swiss society (reacting to a history of successive waves of refugees

---

[12] "What Can the Church Do?" *Social Progress,* March-April, 1964.
[13] KD III/4, § 54ff.

and foreign incursions) tended to seal itself off, hedge-in its family domains and keep foreigners under tight police control.[14] Here Barth would say: "The storied historical existence and task of one's own people cannot be an end in itself for anyone who hears God's command. . . . Freedom is really impressed upon one in this respect."[15]

Where we have had burning questions regarding minority rights or the status and role of women, he would continue to insist on full equality without submission, yet champion their freedom for person-responsive role distinctions, while discounting popular arguments from nature.[16]

Where ours are questions regarding our sexual mores and marital relations, Karl Barth certainly would follow Calvin in reminding us that our bodies are not our own, but a gift in and for mutual grace.[17] Whatever sexual identity we discover in ourselves and whatever structures we embrace, he would have us act in terms of freely committed, loyal relationship; so he would continue to insist that "coitus without co-existence is

---

[14] I witnessed a Student Christian Movement meeting at the University of Geneva, where some of the large contingent of foreign students were complaining that none of them had ever been invited into a Swiss home. The Swiss students present were astonished at the very notion, and protested. Neither had any of them been invited into the sanctuary of each others' homes; for defensive bourgeois privacy had become a national characteristic.

[15] KD III/4 (§ 54), S. 334.

[16] KD III/4, S. 216ff.

[17] CD III/4 p. 327.

demonic."[18] Barth numbered homosexuals among his friends; and he probably would hold that government family aid or tax relief should be proportioned to the number of children or other dependents in a household, without reference to the guardians' or caregivers' identity or gender.

Our openness and readiness to accept and share surely meets its ultimate test, when a human fetus makes its presence felt. Here at our doorstep, an almost miraculous event of astounding proportions confronts us. "The true light of the world," said Barth, "shines already in the mother's womb."[19] The tiny helpless, homeless *viator,* the pilgrim par excellence, challenges who we are and tests our openness within God's all-embracing love. Yet Barth would have us share that same love towards those who have found themselves still unable to accept the challenge and unready to grant every fetus a human birth.

Where ours are questions of national defense and an endless "war on terror," Barth would continue to refute the humanity of "massive assured destruction" and dispute the reliability of nuclear arms even as a mutual deterrent. Meanwhile, he surely would have denounced our government's execution of terrorists without due process by means of unmanned

---

[18] KD III/4, S. 148.
[19] CD III/4, p. 416. See further *in loc.*

drone aircraft not only on evangelical, golden rule grounds, but as self-defeating, since it creates new enemies wholesale, rather than moving us towards peace.

Where ours are economic questions—questions of bitter competition, wealth disparity and sustainable growth. Barth would certainly champion protections for all the stakeholders of our corporations—for their workers and the communities they are chartered to serve, as well as for the stockholders with their executives' remuneration fairly proportioned to that of the common laborers. He would probably oppose laws that permit capital to be divorced from its human face or indebtedness to be bundled and sold out from under any real commitment to support the borrowers.

So in all our practical questions, including those regarding the proper exploitation of natural and human resources or questions of relationship to nature, ecology, energy policy, climate change etc., Barth would have us embrace the political process, and give respectful consideration to all on the scene, since, as peacemakers, we should be ready to make concessions and remain open to compromise. He would not side with one or another class, but call for the tolerance of differences, and the mutual solidarity, that are so sadly lacking in our national arena today.

Yet despite all that, what *he* might have done in the face

of our social-ethical dilemma should not be the salient question for us if we have been attentive to Barth himself. (For that matter, neither should be the pious question, what Jesus Christ did two thousand years ago!) Rather, it is what new thing Christ will do with and through us, as we live out into new situations in direct response to him. That underlying question makes one hungry for whatever creative insight and support others, such as Barth, who are engaged in the same conversation might share. But finally, the Christian imperative, as he kept urging us is this: "You are allowed to be free. *Now be it; do it!*"[20]

Whatever speculations we might indulge regarding what Barth, in our shoes, might have done, he wanted to offer only a stimulus for new reflection and discussion, without claiming prescriptive force. For he eschewed the casuistry that has attempted to establish ethical rules for all times and places.[21] He would have us live out a new drama of Christ-response of our own.

In all of this, Barth would agree with the classical view

---

[20] English Colloquium, Feb. 24, 1959.

[21] See e.g., KD III/4 S. 9 (CD III/4, 6 ff.). It should be pointed out that Barth was not altoghether opposed to Christians' free use of casuistry or other *in renatis* applications of law as aids. But there is danger, lest these become avenues whereby speculations claiming a natural base shoulder their way in to impinge upon Christians' freedom. The contrast here is virtually the same as that which elsewhere distinguishes a theology of nature from natural theologies. The difficulty Stanley Hauerwas sees here is instructive: see *Christian Existence Today*, p. 68f.

that there is a proper *political* use of God's law (even as this is to be most stringently understood as the law of love-based liberty).[22] This means Christians should try to influence and help establish civil legislation that supports both personal freedom and mutual commitments.[23] Our freedom is always to be a "freedom in community."[24]

A CREEPING PHARISAISM ENCROACHES

Having said all this, we must stress that social-ethical formation is only an accompaniment of Christian life and not its substance or final purpose. Wrapped up in our own social-ethical concerns, we risk reverting to a form of Pharisaism that forgets that a living drama of responsive relationship is life's underlying value and goal.

Christian educator, James Smart, who strongly felt Barth's influence, used to stress Jesus' rejection of Pharisaism as a key to social ethics. As Smart put it:

Pharisaism is what always eventuates when sincere and earnest religion passes over from being

---

[22] James 2:12.

[23] The so-called "*usus politicus*" or second classical use of the Law, as opposed to the first, *elenchticus*, which diagnoses our shortfall and catapults us into a living relationship, as we seek grace, and the third use, in the new-born life (*tertius usus in renatus*), as a general rule of thumb for the believer's newfound personal freedom.

[24] KD III/4, S. 216.

what God does in us and through us to being what we do in order to make ourselves acceptable to God. It was embodied in the law-bound life of Saul, the Pharisee, but became the nemesis to his later life as Christ's apostle. Pharisaism was not only a Jewish or Jewish-Christian phenomenon of the first century, but recurs in the Christian Church in changing forms through all the centuries.

So Smart would warn future Christian educators most urgently that in our churches such "Pharisaism is the most widely published form of religion."

Your danger is that you, within your work in the church schools may unconsciously be producing little Pharisees, modern Pharisees, and not modern Christians. All of our *religion*—particularly when we become earnest about it—is in constant danger of becoming indistinguishable from the Pharisaism Jesus confronted.[25]

---

[25] Quoted from a recording of James Smart's Galatians study, in the audiotape library at Union Seminary, VA. Also see his book, *The Teaching Ministry of the Church*, p. 106f.

Still today, earnest people often forget that God in Christ is averse to much that passes as religious practice or spirituality and piety and let a kind of creeping Pharisaism encroach upon the freedom Barth had always enjoined.

If the Christian teacher makes sure that proclamation of grace is well heard, this will indeed evoke in others a desire for significant expression in word and deed. But outward behavior patterns and the social platforms we rig to support them can become seductive and falsely usurp a place as life's fulfillment or goal. For abstract behavior patterns easily can be affected as an ego-cloaking mask, rather than expressing a *metanoio*—a reorientation in love's response to the other. This means the brand of teaching that focuses on the expected display of virtuous action and the habitual structures that sanction it can be sadly misplaced and even counter-productive where the gospel is concerned.

THE MATURE BARTH AND DENOMINATIONAL DIFFERENCES, RIGHT AND LEFT

Despite his reservations here, Barth respected those Catholic Christians, on the one hand, who have institutionalized a legalistic casuistry of outer performance,[26] and those Pietists, on the

---

[26] This was The Council of Trent's treatment of *fides formata*—

other, who rely on their own inner feelings. For Christ's grace embraces us all, even as we misconstrue it. Barth pointedly joined in worship sometimes at the local Roman Catholic church; and Eberhard Busch has shown that even early in his career he was tacitly considerate of pietistic concerns as well.[27] As Busch attests, the mature Barth of our acquaintance during the 1960s was increasingly sanguine regarding the authenticity of Christian patterns of behavior that differed widely from his own.[28] For one must humbly accept that the distortions which persist in our different responses render all of them lopsided and fallible. Yet, we may hope, our diverse flaws may well counterpoise each other and sometimes even become complementary.

So Barth intended the questions he continued to put to Catholics and Pietists to spark interchange between equal brothers in Christ.[29] He would have us all be more open towards "a new Pentecost" of Christ's own Spirit, who will always be distinct from our own spirit and emotions, even as he inspires them. Isn't the salvation he heralds an objective gift for all, regardless of their behavior or psychic state? Aren't we all to become a bit like Moses—who pointed beyond himself to a

---

fully formed faith.

[27] See *Karl Barth and the Pietists* (Downers Grove, IL: Inter-Varsity Press, 2004 [Engl. tr. of Busch's 1978 text]), pp. 275-279.

[28] *Ibid.* p. 300.

[29] *Ibid.* pp. 302-316.

promised land?

If so, even when gifted with a joyful sense of personal rebirth, we must understand such self-experience is not a private passkey but a foretaste of an ineffably larger corporate gift. Accordingly, although he gave increasing attention to believers' sense of spiritual awakening and ethical formation, Barth could never countenance Pietism's tendency to "abolish" the Holy Spirit as a free "partner who is opposite us [or] to so appropriate him that he can be passed off as something that is our own" in splendid isolation from others. Salvation assurance is not to be based on either group identity or private self-experience,[30] but *sola gratia*, on grace alone.

---

[30] *Ibid.*, p. 296. I have been startled by this pietistic tendency in songs recently published for a lucrative "contemporary worship" market. Some gush with thirty or more touchy-feely boasts about our faith's personal advantages in the first person, singular.

Chapter 14

Barth's Liberating Art in Play

Based on nearly fifty years awareness of how aspects of Barth's thought have claimed increasing importance in my own work, the last of the reverberations I want to re-echo here has to do with a general attitude or emotional coloration that Barth felt theology should bring to our lives: "a theology of playful freedom and radiant joy," as I have thought to subtitle this entire book.

Karl Barth really meant it when he used his well-known dictum: "Theology is *the* beautiful science." Of course, as we have noted, our word, "science" doesn't quite capture the meaning of the German "*Wissenschaft,*" which denotes intellectual engagement more broadly than the realm of empirically tested theory. It was obvious that Barth found great joy in beauty.[1] The

---

[1] In his *Evangelical Theology: an Introduction,* Barth remarks that theology is not only the beautiful science, but also, in its playful way, the

aesthetic and the emotional held great importance for him, although faith's intelligence is never to expect or seek clear grounding in our natural aesthetic sense or affect.

Christian theology, however earnest and empathetic to the suffering all around, should always include a stout "*nevertheless.*" We are to be "fools for Christ," as the ancient Church put it, welcoming "Easter laughter" in the face of death and always living into what Allen Verhey calls the New Testament's "great reversal."[2] Faith's great "nevertheless" enables and requires that theology, with eyes wide open, and without a Pollyanna disregard for human tragedy and suffering, find itself nevertheless braced as a zestful, interesting craft—vivid, vital, robust, lighthearted—humorous, even. This insistent "nevertheless" response to all that was dark and ugly was finally a theological touchstone for Barth.

LIFE AS CADENZA: THE PLAY'S THE THING

Although he never trifled in his thinking, Barth's careful exposition of the gospel led him to champion, ever more, the creative freedom which is to be ours.[3] A life of confident response in Christ to God's creation is and should be, in the narrow, quite

---

"most thankful and *happy* science" (p. 12).

   [2] *The Great Reversal: Ethics and the New Testament* (Grand Rapids: Eerdmans, 1984). See e.g., p. 70f. on "the paraenetic tradition."

   [3] Compare Eberhard Busch, *Karl Barth*, p. 490.

technical sense of the word, a life *at play*.

Must this not have been a good part of what Jesus meant by his flat statement that only when you become as *little children* will you see the Kingdom of Heaven?[4] Children can be little monsters sometimes—selfish, improvident, impudent and ornery. But even as such, they all have one thing in common: circumstances may be difficult, but children find themselves at play. I rather think Jesus was signaling a life which, like play, needs no ulterior goals beyond being together and savoring the moment's activity and promise in each other's presence.

In theological terms, if one is indeed living assured of the embrace of God's grace, then (however difficult and threatening the situation, and despite the shadow of our mortality and funereal sorrows) being together with others and celebrating in the moment the *richesse* of all the givens of grace, is to be an end in itself. So a radiant life is to be grasped and freely lived out in response to God in Christ. Even permeating the most tragic shadows there can and will be joy. This human value is received as a gift, *nevertheless,* in the living moment together.[5]

Again, where love is gifted, the other person in the moment is sufficient end-in-self. Temptations to use or manipulate

---

[4] Mk. 10:15; Lk. 18:17; Mt. 18:4f.
[5] Compare Barth's essay published in the Tillich *Festschrift, Religion and Culture,* Walter Leibrecht, ed. (New York: Harpers, 1959), p. 61ff.

each other toward ulterior ends should not intrude. The givens of God's creation (which, as clouded by sin, are always equivocal and death-bound in themselves) in the light of revealed promise, re-present themselves as the Lego blocks of creative life. Their artistic, scientific and intellectual exploration can become—and ethically speaking, should become—cadenzas of creative freedom. That is to say, all the natural stuff of both our external and internal worlds can be reconfigured, re-woven and savored ever-again in celebration of our living moments together in grace—in an interplay that need have no goals beyond the joy of the moments shared. Others are never to be thought of as mere human resources that are simply used.[6]

In his last lecture series Barth had some pithy things to say on how the proper goal of play ironically can be, and often has been, bastardized in the world of professional sports, when athletes' and owners' ulterior goals intrude. And in later years, we saw the *Playboy* and bunny-club mentality spawn ghastly parodies of play, where oppressive and compulsive drives enslaved some, exploited others and made true childlikeness impossible. But ideally, free-spirited art and music and studious thought—even our mundane daily tasks and our nights' em-

---

[6] In this perspective, what can be more indicative of the corruption of our business ethics than the institutionalized treatment of workers as "human resources," rather than as ends-in-themselves?

brace—can become adult and rather sophisticated forms of faith's interplay.[7]

You could certainly find Jesus' metaphors for faith's intelligence reflected in Karl Barth's vision: the *light* or hope of the world[8] makes us its *leaven* and *salt* in the world. We are to reflect it with a savory levity (with salty wit and yeasty effervescence),[9] since the gift of ultimate confidence in grace translates into freedom for creative self-bestowal and self-

---

[7] In this grace-based validation of free play, Barth's grasp of Christian faith shows its greatest contrast to "more natural" mythologies, such as are common in eastern wisdom. For example, the Upanishad's grasp of life (which in part funnels into Theravada Buddhism) sought freedom from the kaleidoscope of mortal life by divesting oneself of personhood's complexity as *mere* play (*maya*) for the sake of a peaceful unity (*moksha*). Gautama could simply declare it all to be *merely* passing illusion. (The root meaning of illusion, of course, is *ludens,* play.)

It is as if for Barth the gospel regards our lives through the opposite end of a telescope. Here the same kaleidoscopic *inter-play* of being there for each other is the very thing God treasures and affirms in sharply focused love, promising to hold onto it and preserve it as of everlasting value. Every playful moment of our drama, all the multifarious complexity of life's *dharma*, is given everlasting significance and worth in divine embrace.

Where Theravada would counsel, "don't cling; don't suffer the burden of all that stuff, let the illusion of separate personhood flow past and sift away; apostolic faith, by contrast, proclaims that the God who loves you clings passionately to your entire story with permanent power to renew and re-create. Here *Deus ludens,* is not the fickle trickster so often projected, for example, in Native American mythology, but one who has covenanted to remain faithfully coherent with himself in an interplay of grace. The most fragile interrelationships of your life, then, are to be restored and preserved for us all and made meaningful in his divine embrace.

[8] Jn. 1:4ff., 19f.; 8:12; 9:5 *et al.*

[9] Matt. 13:33; Lk. 13:21 & Mk. 9:50; Matt. 5:13; Lk. 14:34 *et al.* Hellenistic sources attest that witty humor was thought of as "salty."

expression.[10] Such an unambiguous ground for aesthetic exuberance and laughter is rare in natural experience, which always compels our creative intelligence to wear some sort of blinders or forgetfulness regarding our experience of futility and death.

Discussing life-affirming messianic hopes of the Jewish Scripture, Prof. Amos Wilder asked Barth if he wouldn't take the optimistic vision of natural beauty in the 104th Psalm as "an expression of profane hilarity, or some of the Proverbs as an expression of "sheer enjoyment in man's [natural] intelligence."

Barth responded:

> In the context of the Old Testament, Israel is always falling back; and the high points of positive joy are always overshadowed by new disaster. The goal of the whole? Catastrophe! The Old Testament reflects some joy of life eternal [although ours is] not yet eternal life—yet there are joy and hilarity in an imperfect world— not only a pleasure of this world, but a pleasure in God. There is no logical relation between Da-

---

[10] Thus at the beginning of Anselm's search for faith's intelligence, Barth finds he has both *"den 'beweis' und die 'Freude'"* in view—*"Freiheit für die Ästhetik"*—*"nicht nur **utilitas** sondern auch **pulchritude**,"* associated with *laetificari* and *delectari* [not only evidence for, but the joy and freedom of the aesthetic—not only usefulness, but also the delicious lightheartedness that relates to beauty] (*Fides Quarens Intellectum,* S.14 f.).

vid (or Solomon, etc.) and that which is in the beyond-history. That is something further.[11]

As with all else in Nature, aesthetic joy and beauty are so shot through with precarious ambiguity, that no tenable vision of God's grace can be grounded there. But we find we are given grounds for hilarity *nevertheless*.

IN THE PLAY OF GRACE: MOZART

Despite the Teutonic tonnage of Barth's multi-volume format, his theological subject calls for a round dance of grace. It seems clear that Barth's well-known love for Mozart was reinforced here.[12] The lightheartedness embodied in this music spoke to him of a life that finds its matrix in grace and is thus confident, unburdened and relaxed, despite the mortal darkness that surrounds us.[13] We are minded to reflect our calling in playful freedom and liberating joy. For Mozart plays and does not cease

---

[11] English Colloquium, Feb. 10, 1959.

[12] See CD III/3, p. 297ff. for one of Barth's most glowing assessments of Mozart's music.

[13] Jacob W. Heikkinen put this succinctly in his memorial to Barth, "Karl Barth and Wolfgang Amadeus Mozart" in the *Summer Bulletin, 1969* of Gettysburg Seminary: "Barth affirms the great, free *objectivity* with which Mozart traveled life's way. For him, Mozart is an apostle of *freedom. . .* wonderfully free of the mania for self-expression. 'Mozart invites us to hear what he clearly hears, namely everything which from God's creation presses upon him, rises in him, and wants to spring from him'" (p. 13).

to play."[14] Living such a life, one may savor each moment lightly, unburdened from the overbearing *Sturm und Drang* often evoked by a Beethoven or Wagner. Mozart, above all played freely among the givens of the created order's[15] potential—exploring intervallic relationships, rhythms and cadence with childlike openness, skeining a lighthearted thread of confident humor and joy,[16] without denying the place of dissonance or shadow for a life—"in which the shadow is not darkness."[17]

When the American students wanted to honor Barth with a birthday or anniversary gift, they would try to find some Mozart recording that he did not yet own, knowing that he took great joy in daily listening. For Mozart was not just background for him, but each morning wove the mood which had come to be dominant in his life-work, dimensioned as a play of grace within grace—always to be enjoyed with deep appreciation, through the exploration of gifted relationships within the larger gift of the surrounding world of nature.

As we've seen, Barth's struggle against natural theology in no way diminished his theology of and respect for nature as

---

[14] Autobiographical text cited by E. Busch in *Karl Barth*, p. 410.

[15] From the giftedness of creation Mozart "created order for those who have ears to hear, and he has done it better than any scientific deduction could" (CD/III, 3, p. 299).

[16] Ted Gill once observed that Barth's "ultimate anathema on demythologizing was for its terrible humorlessness" [unpublished paper].

[17] CD III/3, p. 298.

the awesome and astoundingly beautiful matrix for life. For faith's awareness of the giftedness of all things can only heighten the delight we take in the beauty of our ecological surroundings. Our experience of the universe is thus purged of its natural ambiguity, and our mortal fears relaxed. This can be celebrated in the realm of sound with music as parable.

Barth's love of Mozart testifies to the priority in John Calvin's terms of showing honor to God by truly enjoying *"tous les biens,"* all good things, in joyful gratitude as the gifts of his love.[18] This includes respecting all the givens of the natural world (the most fragile organisms and the passionate orgasms, if you will, as well as its sweeping intergalactic expanses). We honor God in enjoying his entire non-personal universe (as well as his own and others' living presence in the Body of Christ).

Understand why Barth's love of Mozart went to the core of his thought here, and you are close to the motive springs of his entire work as a Reformed theologian following in the wake of Calvin, whose similar life-stance has seldom been recog-

---

[18] See le *Catéchisme de l'Eglise de Genève 1542*, Q. 7. The later Reformed *Heidelberg Catechism* expresses this insight by treating on the entire piety and ethic of Christians under title of *"Dankbarkeit"*; i.e., as a free and joyful gratitude motivated by grace (Q. 86ff.). This theme is taken up in the first questions of *the Westminster Catechism* where the chief goal of human life is tied to *enjoying* God forever (which, in recognizing his grace, is tantamount to glorifying him).

nized.[19] It in no way trivializes the earnest gravity of a Reformed theologian's work to insist that it remain playful and show some humor as well. The Puritan work ethic became compulsive and sullen only when this inner wholeheartedness was displaced by bourgeois values (in themselves forms of natural theology and forgetful of grace).

Americans can easily misunderstand Barth's adulation of Mozart, as if he found here an analogical foundation or supplementary funding for his theology. Ted Gill, in his all-too-glowing papers on Barth and the arts, stumbled into this trap.[20] Gill, with his own rather romantic embrace of the fine arts and culture as ancillary sources for Christian thought, didn't make this distinction with anything like the clarity that Barth felt to be necessary. At root here was a confusion between Barth's sturdy *theology of nature* (i.e., a theological grasp of the creation), and a *natural theology* (in Gill's case, a natural aesthetic-based speculation).

---

[19] Wm. J. Bouwsma's attempt to "explain" Calvin's theology as an anxiety-based defense mechanism tends to ignore the free play of confident, prayerful rejoinder to grace that undergirded this Reformer's difficult life. *John Calvin: A Sixteenth Century Portrait* (New York & Oxford: Oxford University Press, 1988).

[20] E.g., Theodore A. Gill, "Barth and Mozart," *Theology Today*, Vol. 43, No.3, Oct. 1986, p. 410. See further pp. 403ff.

WRITING ITSELF AS ARTFUL PLAY

It is important to recognize that Barth's long pilgrimage, his many years of disciplined study and careful reflection, issued for him in a practical dogma which is always both free and joyful. If life itself is marked out to be a cadenza for our free play as grace within all the structures that we find presented to us in God's creation. . . , then our creative thought, our art, our work and our study, can and should become childlike in spirit. For even in these things, as Barth would say, "we cannot be more than children engaged in serious and true play."[21]

Of course the primary play of Barth's own artistic genius was to be seen in his handling of language, although the beauty he found in the art of ordered rhetoric, overcast by his rather weighty German prose, may be lost on many American readers.[22] In Barth's view, theology's beauty, the beauty of God's Word, should be reflected in our words.

A fellow Basel student, Gyula Barczay,[23] used to comment on how Barth's writing had a Baroque swing. Its themes keep swirling back in paisley-like arabesques, to re-echo varia-

---

[21] CD III/4, p. 553. See further *in loc.*

[22] The sort of rhetoric analysis Serene Jones has initiated with the *Institutes* of Barth's great predecessor, John Calvin, could as well be applied to Barth's works. See Jones's *Calvin and the Rhetoric of Piety,* (Louisville, KY: Westminster/John Knox, 1995).

[23] Barczay was a Hungarian refugee student who worked closely with Barth before entering upon a Swiss pastorate.

tions of the key ideas in a kind of self-reinforcing fugal structure. Barczay claimed that despite the enormous breadth of Barth's writings, his thought was not difficult to grasp, since the main themes round back upon themselves with different aspects accented in each reprise. This means one can expect to hear the same insights in variations with added development reverberating coherently across his entire work. So a reader's understanding deepens, as Barth develops his key motifs in various tonalities.

We are observing here far more than a habitual stylistic trait. For this way of working exemplified what Barth intended in his Anselmic stance, whereby one tries never to stray from the sphere of faith's apostolic basis, while exploring the inner coherence between its different articles. Faith seeks an intelligent grasp by systematically suspending one or another article and then uncovering how one's mind must circle back to it again, by following the *logos*, the inner logic of other dimensions of belief—*fides quaerens intellectum*. The ordered fugue reflects affirmation of a basic order shaped by the givens of God's grace in action. Thus Barth's organizational style is reminiscent of the confident way Mozart moved from the Baroque into the Classical, playing with the givens of sound.

The weightiness of large, tightly-argued tomes was prized by German scholars, but this outer format may hobble for us the lightheartedness and levity Barth wanted to recapture for the Church. His Basel colleague Oscar Cullmann, who hailed from the bilingual province of Alsace-Lorraine and lectured every week both at Basel University and the Sorbonne, once confided to me, "The Germans find my books too clear and simple." He was referring to the extra value German readers habitually placed on prolix complexity and a kind of puzzle atmosphere they found stimulating and cultivated. In contrast to his cool French-styled logic (with its straightforward subject-verb-object clarity), even German syntax twists phraseology into a *Rätsel,* a puzzle. For the meaning of the typical German sentence is regularly kept in suspense, until the verb, held to the end, finally unlocks it.

Such a built-in cultural difference over against German habits of mind was even more pronounced for those of us of Anglo-American background. Focused short essays (and essay-like chapters) hold the place of honor for us—plain talk, rather than the exhaustive, *ausführliche, grundliche* treatise of German academic tradition. So we have to shift gears to appreciate Barth's artistry, and its underlying playful dynamic may elude us; and perhaps we'll have to leave it a bit as Mark Twain assured us about Wagner's music, "It's better than it sounds."

PLAY OF GRACE IN THE VISUAL ARTS

The mood that delighted Barth in Mozart's music was not so much in evidence in his grasp of the visual arts. His dismay at the medieval Church's manipulative use of the arts to overwhelm the common worshiper with monumental cathedrals, liturgical pomp and graphic display is well known. Barth was Protestant to the core in his opposition to such ostentation. He did appreciate graphic art, however. A collection of etchings hung in his stairwell,[24] and all have heard how the copy of Grünewald's glowing painting of the Baptist pointing toward the crucified Christ hung as a talisman over his desk.[25] One of Barth's sons had become a painter, and I've heard that Karl expressed interest in German expressionism. But I doubt if he recognized any counterpart to Mozart among graphic artists.

It is clear that Barth gave full weight to the Old Testament's prohibition of any attempt to render God-belief in graven images. And he warned against the heretical one-sidedness that he felt is bound to dog any attempt to portray graphically what is believed about God in Christ. God's Word, we may believe, is self-objectifying. But that word is simply to be heard—heard in the witness to Jesus Christ as God's living

---

[24] Framed prints of plates that appear in his *Protestant Theology in the Nineteenth Century.*

[25] A Reproduction of the Isenheim Altarpiece in Colmar, France.

Word and indicated in the sacraments and proclamation that point toward him. Barth felt that artists' attempts to portray graphically the *subject* of Christian faith, are bound to slide toward a heretical dualism—either towards a spiritualized Christ [docetism] in one direction, or toward a this-worldly image [adoptionism] in the other (suggesting a purely physical man).

Barth could banter about his own rather adamant view here: when a camera-toting student snapped a flashbulb in his face, he chuckled; "Now that's all right if you'll remember the second commandment!"

In his Colloquium, we were discussing the problem of graphic images a short time after I had been to Paris, where in the Musée d'Art Moderne I had been singularly touched by a small portrait of Christ by Georges Rouault. That canvas communicated vividly how the artist had struggled with the impossibility of objectifying on canvas what is believed about Jesus. The image obviously had been re-worked over and over again, until the impasto ridged centimeter-thick on the surface. Hadn't this artist, I asked, expressed thereby the very impossibility Barth saw in trying to portray incarnation belief in painting? I don't know that Barth got the point. In any case, he seemed to feel such expressionism would ask too much of the ordinary viewer and should best be avoided in Christian education. So

405

the ancient image-prohibition should still hold for the modern church.

My erstwhile sister-in-law, Tove Ahlbäck was a gifted painter. Basking in the golden beauty of her Helsinki gallery, I couldn't help wondering whether the relaxed playfulness of Mozart couldn't find its graphic parallel here. But I don't think Barth would have been comfortable with the thought. He seemed perplexed by non-figurative art and tended to bemoan its loss of the clear object.[26] One wonders whether he ever acknowledged that an abstract free-play, in which the artist delights in exploring and celebrating the given potential of rhythmic line and color, may be analogous to Mozart's joyful interplay with tone and harmonies. Not unlike Calvin, Barth retained the traditional view that graphic art should imitate nature; although, faith must remind us that the nature it mirrors, remains in itself ambiguous and often misleading.

In Barth's favor here, I recall the picture on one of those little story-sheets they used to hand out in our Sunday schools showing a flaccid, spiritualized Jesus healing Peter's mother-in-law. I remember it, because as an innocent six-year-old, I thought Jesus looked as feeble as she did and was mystified by

---

[26] Ted Gill stressed this in the unpublished paper and the journal article previously cited. See also E. Busch, *Karl Barth*, p. 411.

my sisters' shrieks of laughter when I commented, "It looks like he needs to get in bed with her." (So effete and sickly was the artist's notion of a spiritualized Jesus!) The golden-haired, white-robed boy carpenter, as he often was romanticized on our Sunday school handouts, could never have had body odor, dirty hands or callused feet.

A LIGHTHEARTED ASCETICISM IN PLAY

Karl Barth remained largely in the almost monastic traditions of continental scholarship, where one steeped oneself in the sources in their original languages. Had he not practiced a scholarly asceticism, he never could have found time, energy and self-discipline to produce his vast work. On one occasion, in his Colloquium, when we were planning to have our next meeting follow a festive dinner, I was struck by how strenuously Barth warned us against serving heavy food or eating too much, lest that dull our minds in the ensuing discussion. However, practical asceticism, as a free self-discipline for the sake of intellectual focus, did not imply a downgrading of the physical side of life. He was, in fact, quite relaxed about physical expression and had always loved to hike in the Alps and ride horseback.

Regarding the physical side of life, his American students liked to re-tell an anecdote that Grover Foley must have

407

told on himself: Grover, a shy intellectual, struck some of us as overly serious—something of a milquetoast, really; but he revered Barth and with his astounding memory assisted him in various ways. On one occasion Grover ventured to ask the professor for personal advice, confessing that he was interested in a certain girl, actually in love, he thought. What should he do? Barth's chuckled response: "Well now, Herr Foley, have you tried kissing her?" Such earthiness regarding sexual interplay coming from his spiritual idol apparently took Grover by surprise.

Given Barth's usual openness, the narrowing of his listening habits to fixate on the classical music of Mozart may strike one as a bit silly, since as most Americans know, fine jazz also can become the playful exploration of God-given potentials that Barth lauded in Mozart, and might be just as parabolic of our liberation in grace. But perhaps his practice of using the same composer's music to set a ground-tone for his work every morning should also be understood as part of the ascetic discipline of a creative scholar, who had found this to be a useful aid in channeling and focusing his energies.

Years later, I made an "a-hah!" discovery in the British Museum rare books chamber, when I found in the middle of the huge tomes of a later generation's Reformed theologian (William Perkins, 1558-1602) this slogan: the Christian's entire life should be "*a continual Sabbath rest.*" Our whole life should be joyfully free of compulsion and thankfully at ease in grace. Right in line with Calvin, as Barth also had re-discovered him! What could be more healing for our own, or any troubled times (and what could be further from either our forefathers' bluestocking Sabbatarianism, or the pressurized success ethic of our day)?

But nature's beauty is itself ambiguous, so art never becomes theology's undergirding frame of reference.[27] Beauty is simply a joyful blessing that comes to us through grace and not its criterion. Here is further instance of Barth's theology *of nature* (in contrast to a natural theology). There is a theology of art or of music) to be discovered and appreciated within the frame of creative grace. Such things can indeed be parabolic. But this is not an arts-theology such as we found Ted Gill fostering—not an aesthetic-based speculation about God.[28] Rather,

---

[27] My sister, Jean Anderson Eakle, who was a graphic artist, once confessed how shocked she was by her own pleasurable aesthetic reaction, to the scrumptious beauty of a gold-vermillion splash of color in a scene that happened to portray a horrifically evil event: the blood-drenched carnage, of a battlefield.

[28] I.e., it is not the sort of basis that was claimed as a corrective or complement to Kantian idealism by such thinkers as J. F. Fries, Rudolf Otto, Auguste LeMaître and Paul Tillich. Gill drew a primal link and parallel between art and religion, convinced that like "Siamese twins" they "are up to the same thing," as they give "available form to individual vision." While he recognized that "Karl Barth would be appalled at the direction" he took, he failed to share Barth's sense of the ambighuity spanned danger of such

409

it is a grace-related, gospel-bound grasp of the entire realm of affect and beauty.

That theology is the *schöne Wissenschaft* does not mean it is simply a beauty-adorned study, for it has as subject, the over-brimming Creator of both unity and diversity, the hidden Source and final Defender of all beauty and joy. Here again, we should not suppose that Barth's struggle against natural theology in any way diminished his theology of nature, which was created, at least in part, as the wondrous and predominantly beautiful matrix for our observant aesthetic life.

Play within the giftedness of all things should also mean concern for our ecological surroundings—standing in delight of intergalactic wonders, and not just of our corporate human personhood in the Body of Christ. As said, the circumstance that the environmental movement was not yet much in public awareness does not mean that Barth's theology was sterile in this direction. Even Barth's love of Mozart testifies strangely to the deep seriousness of honoring God by enjoying "all the good things" of the entire universe, in gratitude as the gifts of his creative love.[29] As we have observed, it means that life itself is to be grasped as dramatic comedy in the technical sense of the

religion and hence missed the point of his religion*less* Christianity. See "Barth and Mozart," *Theology Today*, Vol. 43, No.3, p.406.

[29] As stated in Calvin's Geneva Catechism of 1542, Q.7 and followed by the very first question of the Westminster Catechism.

word; i.e., in awareness that all's well, for it is ending well. It means the long-term triumph of levity, humor and joy that this drama entails.

Of course Barth's frequent reference to Mozart's music as mirroring the confident life in faith was not lost on us. My own decision, upon completing my doctorate, to turn my studies to the special role of play as a most appropriate mode for life in grace, had a root here. When I had just completed my final, *rigorosum* exam for the doctorate at Basel, I went up the Bruderholzallee for a last time to visit Karl Barth. I almost jumped when he addressed me as *Herr Doktor*: "Now, *Herr Doktor Anderson*, what do you plan to do next?" I surprised myself by the firmness with which I answered, "I think I'm going to do a study of the theology of play." The issue for our workforce in a day of industrial overproduction and limited job opportunities was not so generally recognized in 1964 as it should be today. But Barth understood.

SERIOUS WORK AND THE PURITAN PLAY ETHIC

As I have often stressed, the seriousness of free play in grace and power of playful imagination are themes that deserve far greater attention in Christian social ethics than they have received. In a truly Puritan work ethic, the total self-bestowal of hard labor, as we saw earlier, can and should be felt as an adult

411

form of playful self-abandon where one feels free to pour oneself out into sweaty toil.

One is also free to embrace every other form of serious industry in the spirit of playful self-abandon. In a more play-affirming society, people's enjoyment of each other (as distinct from compulsive, self-centered entertainment) is of primary value, and individuals are embraced as partners in free and liberating activities. Persons at work are no longer regarded as mere human resources to be exploited for ulterior production goals.

Materialistic cost-effectiveness and growth idolatry tend to reign in our secular consumer society. As Studs Terkel observed, Americans' work is often so slavish and oppressive it makes them sick. They seek mindless excitement and violent entertainment as an escape. But Christians' most serious work can and should be framed and embraced as a light-hearted free play in grace with and for each other.

Here was the same attitude I had absorbed long since as a boy working at the side of my garden-tending father, who with a staunchly free and full-statured Calvinist assurance would always challenge my brothers and me, "Let's see how much we can do for these folks and not how little." It was never compulsive. For he knew to make twelve hour days feel like an inspired, heroic game we enjoyed—a foolishness for Christ that a Marxist might find woefully unrealistic. But it is true: our work was transformed into an enthusiastic careful gift for those around us—an attitude that carried over into our later lives doing heart surgery, community service and teaching.

This has not been sufficiently recognized as the unalloyed heart of a puritan work-ethic[30]. It stems from a grace-rooted valuation of playful free activity with and for each other. For even boring, onerous tasks, can and should be undertaken without compulsion and imbued with a playful team spirit not unlike that which can energize sweaty workouts for a crew race or ball game.

That Barth saw theology itself as the most beautiful and playful intellectual discipline in no way trivialized the earnest gravity of his work. For a theology that engenders an objective freedom as Christians' life stance, and follows wherever an incarnational ethic of pneumatic response may lead, is bound to remain beautifully at ease.

---

[30] Max Weber's famous thesis regarding "the Calvinist work ethic" which characterized it in terms of the selfish practical syllogism we mentoned above (as a means to prove one's exclusive election) was, sad to say, quite apt regarding many latter day Calvinists, who had missplaced the Reformers' grace-responsive heart of the matter.

413

Afterword

Reflecting Playful Freedom and Radiant Joy

There is no way one can hope to summarize or recapitulate a student's experience of so wide-ranging and lively a thinker as Karl Barth. Yet I have found myself recalling a few leitmotifs that did resonate through everything he taught or wrote, though his genius transposed them into many different tonalities.

These, I think, have shown themselves to be far more than temperamental or attitudinal characteristics of the man; for they root into the nature of the Christian gospel, as he found it before him, and are grounded in the substance of the revelation of God in Christ. This is what has led to his characterization and presentation of theology not just as "the beautiful science," but (following some of his other adjectives) as a "modest, free, critical and happy science."[1]

Seeming to come evermore to the fore in Barth's understanding of Christians' life and thought is a divinely motivated,

---

[1] *Evangelical Theology: An Introductrion*, p. 16.

but completely free, *Person-response*. We have found this insistent ground tone sounding throughout and determining his theology's appropriate stance and modes of expression. Accordingly, I would now hazard to sum up Karl Barth's *Trinitarian* theology (along with its intrinsic ethic), as one of *free, pneumatic counterpoint* in company with Christ.

We have seen how Barth avoided buzzwords, but as he looked back, he did finally come to characterize his own Reformed thought as *theology of freedom*."[2] He would have been comfortable with this description of a *free*, pneumatic relationship, however, only if by "pneumatic" we are pointing to the believed, actual presence of God in Person as the Spirit of Christ; i.e., as none other than the living One who is to be known and clarified in human terms *only* in attentive correspondence with the life and teachings of Jesus of Nazareth.

This is definitely not to be transmuted into a statement about our own human spirit or some general capacity for "spirituality." Our bookstores are full of that sort of thing, but nothing could be further from Barth's insights. Rather, his work speaks to the claim of God's personal presence—we could even say, his "human personality," as he presents himself to be

---

[2] *Ibid.*, p. xii. See the selection of Barth's works published under this title by Clifford Green: *Karl Barth, Theology of Freedom* (Minneapolis: Fortress Press, 1991).

known in our terms. So there is a solely and exclusively christo-logical basis for our awareness of, and intercourse with, the Holy Spirit's presence and for our further discernment of God's will, his inspiration, and his leading.

The one who is both subject and object of theology is to be recognized and embraced, through this personhood. His self-definition and norm are essentially incarnational; and he has pledged himself to remain for us Christ-like in character and intent (as the medieval Church stressed by its insistence on the famous creedal *filioque* clause).[3] Although God's totality is not to be reduced to mere humanity, he may be trusted to remain coherent with his gifted human parameters.

Karl Barth did not claim the last word on anything, but he suggested root correctives that might make the Reformed tradition more appropriate to the living Savior, who is both its subject and object. These, in turn, would move it to reach out and bridge across to other traditions in the extended family of covenant-bound community and engage others in a lively con-

---

[3] The symbol-claim that the divine Spirit comes and accompanies us as the one who proceeds not only from the hidden God, the Father, but also as one who is to be humanly known—as "proceeding *also* from the Son" (*filioque*) and so to be grasped by us only *in his human terms,* and not subject to further speculations of either experiential or mystical bent. This was stressed in Western creeds in line with the scriptural injunction to "test the Spirits" (I John 4:1), largely to ward off christologically-inconsistent claims to new "spiritual" revelation or "discernment."

versation that seeks all the while to be christological.

We are not invited to live with a static fixation on biblical times, but are emboldened always to stride out in a *Christ-accompanied adventure*—hoping each day to discover something new to be shared with him in Spirit and so, as we are prepossessed and preoccupied by his grace, gradually to slough off the destructive compulsions of an unaccompanied ego's efforts at self-security. Since both his accompaniment and our dependence are holistic—expressing intellect as well as feeling—theology is bound to issue in part as a cool, carefully reflected discussion, and not just in a warmer emotional or mystical state of mind.

After his American tour, Barth, in the "Foreword to the American Edition" of his swan song, *Evangelical Theology: An Introduction,* wrote that he meant his *Church Dogmatics,* "not as the conclusion, but as the initiation of a new exchange of views about the question of proper theology, the established knowledge of God, and the obedient service of God among and for men." He thought that a new discussion was, in fact, taking place in America and expressed the "faint hope that this discussion might one day be pursued there in a more fruitful manner than in the . . . somewhat stagnant" waters of European theology. He saw Christ-attentive discourse and life to be represented from first to last by a *"theology of freedom." * For the *"Theos"* of

Christian theology is the liberator of captive people, the source of their each day's manna and the heart of a continual Sabbath-rest.

As his parting word to his American audience he wrote, "What we need on this and the other side of the Atlantic, is not Thomism, Lutheranism, Calvinism, orthodoxy, religionism, existentialism, nor is it a return to [the old 'Liberalism' of] Harnack and Troeltsch (and least of all is it 'Barthianism')." Rather, it is a "'theology of freedom' that looks ahead and strives forward." Only that could be suitable for "the nearly apocalyptic seriousness of our time." For only that can be an appropriate interaction with the living One, who is not only "the foundation," but also the "object and content of evangelical theology."[4] There can be no better American retrospective on the spirit and heart of this man than to carry that Christ-attentive "exchange of views" on into our own time and place. I have made a stab at that.

While I was finishing this book, Gunlög and I were stunned by the sudden death of our son, Martin, a gifted medical engineer and delightful companion. Shortly before this unex-pected tragedy he and I had a long telephone conversation about the hope we are given, that shines like a beckoning beacon

---

[4] p. xi-xii.

through every dark experience: a great God-given, "Nevertheless!" That night I had a strange dream of breathing life into my son's prone body, a dream that was still vivid when we learned of his tragic death a few days later.

Karl Barth, as our teacher, breathed a life-restoring freedom, pointing us toward hope and promise for life in grace that is not our own to control, but bears us on past our dying. But this is no hope at all, unless it is there for all. That is the legacy of the Reformed Church and a ground-tone of joy in the life and works of this gifted theologian, who never made it his pride to be a Christian, but rose each morning with the hope that is given to all of us, to respond as one this day.

Bibliography

Adams, James Luther, *Taking Time Seriously* (Glencoe, IL: The Free Press, 1957).

Anderson, Raymond K[emp], "Christianity is caught, not taught," in *Leibhaftige Ökumene: Berichte ausländischer Mitarbeiter und Studenten in unserer Kirche* (Berlin/Stuttgart: Lettner Verlag, 1963).

-----"Corporate Selfhood and *Meditatio Vitae Futurae:* How Necessary is Eschatology for Christian Ethics?" *Journal of the Society of Christian Ethics*, 23/1 (2003) 21-46.

-----"Corporate Personhood: Societal Definition of the Self in the Western Faith Tradition," *Becoming Persons* (Robert N. Fisher, ed., Oxford: Applied Theology Press, Vol.2, 569-589).

-----*Love and Order—The Life-Structuring Dynamics of Grace and Virtue in Calvin's Ethical Thought: An Interpretation* [Basel Dissertation] (Wilson College, 1973).

-----"The Principal Practice of Faith: How Prayer was Calvin's Key to Living Well," *Christian History Magazine: John Calvin* (1986).

Barnes, Elizabeth B., *An Affront to the Gospel? The Radical Barth and the Southern Baptist Convention* (Atlanta: Scholars Press, 1987).

Barth, Karl, *Die Auferstehung: Eine akademische Vorlesung über I Kor. 15* (München: Kaiser Verlag, 1926) English translation: *The Resurrection of the Dead* (New York: Revell, 1933).

421

-----*Barth: God Here and Now* (London & New York: Routledge, 2009).

-----*Die Botshaft von der freien Gnade Gottes* (Zürich: EVZ, 1947 & Zollikon, 1947).

-----*Credo* (New York: Scribner's, 1962) = *Credo: die Hauptprobleme der Dogmatik dargestellt im Anschluss an das Apostolische Glaubensbekenntnis* (Geneva: Weltbund der Kirchen, 1935).

-----*Die Christliche Lehre nach dem Heidelberger Katechismus* (Munich: Chr. Kaiser Verlag, 1949).

-----*The Epistle to the Romans* (Oxford: Oxford University Press & London: Humphrey Milford, 1933).

-----*Evangelical Theology: An Introduction* (New York: Holt Rinehart and Winston, 1963).

-----*Deliverance to the Captives* [Sermons and Prayers] (New York, Hagerstown, etc.: Harper and Row, 1961).

-----*The Early Preaching of Karl Barth,* Karl Barth and William H. Willimon (Louisville: Westminster/John Knox Press, 2009).

-----*The Faith of the Church: A Commentary on the Apostle's Creed According to Calvin's Catechism* [of 1545] (New York: Meridian, 1958).

-----*Fides quaerens intellectum: Anselms Beweis der Existenz Gottes* im Zusammenhang seines theologischen Programs (2nd ed., Zollikon: Evangelischer Verlag, 1958). Tr. *Fides quaerens intellectum: Anselm's Proof of the Existence of God in the Context of his Theological Scheme* (Richmond,VA: John Knox Press, 1960).

-----*Final Testimonies,* Eberhard Busch, ed. (Grand Rapids: Eerdmans, 1977).

-----*The Holy Spirit and the Christian Life: The Theological Basis of Ethics* (Louisville, KY: Westminster/John Knox Press, 1993).

-----*The Humanity of God* (Richmond, VA: John Knox, 1966; *Die Menschlichheit Gottes* Zollikon: Evangelischer Verlag, 1955).

-----*Karl Barth, Theologian of Freedom,* Clifford Green,

ed. (Minneapolis: Fortress Press, 1991).

-----*The Knowledge of God and the Service of God According to the Teaching of the Reformation.* [Gifford Lectures, 1937 and 1938], (New York: Scribners, 1939).

-----*Kirchliche Dogmatik* (Zollikon-Zürich: Evangelischer Verlag, 1932-1967); Engl. Tr.: *Church Dogmatics*, G. W. Bromiley et al. (Edinburgh: T&T Clark, 1957-1977).

-----*Letters, 1961-1968*, J. Fangmeier & H. Stovesandt, eds. (Grand Rapids: Eerdmans, 1981 [Edinburgh: T&T Clark, 1968]).

-----*La Prière d'après les catéchisms de la Réformation, Neuchatel* (Neuchâtel: Delachaux et Niestlé, 1953); [Engl. Fiftieth Anniversary Ed.] (Louisville, KY: Westminster/John Knox, 2002).

-----*La Proclamation de L'Evangile* (Neuchâtel: Delachaux et Niestlé, 1961).

-----*Die protestantische Theologie im 19. Jahrhundert: Ihre Vorgeschichte und ihre Geschichte* (Zollikon-Zürich: Evangelischer Verlag, 1952).

-----*Selected Prayers* (Virginia: John Knox Press, 1965).

-----*The Theology of John Calvin* [1922 lecture series], (Grand Rapids: Eerdmans, 1995).

-----*The Way of Theology in Karl Barth; Essays and Comments*, H. Martin Rumscheidt, ed. (Allison Park, PA: Pickwick, 1986).

Braaten, Carl E. and Robert W. Jenson, *Union with Christ: The New Finnish Interpretation of Luther* (Michigan/Cambridge: Eerdmans, 1998).

Brown, Robert MacAfee, "Good News from Karl Barth" in *How Karl Barth Changed My Mind*, (Grand Rapids: Eerdmans, 1986).

-----*Saying Yes and Saying No: On Rendering to God and Caesar* (Philadelphia: Westminster/John Knox, 1986).

Busch, Eberhard, *Barth* (Nashville: Abingdon, 2008).

-----*The Great Passion: An Introduction to Karl Barth's Theology* (Grand Rapids/Cambridge: Eerdmans, 2004).

-----*Karl Barth and the Pietists: The Young Karl Barth's Critique of Pietism and Its Response* (Downers Grove, Illinois: Intervarsity Press, 2004).

-----*Karl Barth: His life from letters and autobiographical texts* (Philadelphia: Fortress, 1975; Grand Rapids, MI: Eerdmans, 1993).

Casalis, Georges, *Portrait of Karl Barth* (Garden City, New York: Doubleday, 1963).

Cobb, John B. Jr., *A Christian Natural Theology* (Philadelphia: Westminster Press, 1965).

Come, Arnold, *An Introduction to Karl Barth's "Dogmatics" for Preachers* (Philadelphia: Westminster, 1963).

Corette, J. and Richard King, *Selling Spirituality: The Silent Takeover of Religion* (New York: Routledge, 2005).

Dorrien, Gary, *The Barthian Revolt in Modern Theology* (Louisville: Westminster/John Knox, 2000).

Feuerbach, Ludwig, *Das Wesen der Religion*, 1845.

Fletcher, Joseph, *Situation Ethics: The New Morality* (Philadelphia: Westminster Press, 1959).

Ford, David F., ed., *The Modern Theologians: An Introduction to Christian Theology in the Twentieth Century*, Vol. I (Oxford & Cambridge: Blackwell, 1989).

Gibson, David & Daniel Strange, eds., *Engaging with Barth: Contemporary Evangelical Critiques* (New York, London: T&T Clark, 2008).

-----*Reading the Decree: Exegesis, Election and Christology in Calvin and Barth* (Edinburgh: T&T Clark, 2009).

Godsey, John D., *Karl Barth's Table Talk* (Richmond, VA: John Knox Press, 1963).

Green, Clifford, ed., *Karl Barth Theologian of Freedom* (Minneapolis: Fortress, 1991).

Hauerwas, Stanley M., *Against the Nations* (San Francisco: Harper & Row, 1988).

-----*Christian Existence Today* (Grand Rapids, MI: Baker Books, 1988).

-----*Hannah's Child: A Theological Memoir* (Grand Rapids, MI: Eerdmans, 2010).

-----*The Hauerwas Reader* (Durham, NC: Duke University, 2001).

-----*With the Grain of the Universe: The Church's Witness and Natural Theology* [2001 Gifford Lectures] (Grand Rapids, MI: Brazos Press [Baker Book House], 2010).

Heppe, Heinrich, *Reformed Dogmatics Set Out and Illustrated from the Sources* (London: George Allen & Unwin, 1950).

Hesselink, I. John, "Karl Barth and Emil Brunner—A Tangled Tale with a Happy Ending / The Story of a Relationship" in *How Karl Barth Changed My Mind*, Donald K. McKim, ed. (Eugene OR: Wipf and Stock, 1998).

-----*Calvin's First Catechism: A Commentary*, (Louisville, KY: Westminster/John Knox, 1997).

-----"Karl Barth as Mentor and Friend," in *Faithful Witness,* Festschrift for Ronald G. Goetz, Michael J. Bell *et al* eds. (Elmhurst, Ill: Elmhurst College Press, 2002).

Heussi, Karl, *Kompendium der Kirchengeschichte* (Tübingen: J.C.B. Mohr, 1956).

Hunsinger, George, *Disruptive Grace: Studies in the Theology of Karl Barth* (Grand Rapids: Eerdmans, 2000).

-----*How to Read Karl Barth: The Shape of His Theology* (Oxford: Oxford U. Press, 1991).

Jenson, Robert, *Alpha and Omega: A Study in the Theology of Karl Barth* (Edinburgh, New York, Toronto: Thomas Nelson and Sons, 1963).

----- "Karl Barth," in David F. Ford, ed., *The Modern Theologians* (1989).

Jenson, Robert et al., "Faculty Papers in Memoriam: Karl Barth (1886-1968)," *Gettysburg Lutheran Theological Seminary Bulletin,* 1969, v.49, No. 2.

Jones, Paul Dafydd, *The Humanity of Christ: Christology in Karl Barth's Church Dogmatics* (Edinburgh: T & T Clark, 2011).

Kierkegaard, Søren, *Philosophical Fragments or a Fragment of Philosophy* (Princeton: Princeton University Press, 1936).

Kirschbaum, Charlotte von, *The Question of Woman: The Collected Writings of Charlotte von Kirchbaum*, tr. John Shepher (Grand Rapids: Eerdmans) 1996.

Köbler, Renate, *In the Shadow of Karl Barth: Charlotte von Kirschbaum* (Louisville: Westminster/ John Knox Press, 1989) [Tr. of *Schattenarbeit: Charlotte von Kirschbaum—Die Theologin an der Seite Karl Barths* (Köln: Pahl-Rugenstein Verlag, 1987)].

Krötke, Wolf, *Sünde und Nichtiges bei Karl Barth*, Engl. tr.: *Sin and Nothingness in the Theology of Karl Barth* (Studies in Reformed Theology and History, New Series, 10 (Princeton: Princeton Theol. Seminary, 2005).

McCormack, Bruce L., "The Barth Renaissance in America: An Opinion," *The Princeton Seminary Bulletin,* Vol. 23, No.3, 2002.

MacGregor, Geddes, *A Renaissance in Christian Thought* (Wheaton, IL: Theosophical Publishing House, 1979).

McKenny, Gerald P., *The Analogy of Grace: Karl Barth's Moral Theology* (Oxford: Oxford University Press, 2010).

McKelway, Alexander J., "*Magister Dialecticae et Optimarium Partium*: Recollections of Karl Barth as Teacher," *Union Quarterly Review*, Vol. XXVIII, No.1, Fall 1972.

-----*The Systematic Theology of Paul Tillich: A Review and Analysis* (Richmond, VA: John Knox, 1964).

McKim, Donald, ed., *How Karl Barth Changed My Mind* (Grand Rapids: Eerdmans, 1986).

McLean, Stuart, *Humanity in the Thought of Karl Barth* (Edinburgh: T&T Clark, 1981).

Moltmann, Jürgen, *The Theology of Hope* (New York: Harper and Row, 1967).

Niebuhr, Reinhold, *The Nature and Destiny of Man* (New York: Scribners, 2 vols., 1943).

O'Grady, Colm, *An Introduction to the Theology of Karl Barth* [A Survey...] (New York; Corpus,1968).

Otto, Rudolf, *The Idea of the Holy* (London: Oxford U.

Press, 1928).

Pokrifka, Todd B., *Redescribing God: The Role of Scripture, Tradition, and Reason in Karl Barth's Doctrines of Divine Unity, Constancy and Eternity* (Eugene, OR: Pickwick Publications, 2010).

Price, Robert B., *Letters of the Divine Word: The Perfections of God in Karl Barth's Church Dogmatics* (Edinburgh: T&T Clark, 2011).

Quispel, Gilles, *Gnosis als Weltreligion: die Bedeutung der Gnosis in der Antike* (Zürich: Oreigo Verlag, 1972).

Roberts, R. H. "Barth's Doctrine of Time," p. 93ff. in *Karl Barth: Studies of his Theological Method*, S.W. Sykes, ed. (Oxford: Clarendon Press, 1979).

Robinson, John A. T., *Honest to God* (London: SCM Press, 1963).

Robinson, James M. ed., *The Beginnings of Dialectic Theology,* (Richmond, VA: John Knox Press, 1968).

Rumscheidt, H. M. (ed.), *Footnotes to a Theology: The Karl Barth Colloquium 1972* (Ontario: Corporation for the Publication of Academic Studies in Religion in Canada, 1974).

Schaafsma, Petruschka, *Reconsidering Evil: Confronting Reflections with Confessions* (Leuven: Peeters, 2006).

Shofner, Robert D., *Anselm Revisited: A Study on the Role of the Ontological Argument in the Writings of Karl Barth and Charles Hartshorne* (Leiden: Brill, 1974).

Staehelin, Ernst, *Die Verkündigung des Reiches Gottes* (Zürich: EVZ, 1968).

Sykes, S. W., ed., *Karl Barth: Studies of his Theological Method* (Oxford: Clarendon Press, 1979).

Thurneysen, Eduard, *"Die Bergpredigt," Theologische Existenz Heute,* Neue Folge: Nr. 105, 1936. Translation published as *The Sermon on the Mount* (Richmond, VA: John Knox Press, 1964).

Torrance, Thomas F., *Karl Barth, Biblical and Evangelical Theologian* (Edinburgh: T & T Clark, 1990).

-----"My Interaction With Karl Barth" in *How Karl Barth Changed My Mind*, Donald K. McKim, ed. (Eugene OR:

Wipf and Stock, 1998).

Van Til, Cornelius, *Barth's Christology* (Philadelphia: Presbyterian & Reformed, 1962).

-----*The New Modernism; An Appraisal of the Theology of Barth and Brunner* (Philadelphia: Presbyterian and Reformed Publishing, 1947).

Verhey, Allen, *The Great Reversal: Ethics and the New Testament* (Grand Rapids: Eerdmans, 1948).

-----*Remembering Jesus: Christian Community, Scripture, and the Moral Life* (Grand Rapids: Eerdmans, 2002).

Vischer, Wilhelm, *Bedeutung des Alten Testaments für das christliche Leben* (Zollikon-Zürich: Evangelischer Verlag, 1947).

Weber, Hans Emil, *Reformation, Orthodoxie und Rationalismus,* 2 Sections (Gütersloh: C Bertelsmann, 1937-1951; Wissenschaftliche Buchgesellschaft, 1966).

Webster, John, ed. *The Cambridge Companion to Karl Barth* (Cambridge: Cambridge University Press, 2000).

Winn, Christian T. Collins, *"Jesus is Victor!" The Significance of the Blumhardts for the Theology of Karl Barth* (Eugene, OR: Pickwick, 2009).

Zellweger-Barth, Max, *My Father-in-Law: Memories of Karl Barth* (Allison Park, PA: Pickwick, 1986).

Index of Names and Subjects

430

431

433

434

435

436

Raymond Kemp Anderson

Dr. Raymond Kemp Anderson served for many years as Professor and Chairman of the Philosophy and Religion Department at Wilson College, Pennsylvania and as minister and leader in the Presbyterian Church. He received his Th.D. from the University of Basel and was privileged to have been one of the last American doctoral candidates of the eminent Reformed theologian, Karl Barth, at the University of Basel, Switzerland.